CITIZEN WARHOL

Blake Stimson

REAKTION BOOKS

To Elise and Louise

Published by Reaktion Books Ltd
33 Great Sutton Street
London EC1V 0DX, UK
www.reaktionbooks.co.uk

First published 2014

Copyright © Blake Stimson 2014

Printed and bound in China by Toppan Printing Co. Ltd.

A catalogue record for this book is available from the British Library

ISBN 978 1 78023 192 1

CONTENTS

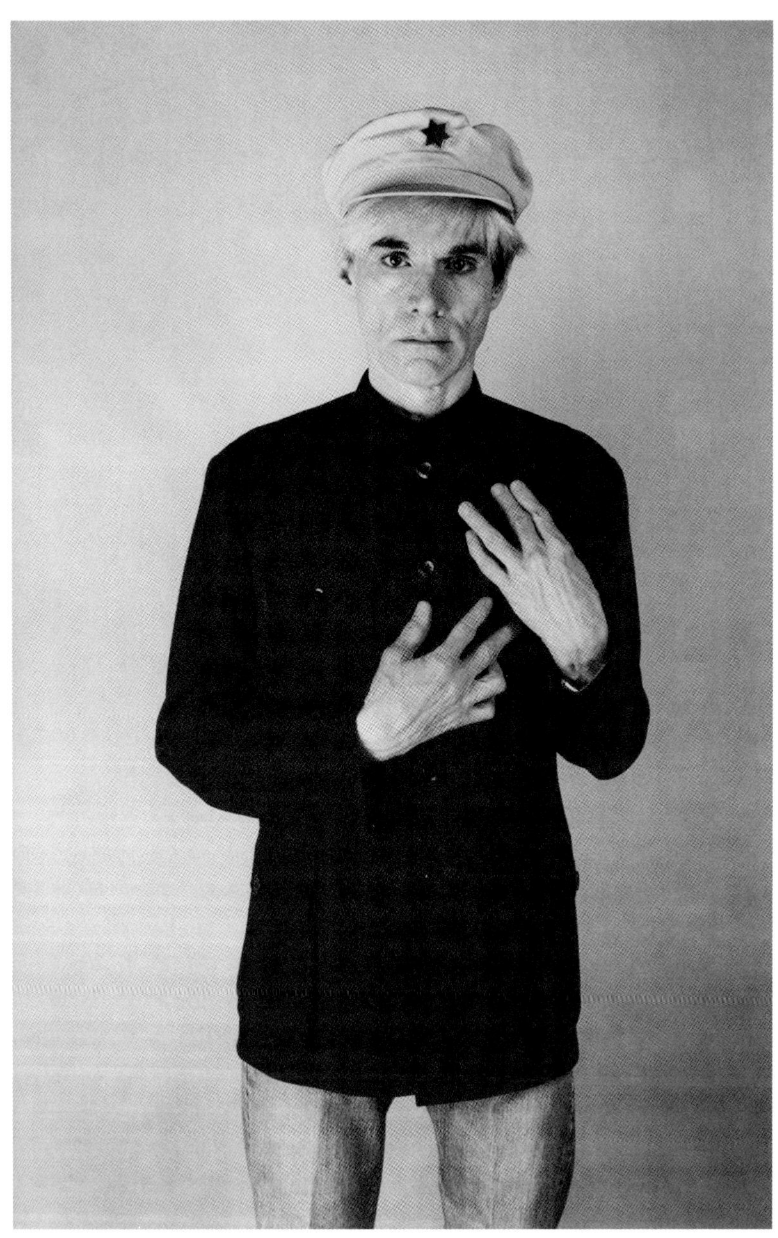

1 Christopher Makos, *Andy in Chairman Mao Suit*, 1982.

PREFACE:
THE CITIZENSHIP
OF ARTISTS

Lamenting who we have become in the context of the social, political and economic changes broadly associated with neo-liberalism, the cultural critic and proponent of public higher education Christopher Newfield offered a diagnosis of what has been lost in that process: 'I think what is missing', he said, 'is the realization of specific, situated experience, the making of interiority as rediscovered in the novel and then publicly forgotten by modernity, which rendered it as real as social facts, or as real as money.'[1] The once vaunted interiority of the novel, or of modern art, of Protestant religiosity, enlightened subjectivity or of liberal arts education, Newfield suggests, has collapsed into an unreflective exteriority no different than that of money. The rich interior specificity of self, given form by the intertwined activity of sustained reflection and public exchange with others about that reflection that was the core dream of the Enlightenment, has been reduced to a mechanical mirror image or 'subject position', to the lesser, delimited reality of a plotted coordinate in a discursively constructed world. This atrophy or entropy of interiority is both modernity's endgame and our postmodernism, but it is not particularly new: as the art historian T. J. Clark put it about Picasso's work, what has long been at stake is 'a finite, enclosed space of possessions, property, enclosure, intimacy, availability' – that is, 'an eminently bourgeois space' that is 'completely under threat from the outside, from a kind of space which does not belong to us'.[2]

'Good riddance', we have thought about that inner life, that eminently bourgeois space, for the half-century since Andy Warhol became a household name. This book is about that eradication and the role Warhol played in helping us realize it. In the old world view structured by the aim of enlightenment, to be a citizen was to conjure an interiority that served as both protective redoubt and purposive incursion into the prevailing rule-bound exteriority of being a subject to God or a subject of a king; to exercise inner-directed reason in public was to activate and occasionally actualize freedom from the subjection of dogma, decorum and the systemic violence of market and state. By contrast, in the post-Enlightenment view that Warhol came to speak for better than anyone else, citizenship was to be less a medium of autonomy and more a register of dependency. For us postmoderns, citizenship augurs its influence less through feelings and ideas and instead measures its sway more by accumulation and possession. Our lives as citizens are increasingly less about inner-directed selfhood challenging and redirecting the externally directed world, and have come ever more to register the external exchange between things and the exercise and realization of our own thingliness. Even the once exalted principle of the universal rights of man has become less an ideal to cultivate and more a possession to hoard: 'The interior man, the indifferent and gentle martyr', as Warhol's contemporary Gilles Deleuze once described the old Enlightenment subject, has 'become the private man, aggressive, worried about his rights, and only in his worry wants to call upon Reason'.[3]

The question of why this shift has happened is a complex one, of course, and as such will be something we can only sketch here. Generally, we might say that postmodernization was successful because it offered us a significant psychological pay-off – a sense of release from the 'gentle', existential, martyr-like burden of interiority, the burden of challenging the world from within, the burden of becoming a thinking, feeling, social subject rather than performing one's role as an object of the will of others or exercising it as a solitary will of one's own. This, in sum, is the tremendous liberty that Warhol's work and persona got so right. It is also a liberty that has found its way deeper and deeper into the fibres of our citizenship over the course of the last half-century. More and more, we have come to experience ourselves as socially situated identities rather than as historically enabled subjects; more and more, we have felt the release from having to carry the weight of the world on our shoulders in the name of the old project of enlightenment. What Warhol represents more than anything else, it might be said, is that Atlas did indeed shrug, and in so doing we came to embrace the pleasures of letting the aged, hoary martyrdom of enlightenment slide.[4]

The ecstatic release that arises from the equivalence of things and thingliness is richly present everywhere in Warhol's work and persona, but one standard expression of the liberation it offers was given in the opening salvo of his oft-cited interview in 1963 with Gene Swenson:

> Someone said that Brecht wanted everybody to think alike. I want everybody to think alike. But Brecht wanted to do it through Communism, in a way. Russia is doing it under government. It's happening here all by itself without being under a strict government; so if it's working without trying, why can't it work without being Communist? Everybody looks alike and acts alike, and we're getting more and more that way.[5]

Instead of the great modernist dream of political subjectivization, of citizenship and comaraderie, in other words, self was becoming a function of economic exchange, and that exchange was becoming the measure of self. This can stand well enough as our working definition of postmodernization.

There are many ways to understand this process but for our purposes it is best considered in aesthetic terms. Where the great longing for enlightenment given by the novel and modern art, by philosophy and the personal relationship to God, by higher education and democratic forms of governance, had been cast as the promise of *beauty* – the promise of self arising out of system, in the sense of Rousseau's 'general will', Kant's '*sensus communis*' or Marx's 'class consciousness' – Warhol's period rejoinder was to turn to the infinite authority of *sublimity*, the experience of system arising from self. In lieu of using 'one's understanding without guidance from another' to redirect public opinion, as Kant famously put it in the opening lines of his popular answer to the question 'What is Enlightenment?', Warhol insisted that both his understanding and his being were guided by a prevailing, generalized, systemic Other, an external system, world or being that he could provide access to but only as its relay or functionary, only as a passive, glittering reflection of its awesome, external authority, its magnificent and sublime Otherness.

He was not alone in this, of course, but, just as Kant had in his day, Warhol provided the clearest, most resonant answer to the pressing question of our time. We could cast that question as 'What is post-Enlightenment?' or 'What does it mean to be postmodern?' but, phrased as such, the question is too abstract and too academic. Our concern is made more concrete if we see it instead as an answer to a more mundane problem that Warhol posed in the same interview: 'It's hard to be creative', he lamented, 'and it's also hard not to think what you do is creative or hard not to be called creative because everybody is always talking about that and individuality.'[6] The task, as he defined it, was to figure out how to release oneself from the social burden of creativity, the social burden of individuality and of determining the direction of the society we live in. 'How to shrug?' is how we might phrase it with Ayn Rand's *Atlas Shrugged* in 1957, or 'How to Stop Worrying and Love the Bomb?', as *Dr Strangelove* put it in 1964.[7] These are the questions that Warhol raised and answered better than any other.

All citizenship really means is contracting with others for the purpose of governance. Schematically, this can be done in one of two ways: either with that contract taking on a life of its own and ruling at a psychological remove from citizens themselves – as God, say, or King, or Nation, or State, or Economy – or with it not doing so, with the contract between citizens serving as an ongoing site of discussion, debate and deliberation about what constitutes the best society. The great promise of enlightenment was that the contract could itself institute the process of thinking for oneself in public, of thinking and feeling as a shared activity, and keep at bay any system that would act in its name. What Warhol's work heralded far better than any other cultural marker is, first, the collapse of the historical promise of citizenship-as-self into the posthistorical inevitability of citizenship-as-system and, second, that differences between such systems matter less than we sometimes imagine. God, King, Nation, State, Economy: each is as anti-modern or postmodern as the next; each is as anti- or post-Enlightenment as the other; each promises a release from the burden of carrying the world on one's shoulders as much as all the rest. Each also projects the internal human capacity for enlightenment on to the external authority of system: 'Russia is doing it under government', as Warhol put it, 'It's happening here all by itself.'

Such projections on to some external Other have always been one part of the domain of art, of course, even as various modern forms did what they could to struggle against that exteriorization. Either art is a matter of laying claim to life, to self-governance, or it transcends life and bestows governance to Nation, State, Economy, God or even Art itself. Exercised by Warhol's 'Brillo box' exhibition in 1964, the young Arthur Danto got this half right as he tried to define the concept 'art world':

> What in the end makes the difference between a Brillo box and a work of art consisting of a Brillo Box is a certain theory of art. It is the theory that takes it up into the world of art, and keeps it from collapsing into the real object which it is.[8]

Danto understood the fetish-like transcendence of art perfectly well; what he misunderstood was the medium or cause of that transcendence. As Warhol had pointed out a year earlier, it was not art theory but, in one case, government that caused that transcendence, and in his own, it was a process that happens 'all by itself'. What he meant, of course, was that people, values, tastes and so on were becoming more and more alike, as Americans – by their own choosing rather than by government or Church dictate, or by the coercive peer pressure of nationalism – turned to the consumption of Coca-Cola, or tuned into the same television shows nightly or ate the same brand of soup everyday for lunch. In other words, the fetishism of Warhol's Brillo box, the way in which its value seemed to exceed the object it presumed to be, was not a function of anything so fanciful and high-minded as art theory but was instead a function of the everyday fetishism of the commodity form elevated to a higher exchange value by its place in the boutique context of an art gallery. In this regard, Warhol's work was all about 'collapsing into the real object which it is', about collapsing the once interiorized category of art into the exterior category of exchange.

In one sense we could say that Warhol was a kind of Marxist, or at least had a working knowledge of the process that Marx came to label 'ideology'. That is, again and again throughout his long career he revealed a fundamental truth about his work as an artist that was the cornerstone of Marx's theory: as soon as something 'emerges as a commodity, it changes into a thing which transcends sensuousness'.[9] Indeed, it is probably fair to say that Warhol's entire life and career was built on the liberty born of that transcendence. His was an art that embraced the relations between things rather than the relations between people, or between people and things. What his genius marked so much better than any other, however, was not the political-economic insight that commodity fetishism exists, nor the psychological intuition that it offers a reprieve from the burden of enlightenment, but instead the historical anticipation that it would eventually dominate so significantly who we have become. In short, Warhol's genius lies in his prefiguration of the far-reaching psychological, social, political and economic implications of the end of the Cold War. For example, by casting our contemporary mode of transcendence – that which we now call 'globalization' or 'neoliberalism', or just 'consumerism' – against the old-world approach of communism in his early interview with Swenson, he put his finger on the means by which we were so effectively seduced by the commodity form, into the world of endless equivalence between things and thingliness, into a mode of citizenship that happens 'all by itself' without shouldering the burden of enlightenment. The question, for our purposes, is a historical one about how such insight into the citizens we would become took hold and found such consequential expression in the life and work of Andy Warhol.

The literature on Andy Warhol is extraordinarily rich. Perhaps more than any other artist throughout art's long history, Warhol has attracted fans, aficionados, enthusiasts, experts and what might best be called 'philosophers' – critics, art historians, bona fide philosophers and many more – who have not just dug up the details of his life and work and reported them, or waxed eloquent on the pleasures they discovered there, but have struggled to interpret Warhol and his enterprise as an enigma. Almost all of these efforts to engage with Warhol and his legacy are valuable – really, enormously so, really *in*valuable – because not only are they unusually earnest, involved and impassioned about their subject but almost all of them see themselves in their subject in some way. These reflections on Warhol's life and art evince something like a 'Warhol effect', a register of the way he made them feel, think or act. In other words, their process for coming to terms with the meaning and significance of Warhol's art, like Warhol's own process, is also one that happens 'all by itself'. My effort here is no different and it too might well be read symptomatically. Hal Foster once alluded to this phenomenon by suggesting that we all make the Warhol we need or get the Warhol we deserve.[10] Reading through the wealth of responses to Warhol, this would certainly seem to be the case. In the end it is this Warhol effect that is of the greatest interest for this study. In particular, we will be concerned with what this distinctively rich response tells us about ourselves, not as individuals or as this or that demographic constituency (gay or straight, say, immigrant or native, secular or religious, rich or poor, and so on) or as generic human beings, but instead as moderns or postmoderns, as subjects inextricable from the gravitational pull of the particular ways the world, and we in it, are changing today.

INTRODUCTION: AMERICA REALLY IS THE BEAUTIFUL

Try as we might, it seems fair enough to say we never escape our origins. Andy Warhol was no different than anyone else in this regard, even if he tried harder than most and in a panoply of ways. Like many children born to immigrant families, the secret to his success as a wannabe American, as an outsider-becoming-insider, was to melt – to dissolve his familial foreignness into the larger pot of American cultural life. He did this by all the usual means of de-ethnicization – by dropping the second 'a' from Warhola, for example, or by reducing his bulbous nose with plastic surgery, or by becoming an enthusiast of all things American (especially our national pastime of shopping), and by adopting some of the trappings of celebrity, including his signature wig, wearing dark glasses at all hours inside and out, and his amphetamine-abetted slim physique. The vagary and psychical turmoil that is sometimes born of the suspension of inherited identity can also be seen in his amorphous and complex sexuality, his tabloid-ready mix of demi-monde and celebrity lifestyles and, of course, his distinctively passive-aggressive personality and artistic sensibility. If we can say that there is one guiding theme that ran through Warhol's life and work, this is probably it: melting, dissolving, the death of the self in order to achieve transcendence as a figure for the overcoming of difference in some larger collective ideal or, more truthfully, some larger collective ideallessness. The term his friend Henry

Geldzahler used to describe Warhol was *recording angel*: 'He used his blankness – his dumb blondness – in everything he did, in film, in painting – to record the world and give it back as art.'[1] He had an angelic quality, of purity or virginity or clarity – of pure contingency, a blank slate or, better, a blank tape – and as such he exuded a sense of being open to anything, of being anything, of being open to the process of becoming without the ancestral burden of the past and without enlightenment's encumbrance.

That said, Warhol's turn outwards from his isolated and interiorized past towards the world beyond was a form of self-creation through self-transcendence, and in this sense was nothing new. For example, it was a gesture or a way of being in the world or an experience of self that draws its main impetus from the old dreams of progress and enlightenment embodied in great modern symbols like the French Revolution's allegory of Liberty or the great modern institutions of art, science, philosophy and democratic politics, or their emblematic expression in re-tooled religious abstractions such as the Washington Monument (illus. 2). More than anything else, Warhol was someone who reinvented himself in public in ways that challenged convention. 'Enlightenment is man's release from his self-incurred tutelage', as Kant famously put it, meaning release from the guardianship of tradition through critique of the powers of reason.[2] Warhol achieved that release brilliantly, not so much by reinventing reigning moral and intellectual principles through the public exercise of critical reason, as

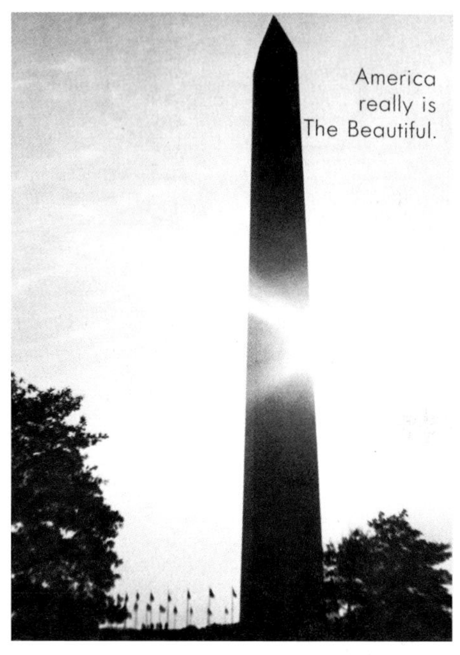

2 Andy Warhol, frontispiece from *America*, 1985.

3 Andy Warhol, film stills from *Empire*, 1964.

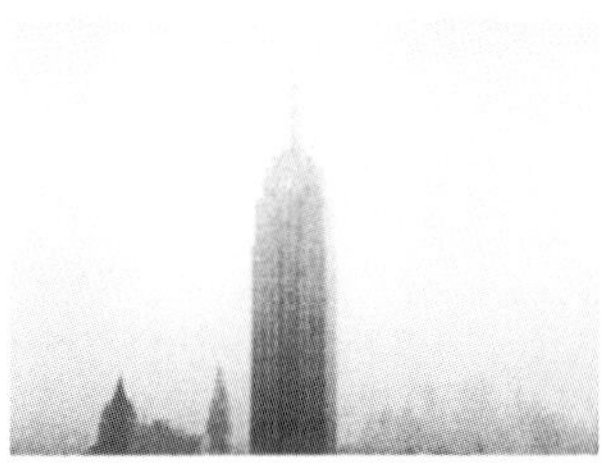

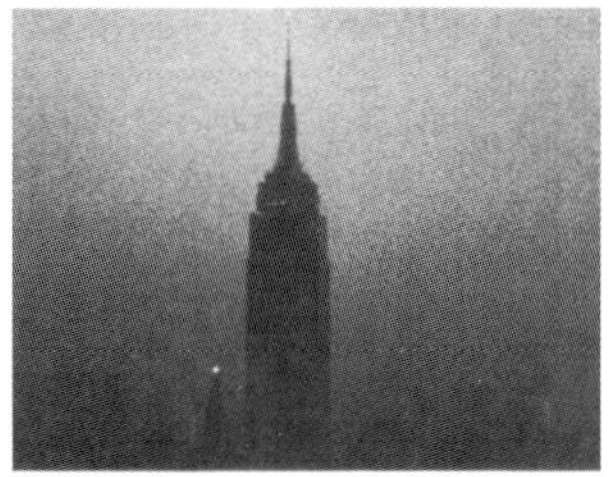

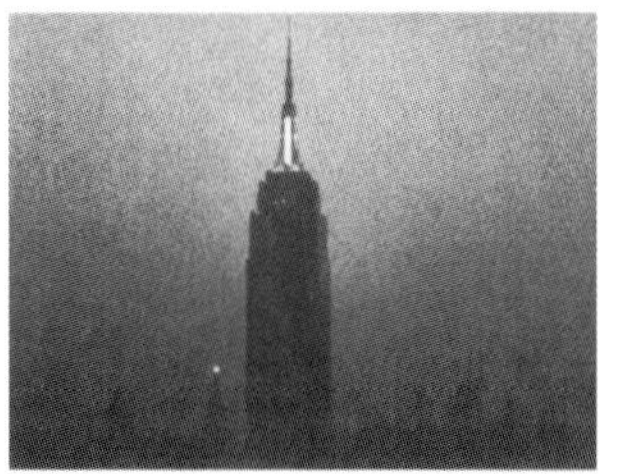

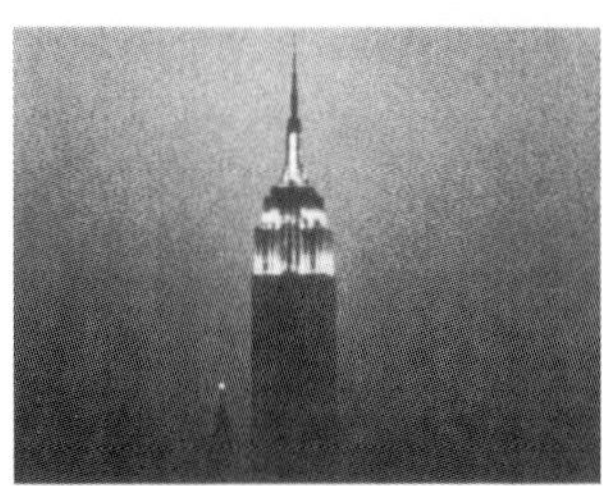

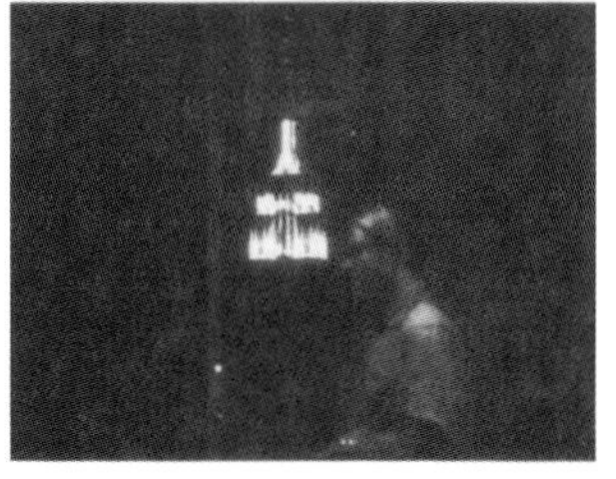

Kant had in mind in the eighteenth century, but instead by consistently and systematically turning his attention away from the tutelage of principles in general – certainly the pre-Enlightenment doctrinal dictates of morality and theology, but also Kant's reflexive principles of reason and critique – by playing the dumb blonde to their presumption of governing authority. This was as true for politics and philosophy as it was for art. 'What do you think of Jasper Johns?', Warhol was asked in a characteristic interview. 'Oh, I think he's great', he responded. 'Why?', the interviewer wanted to know. 'Oh, well, he makes such great lunches.'[3]

Whether given by a cleric as established Church doctrine or raised as a philosopher's challenge to such doctrine in the name of social criticism, moral, intellectual and aesthetic principles of the sort that concerned Kant and his predecessors and heirs have always been designed to constrain, direct or excite human desire towards socially productive ends. Time and again throughout his life, Warhol would address the authority of such principles when asked to do so by interviewers, or simply by the high artistic assumptions of galleries and museums, curators, collectors and critics, only to then turn his attention away towards another path for desire: that of unrestricted, undirected, antisocial play, or at least a kind of desire that was free to casually, unceremoniously and without any enduring commitment attach itself to the world most readily at hand – people in the room, commodities from the store down the block, celebrity photographs, advertisements, news items from the morning's paper. In this way his life and work gave early and formative symbolic form to the world-changing, postmodern principle made programmatic years later by Margaret Thatcher's resounding adage that 'there is no such thing as society' and Ronald Reagan's unwavering dictum that government is a problem rather than a solution.

Put differently, Warhol's was a politics and an ethics of everyday life, of the ordinary against the extraordinary, of the commonplace against the true and the good, of the performative to and fro of daily existence against the progressive unfolding of revelation or enlightenment. Put differently again, his was a world that happens 'all by itself'. I 'prefer to remain a mystery', he said in a 1966 interview, 'I never like to give my background and, anyway, I make it all up different every time I'm asked.'[4] In this way, the tutelage that Kant and his philosophical and political allies vilified was kept at bay, not by turning to the transcendence of universal reason in order to trump the false universality of tradition or doctrine, but instead by turning to the universalism and transcendence of everyday, ordinary desire, of desire for anything and everything in the way that one desires food, say, or money, or company, or sex. It didn't really matter whether that everyday desire was a function of the cycles of nature or was born of the repetitive gestures of work and consumption; what mattered was that the recurrence of everyday desires would eclipse the progressive unfolding of enlightenment.[5]

In this regard, Warhol's appreciation for the Washington Monument as a sign that 'America really is The Beautiful' was akin to his oft-quoted appreciation for the starring role played by the Empire State Building in his marathon film *Empire* (illus. 3): 'It's an eight-hour hard on', he reportedly commented, 'It's so beautiful. The lights come on and the stars come out and it sways.'[6] In a sense, Warhol just reversed the Enlightenment maxim as it had been taught to him at the tender age of nine in Saturday-morning art classes at the Carnegie Museum in

Pittsburgh: 'Art is not just a subject', his instructor Joseph Fitzpatrick is said to have bellowed to a large room full of fifth-, sixth- and seventh-grade art students, 'It's a way of life. It's the only subject you use from the time you open your eyes in the morning until you close them at night. Everything you look at has art or the lack of art.'[7] At some point Warhol simply stopped seeing the distinction between art and non-art, and in so doing stopped vesting himself in the exercise of his powers of judgment. His long-time assistant Gerard Malanga would have him say it this way in a faked interview: 'Human judgment doesn't mean anything to me. Human judgment cannot exist in the world of automation. "Problems" must be "solved". Without judgment there can be no problems.'[8]

For our purposes, thus, we might call Warhol's dispensing with judgment in favour of visibility and success the American Dream or the Pursuit of Happiness, and cast it against the kind of ideals that concerned Kant and his ilk – *Liberté, égalité* and *fraternité*, for example, or 'publicness', or enlightenment itself. Certainly it was a glorious dream for Warhol but we could also, and with equally good faith, flip that dream on its head and call it the American Nightmare. Which way it turns really depends on what we think about all those distant vaunted principles – God or man, faith or reason, revelation or enlightenment, the Word or truth, sanctity or beauty, and so on. In Warhol's world they exist, and powerfully so, but only to be casually and routinely undone in the name of the most ordinary of desires, the desires we associate with consumer satisfactions of transient bodily and material needs as easily available substitutes for larger callings.

Consuming rather than philosophizing or praying: this is the delight of Warhol's work and even of postmodernism generally, either as dream or nightmare. It relishes the drip-feed of *jouissance* given by its own governing and ever-recurring 'incredulity towards meta-narratives', as the philosopher Jean-François Lyotard once put it, and we in turn cannot help but rejoice in the new liberty such incredulity provides, even if we do so with some melancholy and foreboding at the prospect of being cut loose from our old moorings or, rather, from any moorings at all.[9] Really, the dream-cum-nightmare of the consumer and the nightmare-cum-dream of the citizen are inseparable – just as with the pre-modern couplet, faith and doubt – and they have gone hand-in-glove since modernity's early days, the one serving as symptom to the other's triumph. 'The double nature of humanism', as one account puts it, is 'the defiant boast of the modern ("I take value from myself alone!") and its hollow cry of anguish ("I am so lonely in this universe!").'[10] Warhol's great postmodern accomplishment was to unite these two qualities, to mute the modern's boast and cry by having each cancel the other out in the cheery tone and anxious metre of the postmodern consumer's everyday life.

We will follow the ups and downs of this liberty and its accompanying anguish as they develop in Warhol's life, from his childhood in the grisly working-class Pittsburgh of the 1930s through his art school training and various professional accomplishments and on to his high-profile later life as a full-blown American icon in league with the movie stars and politicians he fawned over and who he turned into expressions of his own distinctive style and its corresponding conception of the world.

If there is one key problematic that can be said to carry through our inquiry as a whole, it concerns the commingling of liberty and anguish and the corollary possibility of freedom without anguish, freedom without loneliness. To speak of 'Citizen Warhol' is already to imply a political philosophy, a system of governance and a set of ideals that authorizes and enables that citizen status. Our concern will not only be to see and understand that distinctively postmodern, post-theological, post-Enlightenment, post-political citizenship in the life and work of Warhol – a citizenship without trust in God, without belief in society, without faith in government, without the old political longing for a better future world, a citizenship, in other words, without the usual trappings of a social contract – but also to critically appraise it. In this way, Warhol's life represents not only a story to be narrated but also a symptom to be diagnosed or vital sign to be gauged and developed. Our diagnosis, in the end, will fall on the side of death rather than vitality or life, but our concern will be with the ways in which a new form of citizenship – the form we find ourselves cleaving to today – arose from the ashes of what it had once been.

The terms 'postmodern' and 'modern' mean many things, of course, but in one sense they have always been a conterminous couplet representing two views about the human consequences of industrialization. The history of modern art has always been a contest between these two views, these two notions of becoming, where one is understood to be liberalizing and the other enlightening, one associated with the principle of freedom from authority and the other with freedom to participate in and direct that authority. The original philosophical roots of this contest are clear enough: on one side John Locke and David Hume had it that 'Reason is, and ought only to be the slave of the passions, and can never pretend to any other office than to serve and obey them', while on the other we have Rousseau and Kant, with their world-changing understanding of 'the freedom to make public use of one's reason in all matters'.[11] Where one side privatizes the other makes public; where one isolates the exercise of reason in individual experience, the other socializes reason by making it a civic process, a process not of the body alone but instead of the body politic. Where one speaks in the voice of the labourer or the consumer or the property-owner or the slave, the other speaks the language of the citizen.

Such a distinction between private and public reason and their attendant freedoms was a significant issue in the labour- and

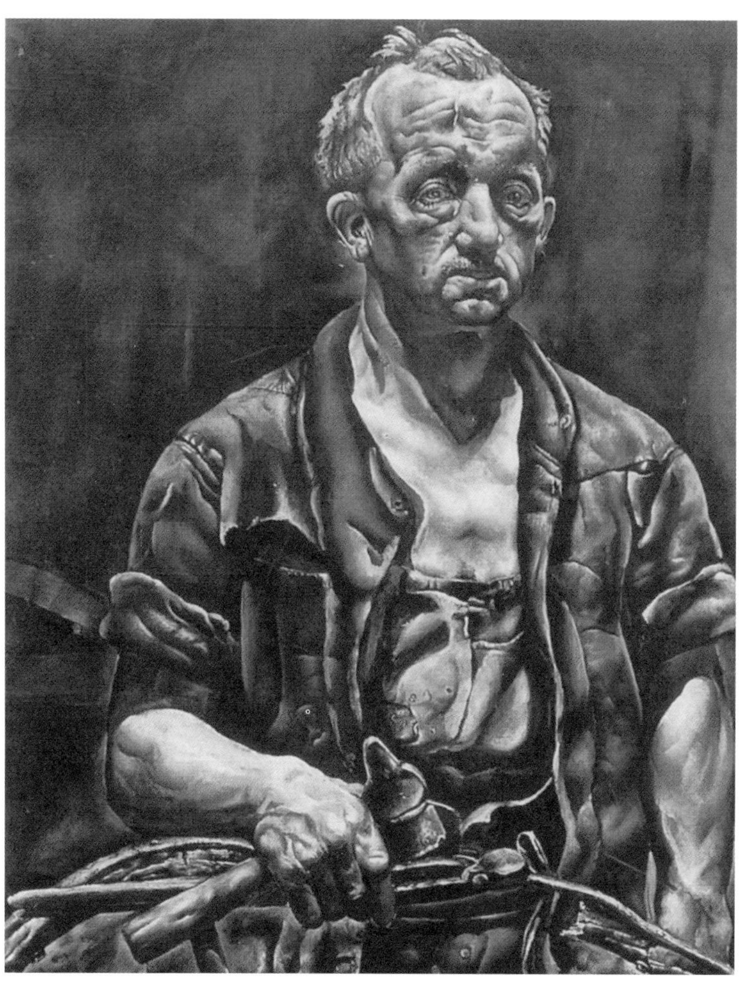

4 Ivan Le Lorraine Albright, *Among Those Left*, 1928–9, oil on canvas.

5 Diego Rivera, *The Making of a Fresco Showing the Building of a City* (detail), 1931, fresco.

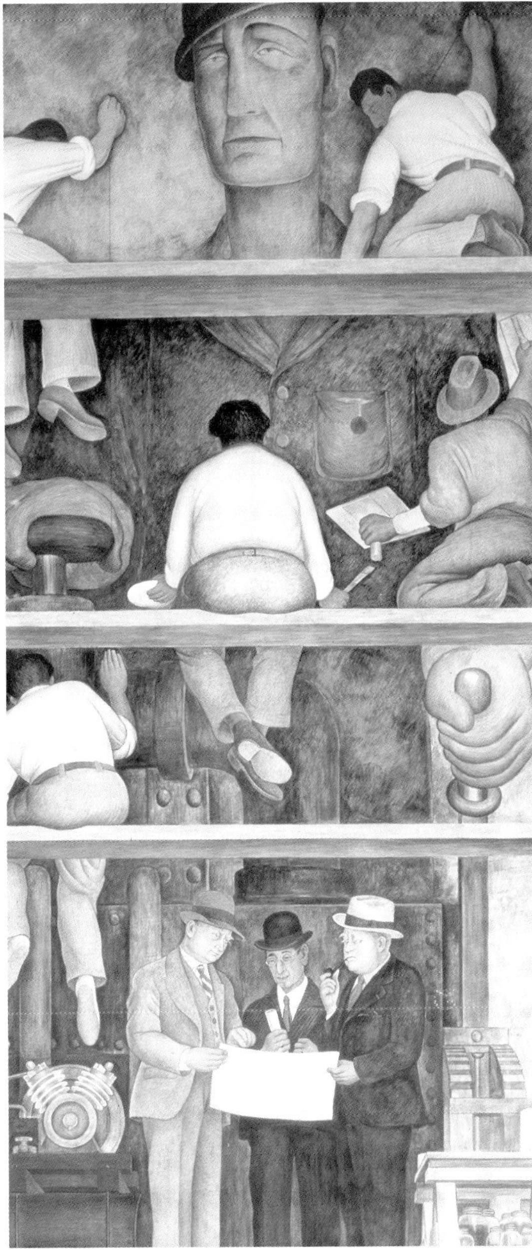

smog-infused atmosphere of industrial Pittsburgh during the 1930s and '40s, when Warhol was growing up. Man was at a crossroads, as the title of Diego Rivera's Rockefeller Center mural put it in 1934, and that intersection centred first and foremost on the figure of the industrial labourer as the pivot point for that future. Its crux was the crisis industrialization has always brought to the fore: the loss of artisanal skill to cog-in-the-machine alienation on the one hand, and the gain of new powers of economic, social and political cooperation enabled by that same alienation, on the other.

One artist concerned with such old-world losses whose work Warhol would have been familiar with was Ivan Albright. In particular, he would have known Albright's painting of a forlorn blacksmith, cast as a vestige for the new industrial age, *Among Those Left* (1928–9), exhibited in the 1939 Carnegie International and purchased for the museum's permanent collection in 1949 (illus. 5). He would certainly have also known the work of Rivera and his fellow Mexican muralists, less from having seen the murals in person and more from their place in the news and in the esteem of his art school instructors. Rivera more than his colleagues was a media staple until his death in 1957, with puff pieces about his artistic genius mixing routinely with reports about his health and illnesses, marriages and divorces, and his battles and repeated efforts to make up with Leon Trotsky, the Communist Party and his various patrons and supporters. In particular, Warhol would have been keenly aware of what *The New York Times* called the 'chief vice of the new art'. 'Everybody' in the art of the late 1930s, the paper reported,

> looks like a Mexican, nearly always like a Mexican peon. It is the influence of Diego Rivera carried to the point of blind imitation. Now it is well enough to borrow Rivera's proletarian gospel and make everybody look like a candidate

> for the barricades . . . [and to] do it with an air of having just read Karl Marx's *Kapital*.[12]

While this report was overreaching in its claim about figurative art of the 1930s, its account of period body types and political attitudes is fair enough. Substantial bodies, labouring hands, determined gazes, cooperative interaction, public-scale art – this was the 'air of having just read Karl Marx's *Kapital*', the air of making 'public use of one's reason' rather than making it a 'slave of the passions'.

What the influence of Rivera and his ilk meant, more than anything else, was the Rousseauian or Kantian promise of enlightenment, the promise of a social subject born of that public exercise of reason. It was this expectation that Warhol was especially effective at deflating. What else did his downward recontextualization of Mao and Lenin and Christ or his upward recontextualization of soup cans and Brillo boxes and Coke bottles and dollar bills mean socially, politically, historically, artistically? By bringing the high ground of faith and conviction-driven world-building together with the low ground of immediate market-based satisfactions in the nebulous mid-ground of art, these gestures offered his viewers the release of social death. This was the great pleasure of Warhol's life and work: a reprieve from the inherited demand to build and embody social institutions; deliverance from the weighty desire for enlightenment and the residual guilt still tethering social norms to an earlier moment's Protestant work ethic; and a newly liberated, freshly emboldened turn to the smaller but more frequent and tangible pleasures of ownership and being owned.

In addition to our origins, of course, we are all made up of a confluence of external influences and aims that often contradict, complicate and interfere with one another while still allowing us to become something more (or less) than the life we were born into. Such was the case for Warhol as much as anyone else. This study is broken into two larger sections. 'Part I: Interiors' is devoted to those of Warhol's influences that would eventually take him beyond his origins by helping him remake the idea of modern art: his devout religious upbringing (chapter One); the distinctive immigrant, working-class environment he was raised in (chapter Two); his role as a child fan (chapter Three); his first foray into artistic transgression (chapter Four); and the suppression and redirection of that transgressive impulse by his art school training (chapter Five). Each of these, it will be argued, helps us to see the contours of his interior life that he would come to be so effective at hiding. 'Part II: Exteriors' focuses on the resulting desires, aims, roles and exteriorized expressions that confirmed Warhol's arrival in that 'beyond': his making of the nondescript into an endearing style or sensibility unto itself (chapter Six); his transformation of that sensibility from an expression of youthful innocence into a disaffected worldliness (chapter Seven) and a two-edged, passive-aggressive mix of sweetness and malevolence (chapter Eight); and, finally, into the greatest of all expressions of the Americanization of, and thereby the globalization of, civic imagination and social belonging (chapter Nine).

In this respect the story of Warhol's development, as we will follow it, is roughly chronological, but it will not be narrated with a 'first this happened, then that, then this' approach. Instead, each of these key moments in his life is considered as a portal into larger historical questions so that a fuller understanding of the significance of his work can emerge, particularly as these open up the meaning and significance of the key influences on his life and work. Each of these contextual studies draws out an important facet of Warhol's distinctively influential sensibility more than any event-by-event narration of his life could provide, and in this sense this book is better understood as a work of art history, social history or intellectual history than as one of conventional biography.

That said, Warhol's life followed the pattern of many who successfully realized the American Dream in the twentieth century, and its key developments can be lined up pretty quickly. His parents were part of the big wave of immigration at the beginning of the century, leaving their home in Miková, Slovakia, a Rusyn village of approximately 150 residents in the Carpathian Mountains, near the borders of Poland and Ukraine. Like many other Central Europeans they settled in Pittsburgh; the family lived in an ethnic ghetto and Warhol's mother Julia aimed to preserve much of their cultural heritage as a buffer against the battery of urban, industrial life, while his father Ondrej supported them as best he could through work in construction. Andrew Warhola was born in 1928 and was raised with the split sensibility of many children of immigrants: on the one hand, he spoke Rusyn at home and was deeply integrated into the old-world Byzantine or Eastern Rite Catholicism of his parents, and on the other he was schooled in American popular culture through movies, radio and comic books and in the distinctive artistic culture of Pittsburgh that flowered from the lavish patronage of Andrew Carnegie. He was a bright, sensitive and shy boy who was most comfortable in the company of girls, his mother Julia or alone, drawing and entertaining himself with popular culture. By all accounts his first real attachment outside the family was with the Hollywood persona of the child star Shirley Temple in 1936, when they were both eight years old, an attachment, needless to say, that was never reciprocated. Warhol suffered several childhood traumas that helped structure his ambitions later on: by his own report, he was introduced to sex at the age of five, when he witnessed one young boy being forced to perform fellatio on another by a group of older children; when he was eight he was temporarily stricken with a severe nervous ailment that kept him out of school for several

months; and when he was fourteen his father died, an event
that further complicated the young Warhol's already fraught
emotional life by creating a greater economic burden for the
family as a whole.

Even though his own personal and artistic inclinations were
generally consumerist and thereby anti-social, he was trained
in an artistic environment unusually focussed by Carnegie's
strong theory of the social value of art, from the time of his
first Saturday art classes at the age of ten and through his
college education. Warhol tried rebelling against this dominant
emphasis on social aesthetics and social self-understanding in
various ways but was forced back in line by instructors and,
during his time as a freelance commercial artist in the 1950s,
art directors. This led him to develop a distinctively duplici-
tous approach that effectively deflated the high-minded dream
of collaborative labour turned to collaborative politics expected
by his teachers and supervisors who came of age in the era
of industry, unions and socially minded art. In its place,
Warhol helped to reassert the anti-social imagination that
arises from the consumer's fetishization of things that would
take on new global significance in the wake of the Second
World War. More than any other artist or cultural figure of
the time, Warhol thereby gave expression to the underlying
transition from a Fordist industrial economy to a post-Fordist
consumer economy and the resulting transformations to our
affective way of being in the world. In other words, Warhol's
was an art of consumers not producers, of passive reproduction rather than active transformation, of performativity rather
than enlightenment. This meant that his role as a vanguard
artist, as a latter-day bearer of modernism's 'shock of the
new', could only ever be indirect, could only ever be passive-
aggressive. This indirection is the psychosocial measure of
the citizenship, and of political being generally, that he has
bequeathed to us.

Such a passive-aggressive, oblique or two-sided approach would be the basis for the organization both of Warhol's professional identity and his mature work as an artist around a single, profoundly influential theme: the increasing enclosure of human experience within the commodity form or consumer's experience of life. First and foremost, this sense of enclosure meant that the double-sidedness at issue would be defined by the distinction between inside and outside, self and world, and that its measure of success would be the degree to which the boundary between the two could be made crystalline, inviolable to conveyances from the outside in, to be sure, but also from inside out. Instead, the two sides would meet at the mirror that separated them. The boundary between self and world – the 'skin ego', as it is sometimes called – would become Warhol's topic more than anything else.[13]

This progressive splitting and mirroring between self and world was highlighted at key moments during Warhol's professional career: when he won Art Directors Club awards, first for his role as a 'cheaper Ben Shahn', drawing big, clunky, labouring bodies, and later for the cartoonishly exaggerated, thin and linear elegance of the shoes and feet he drew for the I. Miller shoe company; his first successful art exhibitions featuring soup can paintings and Brillo box sculptures that seemed at once to be both fine and commercial art; his rendering of shocking human tragedy and the most heated social issues of his day as if they were somehow the same as soup cans and Brillo boxes in his 'Death and Disaster' exhibitions and related projects; his increasing social success as a flattened, tabloid-ready image complete with wig as a signature fashion accessory; his successful reincarnation as an avant-garde movie mogul, rock music impresario and lifestyle magazine publisher; his single-handed resuscitation of society portraiture as a viable upmarket vanguard art form; and his despoliation of political portraiture as a socially significant form of cultural expression. In each of these instances what came through increasingly emphatically was the sensitivity and genius of Warhol's artistic impression of how modern life had changed, already in the early, heady days of the American century and all the more in the later decolonizing and 'Coca-colonizing', de-Europeanizing and Americanizing, post-war, post-Fordist, globalizing world.

While the method of this study is episodic and burrows deeply into the contexts surrounding key moments in Warhol's life, its overarching narrative is oriented in a conventional biographical manner, towards the realization of the artist's own aims: towards his 'superstardom', as he called it, his 'becoming-image' or 'becoming-commodity' as we might call it, and all the horizontal extension and vertical deterioration of the basic aspects of his humanity that such a role entails. The tragicomic aspects of his story (like those of most people perhaps) turn on the conflicted character of his aims even more than the contexts that spawned them. It doesn't seem too super-cilious to say that how we imagine and sometimes achieve our own glory is regularly a funny affair. Often this amounts to being too full of ourselves, too enamoured with our own distinctive identity as we see it reflected in the faces of friends and family, enemies and competitors, itemized on a résumé or in the rippling waters of the mass media and other forums for public recog-nition. In Warhol's case, however, the humour lies mostly in his aspiring to become somebody by being nobody, of summoning up all that he had within himself to lose his identity, to become 'The Nothingness Himself', as he liked to put It.[14] In Truman Capote's words, 'He would have liked to have been anybody except Andy Warhol', and in a sense he got exactly what he wanted: to become a superstar by being anything and every-thing but himself.[15]

Our primary burden in these pages will be to make sense of that nothingness, to understand what it meant as a historical category in the same way we might make historical sense of categories such as 'enlightened', say, or 'modern', 'religious' or 'secular'. In this regard we will need to delve deep into the historicity of nothingness as a category of experiencing oneself by considering what it meant in the contexts out of which it arose – its meaning for Warhol as a devout Byzantine Rite Catholic, for example, or for Warhol as a 'Hunky', or Central European working-class immigrant, or as a sensitive, gay boy in a rough-and-tumble industrial city, or as an obsessively, even pathologically devoted fan in an era of burgeoning mass culture, or for Warhol as a deeply private artist subject to the public-interest values of an art world still under the sway of Roosevelt's New Deal. In the end, what makes the nothingness of The Nothingness Himself so compelling is not its psychology or idiosyncrasy but instead the way in which it was formed historically as a point of confluence or convergence of a variety of social pressures, and thus tells us something not only about Warhol's world but also about the world we find ourselves in today. In this regard we will try our best to avoid the cult of personality that Warhol's life and work might otherwise (and regularly does) inspire, and instead abide by the rudimentary critical premise, as Friedrich Engels once put it, that history is never simply the product of great individuals and cannot be narrated in simple biographical time but instead arises from 'conflicts between many individual wills' or 'an infinite series of parallelograms of forces which give rise to one resultant – the historical event'.[16] The event that Andy Warhol marks better than any other is the historic transformation of political subjectivity from modernity into our own day.

As such, it might be said that our interest in Warhol's life arises most productively (and most honestly) from a desire to see how we are reflected there, to take him as the mirror he claimed to be: to read his place in history like an oracle in order to see who we are and what we believe, and to see Warhol, and by extension ourselves, as Engels's 'historical event'. 'I am like a

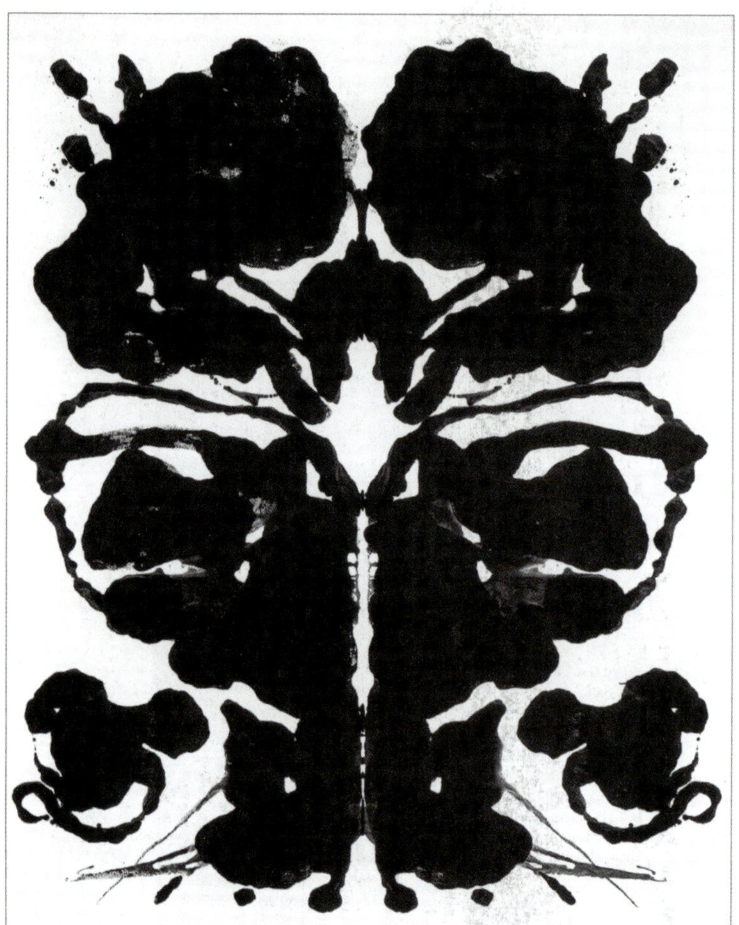

6 Andy Warhol, *Rorschach*, 1984, acrylic on linen, 416.6 x 292.1 x 5.1 cm.

Rorschach test', Barack Obama said at one point during his presidential campaign in 2008, 'even if people find me disappointing ultimately, they might gain something'.[17] Warhol's role has often been much the same and, like Obama, his reflection of who we are has played an active historical role, somehow enabling us to be that which we otherwise would not allow ourselves to be, even if it may have done so to unintended effect. Emile de Antonio, the film-maker and star of Warhol's

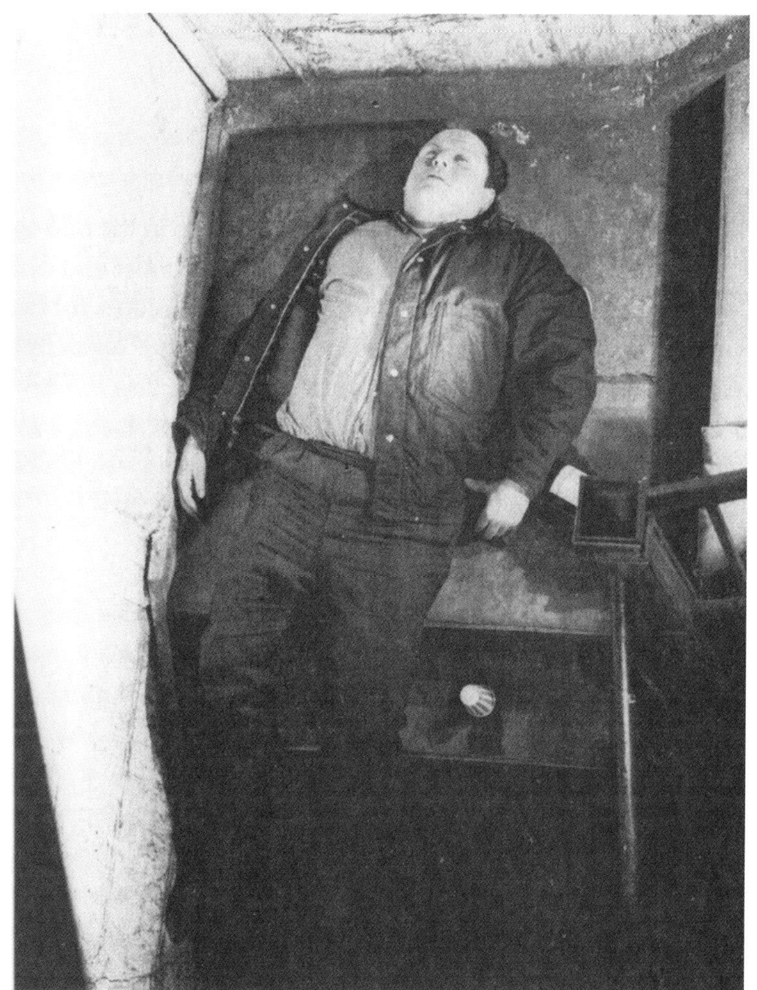

7 Billy Name, production still from Andy Warhol, *Drunk*, 1964.

never-released film *Drunk* (1965, in which he sat in a stairwell by himself, drank a quart of scotch in half an hour and passed out: illus. 7), put it this way: 'Andy's like the Marquis de Sade in the sense that his very presence was a releasing agent which released people so they could live out their fantasies and get undressed' – or, we might add, get really, really drunk – 'or, in some cases, do very violent things to get Andy to watch them'.[18]

Warhol, it might be said, has the same effect on us: he is also our releasing agent, which brings us back to the face-off between the two great modern secular ideals, between the collective's progress towards enlightenment and the individual's pursuit of happiness; between principles that bind us together and the overturning of principles that sidetrack our desire; between the social and cultural implications of socialism in its broadest sense and those of capitalism understood as a way of life; between liberty with anguish, and freedom without. It was America and Americanization that Warhol represented to the post-war world more than anything else, so there is no little inevitability to the view of ourselves that we will see reflected there. Frank Stella may have summed up this sense of where history was heading most concisely on 5 June 1968, the day that Robert Kennedy was shot in Los Angeles by Sirhan Sirhan and two days after Warhol had been shot by Valerie Solanas in New York: 'Bobby's going to die and Andy's going to live', Stella said, 'That's the way the world is.'[19]

Indeed, it might be said, that is the way the world was, and it has been the direction of history for a long time now. Warhol's life and the attributes we most associate with it – the

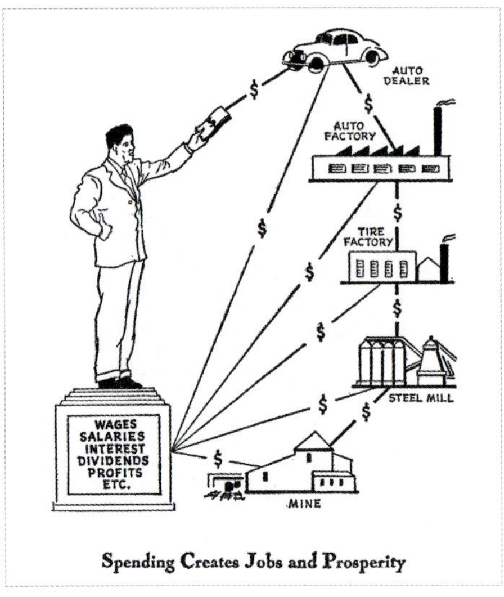

Spending Creates Jobs and Prosperity

8 'Spending Creates Jobs and Prosperity', from Robert Nathan, *Mobilizing for Abundance* (1944).

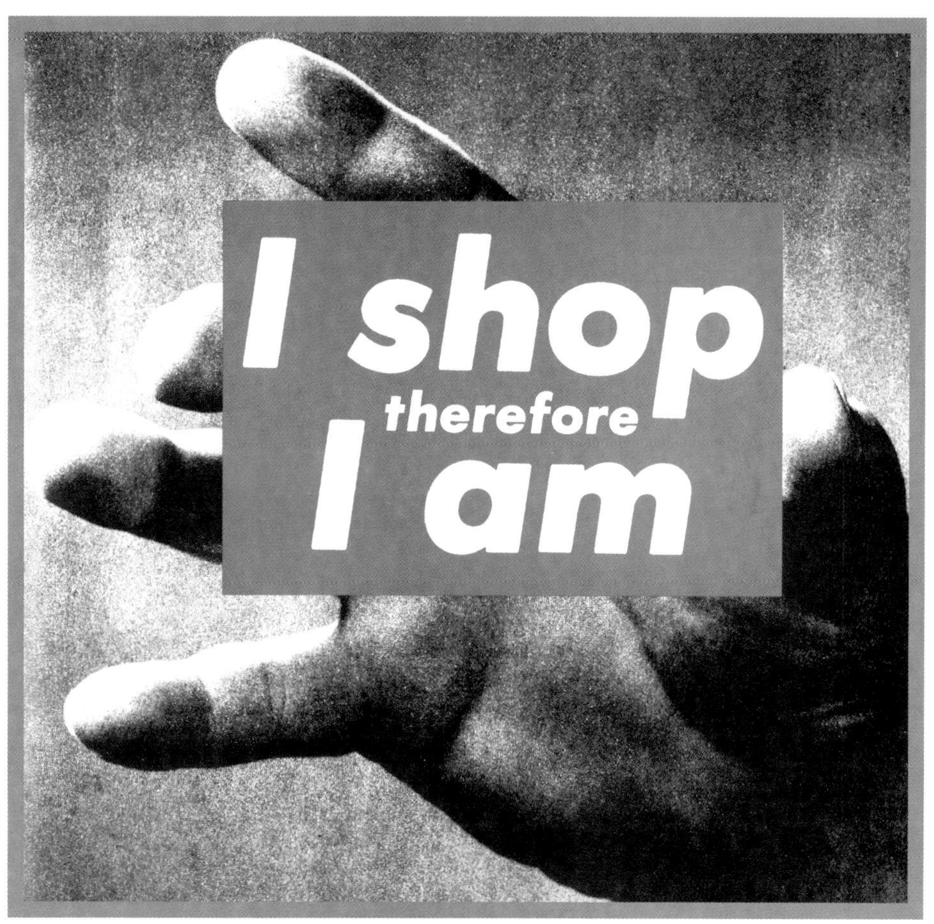

9 Barbara Kruger, *Untitled (I shop therefore I am)*, 1987, photographic silkscreen/vinyl, 281.9 × 287 cm.

unrestrained consumption of things
and images, for example, or the
freeing of sexuality, lifestyle and
belief from traditional constraints,
or simply the great, unbridled promise
of self-creation – are inseparable from
the magisterial 'Pax Americana' of
the second half of the twentieth
century, with its spread of Coca-
Cola, Hollywood films and nuclear
bomb technology around the world,
and the multidirectional, multidimen-
sional globalization that would flower
from it at century's end. It is also at
odds with the 1960s dream of shared
responsibility for remaking the
world in an emergent-socialist form
associated with Jack and Bobby Kennedy, Martin Luther King,
Jr, Dag Hammarskjöld and many others and summed up by
memorable speech lines such as King's hallowed dream of
finally realizing the yet unattained promises of democracy,
and Kennedy's resounding plea to bypass the whole question
of social entitlement and go straight to the promise of civic
responsibility for reimagining the social and political world.

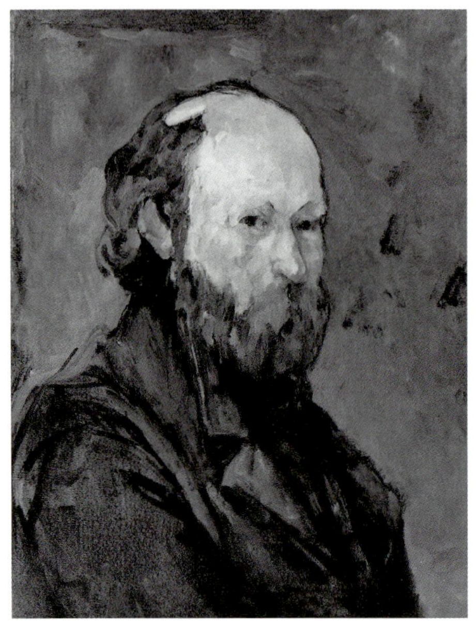

10 Paul Cézanne,
Self-portrait,
1878–80,
oil on canvas.

The high-minded democratic universalism of the 1960s
was fleeting, however, and, broadly understood, anachronistic.
Cultural particularism would dominate throughout the Cold
War period as a proxy for post-war political and economic
realignment and as the new, fluid medium of the Pax Americana.
The momentary appeal to universalism in the speeches of King
and Kennedy would be lost to the overriding particularism of
the age, which would triumph through an unanticipated alliance
between the social liberalism of the New Left and the economic
liberalism of the new right.[20] It was the post-war concept of

culture more than anything else that enabled this unconscious convergence, and which Warhol came to represent better than anyone else. 'Suddenly', as one scholar has put it about the coming into consciousness of the new way of the world, 'everyone discovered that culture had been mass produced like Ford's cars: the masses had a culture and culture had a mass. Culture was everywhere, no longer the property of the cultured or cultivated.'[21] Such was the great postmodern way out of the old modern trap of national identity and the travesty it came to represent most profoundly in the Second World War: by making the shift from Culture with a capital 'C' to culture with a small 'c', from culture as the property of the cultivated elite to culture as the property of each and every consumer, from Western civilization to globalizing multiculturalism, identity could be de-normalized, radically pluralized, and detached from singular aims of nation, community, family, blood, reason, God.

11 Christopher Makos, *Andy Warhol at the Pergamon Museum*, 1982.

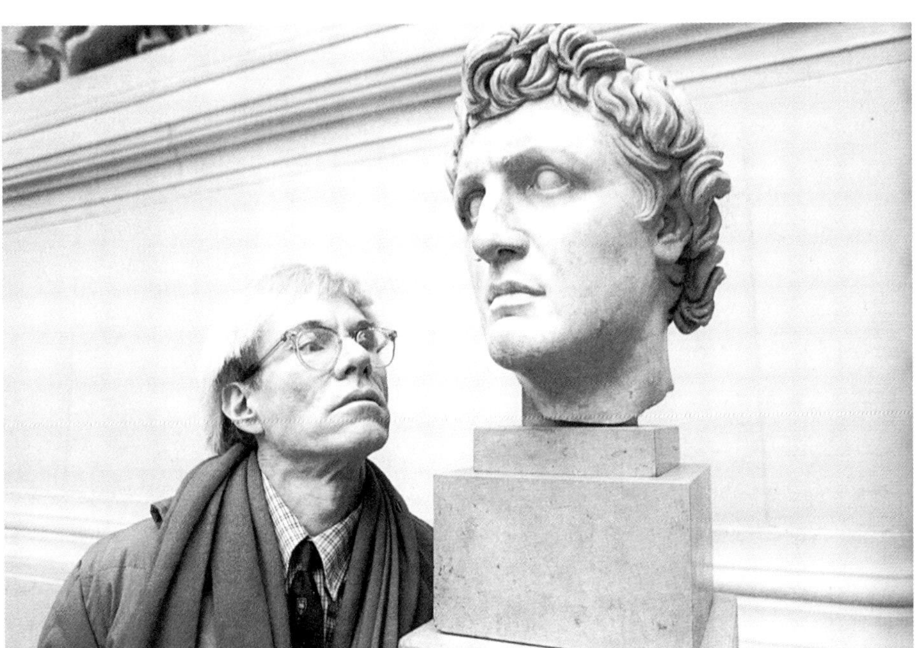

This is just to say that culture was commodified, routed from its prior monopoly status as the taste of an elite that may or may not trickle down to that of the universal bourgeois or universal worker, to a new role designating an equivalent unit of exchange within a competitive marketplace of images, attitudes and ideas. Culture came to stand for localized identity rather than for civilization as a whole, for attitude or neighbourhood rather than tradition or enlightenment. Warhol stands as the pre-eminent artist of this transformation in the same sense that, say, Leonardo da Vinci can be said to be the most exemplary artistic representative of the dramatic historical changes associated with the Renaissance, or Jacques-Louis David the artist who developed the best visual vocabulary for the revolutionary bourgeoisie, or Albert Speer the figure who best gave form to the visual and spatial language of Nazism. In each of these cases art exercised its specific value not only by reflecting but also enabling historical change.

Artists are concerned with form, and the primary formal problem they face is representing the governing model of supersensible transcendence, or the social and epistemological infrastructure of understanding and experiencing the world. 'I call all cognition *transcendental* that is occupied not so much with objects but rather with our mode of cognition of objects insofar as this is to be possible a priori', insofar as we can know objects before we experience them, is how Kant explained this concern.[22] One form of supersensible transcendence is not necessarily the same as another, however, just as one formal expression of transcendence or one mode of cognition is not like all others.

We will be addressing the ways in which Warhol's work gives expression to the last of four great, broadly overlapping periods that define modernity, each giving form to those conditions of knowing or experiencing the world: a vast pre-modern period in which one notion or another of God provides the terms for that transcendence; a second period spanning from the Renaissance to the Enlightenment, in which the concept of the aesthetic emerges and effectively hollows out the religious world view by providing an alternative frame for experience; a third that spans the long nineteenth century, in which the vulnerability and productivity of labour provide the basic philosophical organization of experience; and a final period that begins in the nineteenth century but finds its ultimate geopolitical justification after the two world wars, in which consumerism comes to be the ordering principle that gives us the way by which, as Kant said, we can know objects before we experience them. In other words, we in the West and the Westernizing world have come to experience day-to-day existence primarily through the a priori of shopping. As *Fortune* editor William H. Whyte could announce over a half century ago in 1956, for example, 'thrift is now un-American', and so it continues, at least up through the present economic recession (illus. 8).[23] The economic, political and intellectual history of the emergence of this world view is complex and multifaceted but, for our purposes here, we can simply acknowledge that consumerism has been our cosmology, our taste, our version of modernity, and that other concerns we might have about the world fall in line behind it. The old Barbara Kruger adage 'I shop therefore I am' stands as a suitable summary statement for who we have been for some time now, for who we have become (illus. 9).

Andy Warhol is the artist who allows us to reflect on that condition in the broadest, deepest and most detailed manner. He is our Leonardo, our David or our Speer. More than any other cultural icon, he helped to effect the transition from the old worlds of God, reason and labour to the new world of consumption we still find ourselves in today. In this way he has helped make us who we are. As Roland Barthes put it in 1980, 'however much pop art has depersonalized the world, platitudinized objects, dehumanized images, replaced traditional craftsmanship of the canvas by machinery, some "subject" remains. What subject? The one who looks, in the absence of the one who makes', the one who consumes in lieu of the one who produces, the one who shops instead of the one who thinks, the one who desires instead of the one who believes.[24] Of course, our world now may be becoming something else again under pressure from globalization and its resultant rise in the economic status of China and India, for example, or the increasing political prominence of Islamic fundamentalism and other forms of neo-religiosity or, even, the technologically enabled acceleration of our capacity to 'organize without organizations', as one commentator puts it.[25] But this only means that getting the epoch of the consumer – and the artist that has best represented it – understood correctly is of all the greater importance. Such, at any rate, is the premise of this book.

That epoch, again, first arose in the last years of the nineteenth century as a later-born twin to the epoch of the industrial labourer, and cannot be separated from the rise of modernism as a response to the new, fantastic, increasingly endless and incessant world of industrially produced commodities. Above all, this meant the production of the new as such. Modernism responded to this state of affairs ambivalently, incorporating the promise of newness into itself but locating that newness primarily in form, as a way of distinguishing its version of the novel from that of the world that surrounded it. 'It was a kind of internal exile, a retreat into the territory of form,' one scholar has written, 'but form [that] was ultimately a crucible, an act of aggression, an abyss into which all the comfortable "givens" of the culture were sucked and then spat out.'[26] The traditional institutional authorities of Church, state, family and so on were part of what was sucked into this crucible, of course, but the single most significant 'comfortable "given"' to be incorporated and then expunged by modernism was the new, extra-institutional authority of the shiny and alluring commodity, which was increasingly reorienting experience to a novel world of fluctuating relations and abandoning the old world of established, immobile things.[27] By incorporating the world into itself and remaking it in form, the artworks of modernist artists like Manet or Cézanne or Picasso were able to provide a kind of rejoinder to the rapid shape-shifting of modernity (illus. 10). The primary result of this approach was a kind of agonized inwardness wherein the uncertainty about the rapidly changing world 'out there' was taken up as a new uncertainty about the world inside, and the art that resulted played out one version or another of alienation or doubt or despair.

What will be of interest for our purposes are the ways in which Warhol carries forward the modernist legacy of subjective complexity born of objective circumstances, without the modernists' internal exile or retreat into the territory of form and its complementary outward expression as public displays of alienation, doubt and despair. More important than simply observing this hardening of the modernist divide between self and world as a marker of his postmodernism, however, will be the questions of how and why he was able to make this shift. Much of the analysis that will give us access to these greater questions will necessarily turn on various biographical details – his immigrant upbringing, for example, or his complicated sexuality or, more important still, his distinctive religiosity. But what will be of greatest interest for us is not the biographical details themselves, or even how they helped to form and direct Warhol's mature artistic sensibility, but instead how those details and their influence affected the world that, in its turn, made him into the superstar he longed to become.

Like anyone's life, many of the details of Warhol's were banal, uninteresting, minimally consequential for the meaning and significance of his life's work. This was as true of the glittering

Warhol featured in the society pages as it was of the nuts-and-bolts Warhol doing his shopping, paying his bills and taking care of his rudimentary daily affairs. In the end, in other words, what is most deserving of our attention is not Warhol himself – just as is the case with Leonardo, David, Speer or any other – but instead the deeply historical picture of ourselves that he can give back to us.

PART ONE
INTERIORS

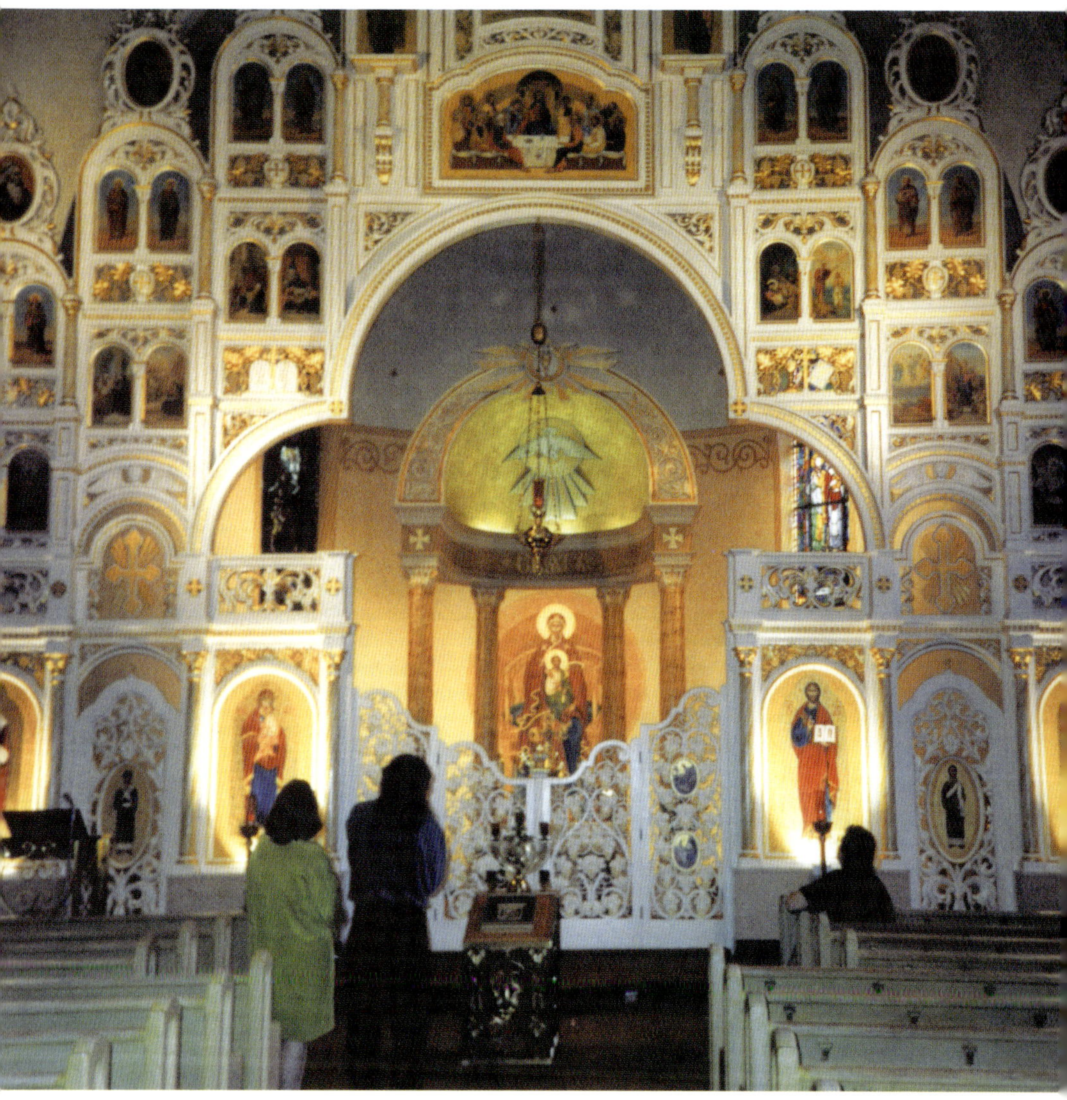

12 Iconostasis, St John Chrysostom Byzantine Catholic Church, Pittsburgh.

1
JESUS CHRIST

According to the Warhola family, Andy's mother Julia was his single greatest influence: 'Her creative talents were the main source of Andy's artistic genius', they say without qualification on the family website devoted to Warhol's life and career.[1] Indeed, by all accounts Julia came from a background rich in art making and appreciation. She was known within her family particularly for her love of drawing, decorating, and collecting images, and it seems without a doubt that she passed her talent and enthusiasm on to her youngest son Andy more than to her older sons John and Paul. She would also later serve as his assistant during his years as a commercial artist, specializing in lettering, among other things, including signing his name. She even won a prestigious Art Directors Club award under the name Andy Warhol's Mother, for an album cover design composed only of her lettering.

This affinity for and facility with art making and collecting is important for any understanding of Warhol's work, but we might also raise the broader question of what art and creativity meant for Mrs Warhola and what part of that meaning she, in turn, passed on to her son. After all, even modern art, with its emphasis on formal innovation and its disassociation from the will of its patrons, was never simply craft but instead gained its status as art qua art by being vested to a certain degree with larger desires and beliefs. For example, modern art has drawn inspiration and purpose from politics – think of what art meant to Jacques-Louis David or Gustave Courbet, or to Albert Speer or Vladimir Tatlin, in the context of the political transformations they lived through; art has also sought to represent the ideal of personal liberation from social norms – consider Caspar David Friedrich's *Wanderer above the Sea of Fog*, or Manet's *Le Déjeuner sur l'herbe*, or pretty much any work by Paul Klee; and so too, albeit less commonly since the eighteenth century, it has served devotional purposes – for example in the work of Maurice Denis or Georges Rouault, or even Barnett Newman. Pinning down exactly the specific meaning of art for this or that artist is less important than simply acknowledging that there is some larger meaning there, some larger unfulfilled desire or ambition, and understanding how that desire motivates and animates the work that they create. Typically, we might assume, that desire attaches itself to a confused mix of meanings and unfulfilled desires, with early attachments often shifting with the winds of historical change and the onset of new needs and influences.

By every account, Julia Warhola was a very devout woman, praying regularly, attending church services many times per week and covering the walls of the family home with a rich assortment of religious imagery, including, most importantly for our purposes, icons. This was nothing unusual for working-class immigrants, particularly in a multi-ethnic environment like Pittsburgh. Much more so in the first decades of the twentieth century than now, much more so in Pittsburgh than many other places, and much more for Eastern Europeans than many others, religious life not only provided a protected enclave of familiar rituals and the comforts of common belief but, just below the surface, it was also a site of geopolitical negotiation and conflict for a rapidly changing world. For example, just as American Jewish organizations and European Islamic groups and the forms of religiosity they cultivate today play a significant role in the larger geopolitical tensions, strife and occasional resolutions thereof in the Middle East, so too did rapidly growing institutions like the American Byzantine Catholic Church play a significant role in the tensions leading up to and following the First World War.[2] Julia Warhola's religious life, in short, represented a complex, deep-seated and living relationship to belief rather than being a merely nostalgic cultural residue leftover from her former life in a rural Carpatho-Rusyn district in northeastern Slovakia.

According to reports from his siblings, Andy Warhol had special status in the family for taking after his mother in this regard as well: while his brothers and father would go to church dutifully for the high service on Sundays, for example, Andy would go with his mother to a Saturday evening service and three on Sunday. Given the general impression of Warhol's work and public image, this degree of religiosity is mildly surprising, if understandable for a child, but there is a lot of testimony from his friends and associates that confirms it carried on throughout his adult life. His art school friend and first roommate in New York, Philip Pearlstein, for instance, noted that 'All the time I lived with Andy, he was very quiet and went to church a couple of mornings a week.'[3] Reports from friends visiting the first apartment Warhol had on his own focus on the religious imagery they saw there, one noting that it was furnished with 'a picture of Christ pointing to his Sacred Heart, and that's about it', and another providing this description:

> It was very small, two rooms, and just candle-lit. The walls were painted like a Rousseau jungle – the entire thing, ceiling, walls – so that you were in a lush Rousseau jungle right down to the little tigers staring at you. A candle swung on a chain, suspended, and as it swung, it illumin-ated a portrait of St Barbara, the black saint, with her

slashes. I asked, 'What's she doing there?' He said, 'Well, look at all the slashings. Read up on her'.[4]

In all likelihood, the image referred to was not a portrait of St Barbara but instead a reproduction of the well-known and much-venerated Black Madonna of Częstochowa, said since 1656 to be 'Queen' and miraculous protector of Poland, a status attributed in part to the slashes on her cheek (illus. 14). Warhol's rejoinder to look at the slashes and read up on her was, no doubt, meant to refer to this divine protector status.

13 Armoury Chamber Master (Kirill Ulanov?), *An Important Icon of the Mother of God of Jerusalem with Selected Saints in a Silver Oklad*, 18th century, 37 × 31 cm.

So too his eulogist, the art historian John Richardson, reported that Warhol made a habit of dropping in on his local Dominican parish, St Vincent Ferrer, several days per week until shortly before he died, and regularly helped out serving meals to the homeless at an affiliated soup kitchen on holidays.[5] Warhol also kept a Byzantine Orthodox prayer book by his bed and other related devotional objects and imagery nearby. One intimate and longtime assistant, Ronnie Cutrone, when asked what Warhol should be remembered for, said this:

I always say one thing, and it's the weirdest thing. What impressed me most about Andy was his belief in God. It's the one thing that really sticks in my mind. I think when an artist believes in God, he knows he's not God and that makes him a better artist and a much more humble person.[6]

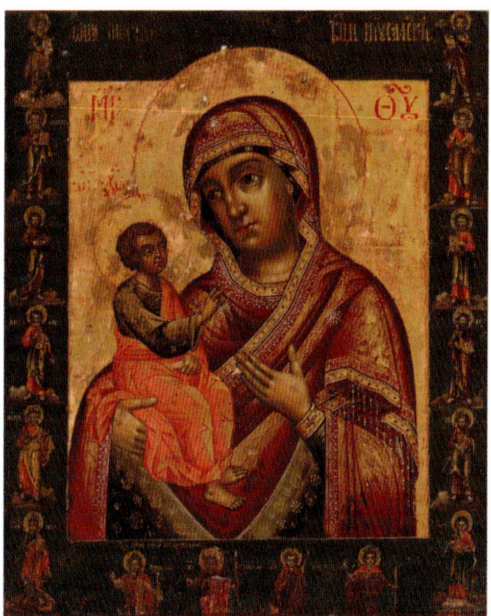

14 The Black Madonna of Częstochowa, Poland.

Something like this account about the centrality of belief for Warhol is consistent among most of those who knew him best.

That said, there is also a long history of Warhol hiding his religiosity from view. 'His religion was a very private part of his life', the photographer, Factory habitué and Warhol familiar Christopher Makos put it.[7] Richardson called it 'his secret piety', saying that Warhol was 'an artist who fooled the world into believing that his only obsessions were money, fame, glamour, and that he was cool to the point of callousness'. Cleverly reversing the polarity of the single greatest truism that runs through nearly all the many accounts of Warhol's life and work – that there is no deeper meaning or conviction motivating Warhol's often provocative statements of personal belief – Richardson concluded, 'Never take Andy at face value.'[8]

We can see early visual evidence of this secretiveness in a well-known work that Warhol completed on assignment in art school as part of an art-cum-visual-sociology exercise completed for his teacher, Robert Lepper. His task was to choose a neighbourhood at random, then a street, then a house, draw some conclusions about what sort of people lived there from the evidence available and then make an image of their living room as he imagined it. Although he did not say so, Warhol chose his own house and his own living room, representing it accurately but effectively de-ethnicizing it by leaving out one sociologically significant detail: the plethora of religious icons that adorned the walls (illus. 15).[9]

All that was left was a single crucifix, a decision that in effect removed his home from the relatively marginal and exotic domain of Byzantine piety that he had grown up with to the more familiar and widely available domain of Roman Catholicism that would be recognizable to teachers, fellow students and friends.

The adult Warhol's praying, church-going, soup-kitchen volunteering and the like rarely made it into his endless accounts of the mundane details of his daily life. This is particularly striking because while Warhol was very reserved about his emotional life – he said that he did not have one – readers of his many reports rarely get a sense that he is withholding the 'who, what, when and where' factual information that served as line items for his daily existence. The man who is best known for his tell-all style, for taking the private form of the diary and making it into a public form of expression, for seemingly trying to have everything and anything enter into representation, maintained some kind of ban or prohibition – some sort of iconoclasm, we might even say – when it came to the details of his religious life.

Negation or refusal of this sort can mean many things, of course. Sometimes it means disavowal, for example, and certainly this was a big part of Warhol's self-creation, his effort to realize the American Dream and create himself anew as 'The Nothingness Himself', embodying the universalism of the commodity form at the expense of his decidedly ethnic past. It can also mean other things, however, and several of these may be more helpful in making sense of the seeming contradiction between the reports of Warhol's deep-seated but very private religiosity on the one hand, and his very public role as emblem for the consumer age on the other.

Of particular value for our purposes as we try to make sense of this negation or refusal, to make sense of his choice to not directly represent his religiosity in the context of his otherwise confessional style, is the distinctive character of Warhol's Byzantine or Eastern Rite Catholic upbringing. This distinction will also be crucial for our understanding of Warhol's mature work as an artist and film-maker. In what follows, we will trace two histories of that negation or refusal: its place in the Eastern or Byzantine Rite theology that was so much a part of Warhol's childhood, and the role it played in the Catholic intellectual tradition that framed his emergence as an adult artist. These are complex histories that we will need to explore in some depth in order to fully understand and appreciate the significance of Warhol's religious upbringing for his mature work.

Generally, Eastern, Byzantine or Constantinopolitan Catholicism is not well understood in the West. While institutionally it is aligned with Western or Latin Rite Roman Catholicism, liturgically it shares the Byzantine Rite, or Rite of Constantinople, with the Eastern Orthodox churches. There are many ways to characterize the distinctive practice and theology that arises from its peculiar place betwixt and between these larger religious traditions – its married priesthood, for example, or its continuing emphasis on monasticism, or the more active role of the congregation, standing throughout the service, chanting and prostrating themselves – but one approach that is useful here is to focus on its unique relationship to images.

There is a long history to this relationship, but its single most important foundational moment was the Byzantine iconoclasm controversy of the eighth and ninth centuries. The iconoclasts' main charge was against the worship of idols, or false gods, in the form of images. Of interest for our purposes, however, was the iconophiles' defence against that charge. Their successful strategy was to incorporate their opponents' iconoclastic critique of the image into the images themselves as a kind of homeopathic ingredient that would ward off the charge of idolatry. It is this distinctive self-protectiveness or defensiveness – the defensiveness of an image that denies its own status as an image – that we will find at the heart of Warhol's mature artistic enterprise.

At the centre of this solution, developed more than a millennium ago, was the theological issue of whether or not images can represent or constitute the multiple states of being associated with Christ – human and divine, or those of man, God and Holy Spirit – and its resolution in the Byzantine theory of the icon, which lives on today first and foremost in Eastern Rite churches such as the one in which Warhol was raised (illus. 16). As one scholar describes the controversy, the iconoclasts failed to recognize what the iconophiles saw in the image: that an icon does not represent 'His divinity or His humanity, but His Person, which inconceivably unites in itself these two natures without confusion and without division.'[10]

15 Andy Warhol, *Living Room*, 1946–7, watercolour and tempera on illustration board, 38.1 × 50.8 cm.

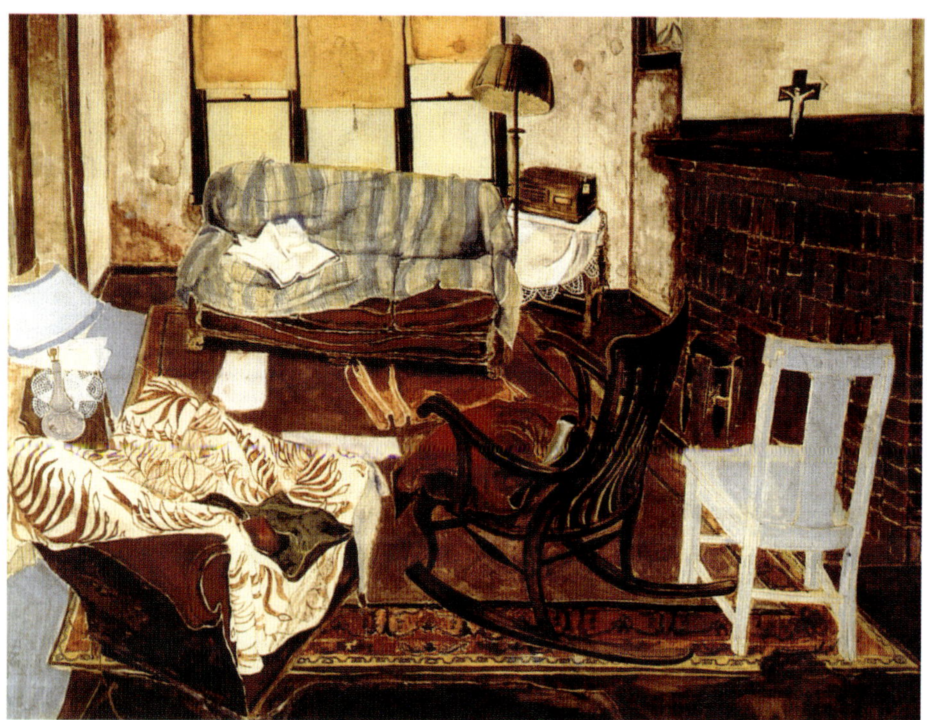

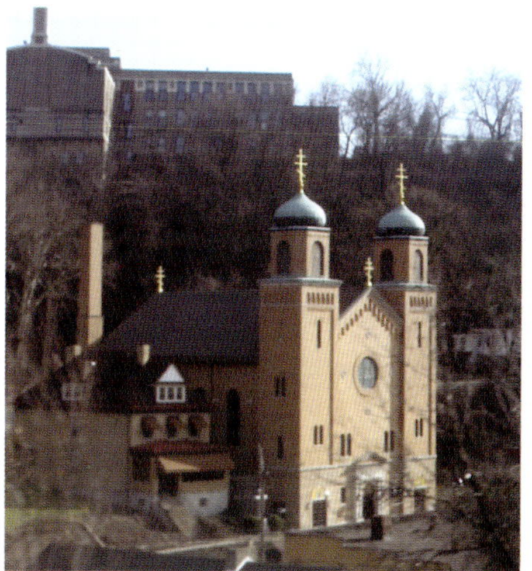

16 St John Chrysostom Byzantine Catholic Church, Pittsburgh.

This theory of the image that finally won out based its claim on the older doctrine of a hypostatic union, or unity of multiple states of being in one entity, but what was new was the theological work of the icon as a material realization of that unity. The resolution of the iconoclasm controversy in the ninth century, a resolution that remains today, was an incorporation of this theological principle into the theory of the image and the experience it provides.

For this study, comparing east and west in order to draw out an understanding of Warhol's distinctive and challenging aesthetic sensibility, the distinguishing characteristic of the iconophilic Byzantine tradition that grew out of this historic debate is the way the doctrine of multiple states of being lived on and was experienced in the material presence of divinity in the icon, rather than in the Word as an immaterial relay from God. The upshot of this Eastern difference is a distinctive relationship with images and a unique model of aesthetic experience – a difference that would come to be the single most significant marker of Warhol's transformation of modern art. Christ's divinity could be represented positively in the Word without fear, but when represented in imagery it was subject to the charge of idolatry.[11] The solution to this problem for the Byzantine Rite liturgical tradition was to privilege apophasis, or a negative theology, in which the image-cum-icon is understood to be more than just a representation. The icon took on a special status distinct from representation by becoming a material incarnation of a theological truth, housing divinity inside or behind its flat surface as a negative or unrepresented interiority or otherness and, thus, as a figure of the doctrine of hypostatic union. Divinity existed as a secret truth or covert life of the icon, as a part of what it was rather than a part of what it represented. As such the icon is not based on a concept of representation at all but instead on a manner of substitution or extension, inhabitation or possession.

It is this idea of inhabitation or possession that we will see in Warhol's work, and it will be at the heart of how we characterize his postmodernism. Take, for example, the art historian Hans Belting's casting of the residual Byzantine view of the icon against the understanding of religious representation that emerged first with the Renaissance, then with the Reformation, the Enlightenment and on to our present day: 'The modern subject, estranged from the world, sees the world as severed into the purely factual and the hidden signification of metaphor', he writes, summing up neatly the tradition of representation that Warhol's work would do more than any other to refute. By contrast, Belting continues, the iconophilic image 'rejected reduction into metaphor' and instead 'laid claim to being immediate evidence of God's presence revealed to the eyes and senses'.[12] Or, as another scholar addressing one aspect of this difference has phrased it (providing us with a more available handle to grasp what is at issue): 'In contrast to our Western notion of mimesis as the imitation of form, Byzantine mimesis is the imitation of presence.'[13] It is precisely that 'imitation of presence' rather than 'imitation of form' that we will see driving Warhol's extraordinary work, but in order to understand how it functions we need first to make sense of how that notion of presence is produced by distancing techniques, how presence cannot be realized and experienced until a eparate space psychologically distant from our own is created for it to inhabit.

This archaic, Byzantine way of relating to images and by extension to the world at large is a form of visuality and a form of spatiality, a historically determined attitude or belief system about seeing and being in the world generally. All such visual and spatial conventions have their tricks or techniques that cultivate specific values and attendant bodily relations or comportments towards the image – an important one of ours, for example, is linear perspective and its legacy in the illusion of three-dimensional space presented on a two-dimensional surface by photography and film. Linear perspective, like photographic vision, creates the illusion of access to a separate world on the other side of the picture plane. What Byzantine seeing required in order to make its claim as immediate evidence of godly presence, by contrast, was a distancing technique, a way of producing a barrier or membrane between the viewer and the realm of the sacred, creating a sense of blocked access. Several Eastern Rite artistic and architectural conventions carry on today that realize this aim – first and foremost the icon itself, and second the iconostasis or screen separating the sacred area of the altar from the congregation – and these conventions were the basis of Warhol's earliest, and arguably most formative, relationship to art.

The iconostasis realizes its purpose very simply, by blocking vision, often by reflecting it back to the viewer through the use of a metallic surface, much like the foil-covered walls of Warhol's studio (illus. 17) or the metallic-painted surfaces of many of his paintings (illus. 18), or even the way in which he cast himself as a mirror to the world, thereby opening up to imagination what is hidden from view. 'The iconostasis is a boundary between the visible and invisible worlds, and it functions as a boundary by being an obstacle to our seeing the altar, thereby making it accessible to our consciousness by a unified row of saints.' In so doing, it 'points out to the half-blind the Mysteries of the altar, opens for them an entrance into a world closed to them by their own stuckness', their own entrapment in the brute here and now of facticity. 'Destroy the material iconostasis and the

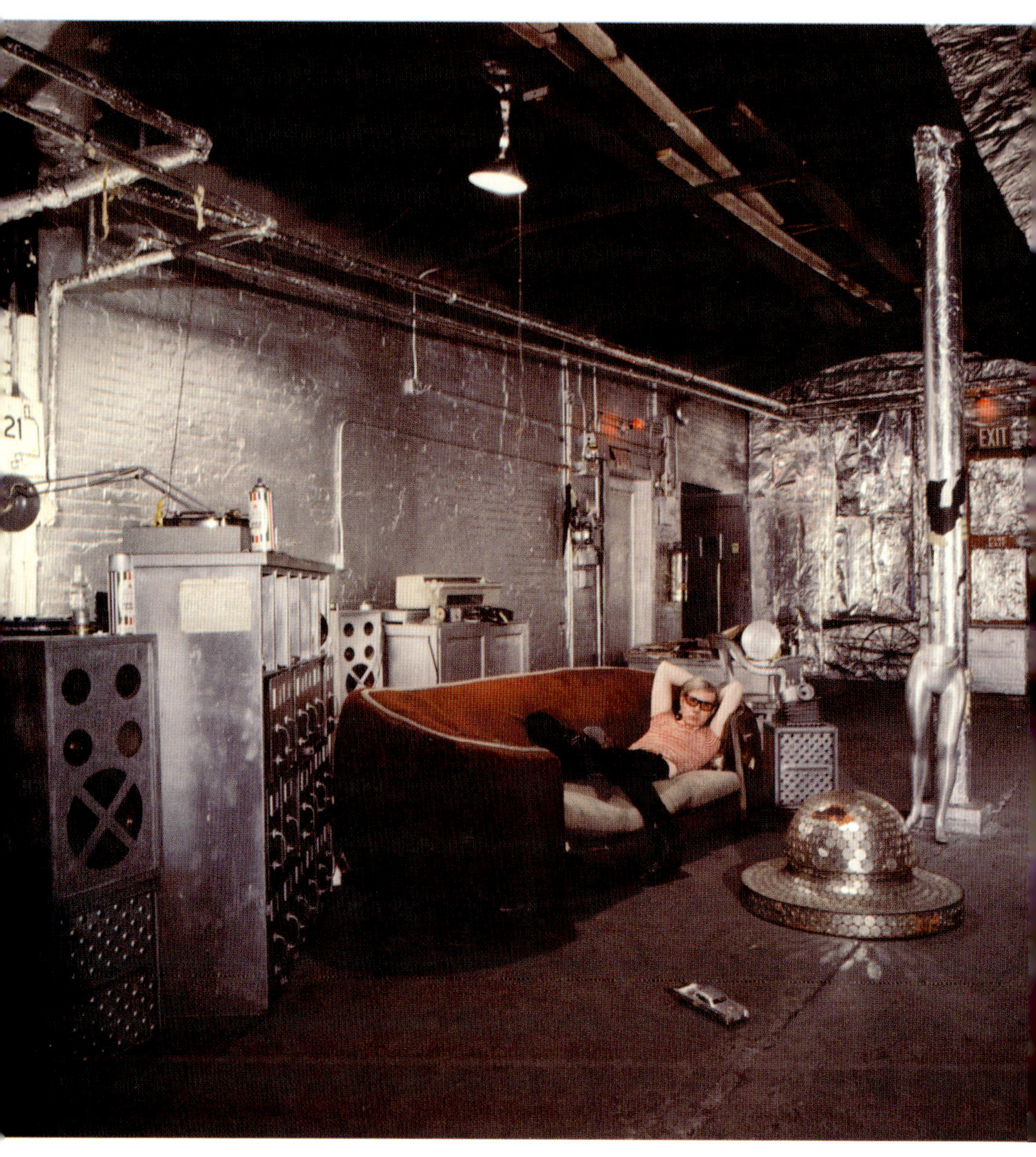

17 Jon Naar, *Warhol at the Silver Factory, East 47th Street, New York City*, 1965.

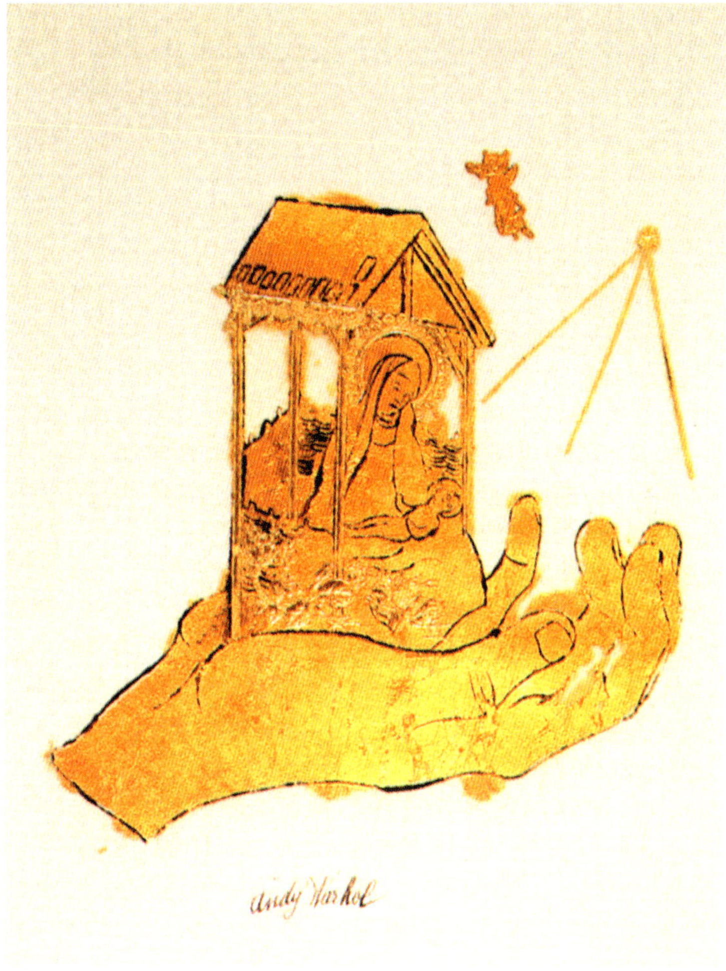

altar itself will, as such, wholly vanish from our consciousness
as if covered by an essentially impenetrable wall.'[14] The iconostasis served as material evidence of divinity because it materially
separates sacred space from profane space, thereby physically
producing the realm of the sacred and forcing the beholder back
on their imagination and their desire rather than leaving them
with only the brute, worldly facts of vision in front of them. As

we will see, this is precisely the trick that Warhol would come to adopt, a method that would in its own way confound and enchant his audience with the same mechanisms used to conjure the experience of faith.

The icon accomplishes the same Wizard-of-Oz effect as the iconostasis, albeit in slightly more complex fashion. The distancing necessary to physically demarcate sacred space is produced through a variety of techniques, but we will focus on just one set of means here: the effect of gilding, mosaic and, particularly, revetment (attaching a metal plate to the surface of the image), to draw attention back from the pictorial illusion of depth and back out to the surface of the work. Through this spectrum of methods the surface of the Byzantine icon put up its guard with a jewelled or reflective or even armoured surface, fending off any possibility for the beholder to enter the space that surrounds the icon, instead drawing him or her up short in the theological message itself, in its demand to believe rather than know, in its insistence on the faith/doubt couplet: there may or may not be something there behind the surface, but either way it cannot be known.

Even stronger, the reflective or defensive surface of the icon could become its primary meaning, something that is particularly effective when icons are experienced *in situ* rather than in the brightly lit, white-walled, sterile zone of a museum. As one perceptive account states, 'When illuminated by the trembling flicker of candles and oil lamps rather than the steady and harsh spotlights of museum displays, the painted holy face on the revetted icon sinks and disappears in the shadow', with even the pictured subject itself coming in and out of visibility, locating the primary effect with the surface ornament. In so doing, icons 'deny the tangibility and even visibility of the sacred image, while they appeal to the sense of touch through the textured surface of their repoussé and enamelled-filigree metal revetments', so relocating the site of experience from seeing and knowing to feeling and imagining, from positive sensory and cognitive access to the sacred to access by apophatic or negative theological means.[15] Put in the most direct terms, these techniques were part and parcel of a particular form of visuality that defined its authority through curtailing knowledge by restricting visual access to the realm of the sacred.[16] This was its peculiar form of negation, its distinctive response to the iconoclasts' charges, and it is only by exercising that negation that its theological content can be made manifest.

Warhol did not have the advantage of the trembling flicker of candles or shadows born of poor illumination to enter into this process of creation by negation, but he did have other means at his disposal. The best account of this alternative method of negation is still Marx's understanding of commodities, 'sensuous things which are at the same time suprasensible', things that we can only make sense of by taking 'flight into the misty realm of religion'.[17] Herein lies the formal basis of Warhol's postmodernism.

The Renaissance, the Reformation and the Enlightenment after that attempted to reverse Byzantine and other medieval forms of negation by giving direct individual access to the heady realm of the sacred, by cutting through the thick, reflective surface of the image with the vision and reason in a way that would allow the mind to occupy the terrain of the gods on the other side of the painted surface, even if it did so by a variety of means. This, of course, was a very different form of visuality – 'modern', we can call it with Belting or, as we will see below, 'Protestant' – but its long history concerns us here mostly as a foil for the pre-modern, Byzantine vision that came before it and the postmodern rejoinder that followed it. It hardly needs saying that Warhol was not the first to respond critically to the penetrating power of modern vision and reason, and we can see various expressions of dissatisfaction with the use of vision to split apart body and mind cropping up since the advent of that split – modern art itself not the least of them – but the intensity with which Warhol's vision stuck to surfaces and threw off the exercise of reason was undoubtedly the single most influential exemplar of the postmodern turn.

One incomparably powerful strain of reaction that would eventually come to drive postmodern visuality generally, and that of Warhol in particular, first emerged around the thought of the philosopher Henri Bergson at the end of the nineteenth century and the first decades of the twentieth. Bergson's attempt to rid both philosophy and common sense of static, snapshot-like 'picture thinking' in favour of a fluid, embodied, lived temporality came to be a central influence on various avant-garde movements

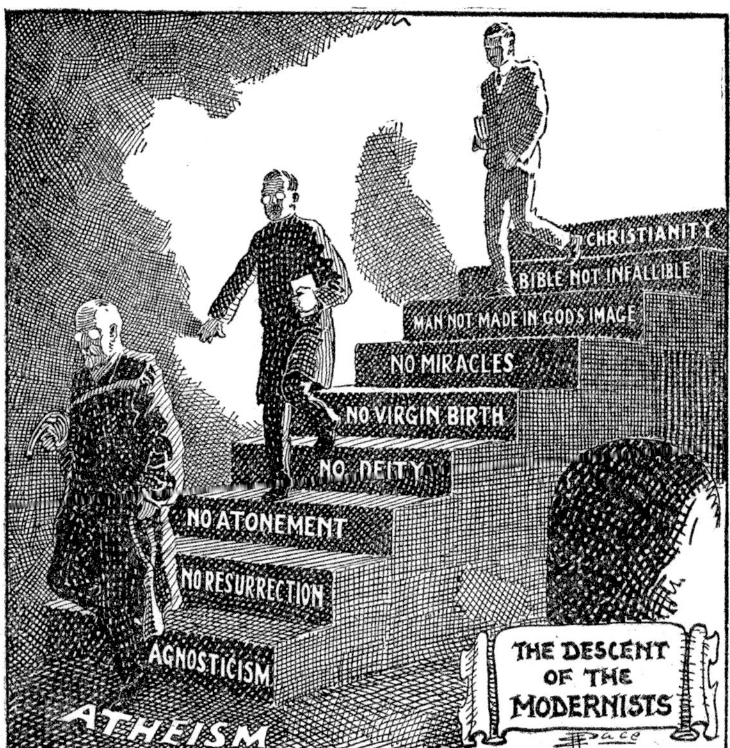

19 E. J. Pace, 'Descent of the Modernists', first published in *101 Christian Cartoons* (1922).

– most notably Cubism, Futurism and Dada – and their legacies in the neo-avant-gardes of Warhol's day, but it also gave rise to a Catholic intellectual tradition with a radically different notion of the image and aesthetic experience. By understanding the distinctiveness of this counter-Bergsonianism together with the legacy of Byzantine visuality we will begin to make sense of the deep-seated religiosity at the centre of Warhol's aesthetic sensibility.

Two of our three spokesmen for this alternative aesthetic tradition came directly out of deep engagements with Bergson's writing but took his central critique of modern rationalism and turned it on its head by developing what might be best labelled a 'modernist orthodoxy': Pavel Florensky, a Russian who taught in the famed early Revolutionary-era art school Vkhutemas, and Jacques Maritain, a French immigrant to the United States who occupied pride of place as its leading 'Catholic philosopher' through the middle of the twentieth century. The third, Marshall McLuhan, comes from the same modernist-cum-Orthodox line of thought, if slightly later. Florensky was likely unknown to Warhol, Maritain was surely known and McLuhan definitely, but all three will serve here to help understand a powerful (even if sometimes not adequately recognized) counter-current through-out much of the twentieth century that framed Warhol's mature enterprise – indeed, that provided a substantive basis for his remaking of modern art. Despite various differences between their Byzantine Rite and Roman orientations, all three thinkers helped to define a substantively consistent position on the role of images and vision and were very clear about what they opposed. All three agreed that it was a tradition stemming back through Kant and Luther to the Renaissance that mucked things up. As one historical account has bluntly put it, Kant gave the 'strongest critical support to the drive towards "subjectivism" implicit in Luther's doctrine of faith', and as such, 'Neo-scholastic theolo-gians and philosophers frequently used the term "Kantian" as a pejorative label much as McCarthyite Americans used the word "communist".'[18] Warhol was not typically so high-minded in anti-subjectivism, but the effect was the same.

Florensky, in one of many similar statements, put it this way: 'Now, it is a truism to note that German idealist philosophy (especially Kant) eliminated sensuous space from philosophic thought. But were Kant and Hegel, Fichte and Cohen, doing anything other than what Dürer had done in engraving? Not at all.'[19] Indeed, he argued time and again in writings from the heyday of the Russian and early Soviet avant-garde, the delineation of space made possible by the new compositional advances of the Renaissance and the philosophical body of thought that came with it undid the advances of the Middle Ages, and that undoing was a perversion of human nature. Engraving 'manifests the very deception at the heart of Protestantism – its cry for freedom of conscience in its denial of the Church tradition – more: in its denial of the universally human tradition', he could say without qualification, for example.[20] By privileging the capacity for human understanding, human description and the like, a kind of deluded arrogance – the 'Kantian arrogance of Protestantism', Florensky called it – emerges: 'Reason comes to enslave everything surrounding it, for, in exercising its freedom of self-determination, it violates the self-determination of the world.'[21] So too the visual form of reason, linear perspective, which he cast as 'a machine for annihilating reality, an infernal yawn that swallows everything wherein the vanishing point functions'.[22] The misunderstanding of modern rationalism was to assume that human beings can fully comprehend their world: 'To cite Bergson', Florensky concluded, '"*la vie déborde l'intelligence* – life transcends rationality". And that is *always* the case', even though he no longer agreed with the specific character of that transcendence as it had been developed by Bergson.[23] Warhol too would offer a form of life that transcended the exercise of reason, even if it would also be different in kind.

Jacques Maritain put forward a similar set of concerns, born of the same philosophical pedigree, many times over throughout his long career, beginning with his study *La Philosophie bergsonienne: Études critiques* (1914), the specific critical angle of which was made more explicit in its later English translation, as *Bergsonian Philosophy and Thomism*. Maritain rarely shied away from making his critique plain and partisan: 'in order to save our race and intelligence', he said at one point early in his career, 'we must come back to a civilization purely and integrally Catholic. And with respect to that which concerns philosophy in particular, it is not Victor Cousin, nor Auguste Comte, nor Descartes that we must take as our masters, but rather Saint Thomas [Aquinas]. *Saint Thomas against Kant!*'[24] So too with his first big book on art, *Art and Scholasticism* of 1920, in which he would lay bare the core anti-humanist distinction driving his philosophy and aesthetics: 'Man created more beautiful things in those days' – that is, the days of Aquinas and scholasticism – 'and he adored himself less.' The problem was that the humanist arrogance that arose with the Renaissance

> was to drive the artist mad, and to make of him the most miserable of men – at the very moment when the world was to become less habitable for him – by revealing to him his own peculiar grandeur, and by letting loose on him the wild beast Beauty which Faith had kept enchanted and led after it, docile.'[25]

The new form of humanism that had arisen with the Renaissance, Protestantism and the Enlightenment – and with the capitalism that fuelled them – 'proved itself inhuman' by taking on a God-like sense of self-importance, by a form of idolatry that made its own image into the central symbol and object of worship for its distinctively modern cult.[26] Its all-seeing gaze given formal expression in linear perspective was at the centre of that arrogant inhumanity.

McLuhan also understood Bergson to have been correct in his basic philosophical presupposition that life transcends rational understanding and, in a manner similar to Florensky's and Maritain's critical Bergsonism, he turned to the body and its extensions in various technologies to work the limits of reason with the transcendence on offer from religious experience. His writings are full of examples – his much-touted prefiguration in 1969 of internet-based cyber-utopianism in the pages of *Playboy*, for instance, was taken to be 'merely a new interpretation of the mystical body of Christ', because Christ, 'after all, is the ultimate extension of man'.[27] In McLuhan's case it was Gutenberg more than Descartes or Dürer who led the way to Protestant and Enlightenment disenfranchisement of the human capacity to appreciate its place in the world, but the principle was the same: 'man's humanity is his freedom in community'; something is 'not a matter of concepts: it's precepts, a matter of immediate reality'.[28]

The problem with the Protestant outlook, McLuhan insisted, was that it judged the world according to concepts. 'It took

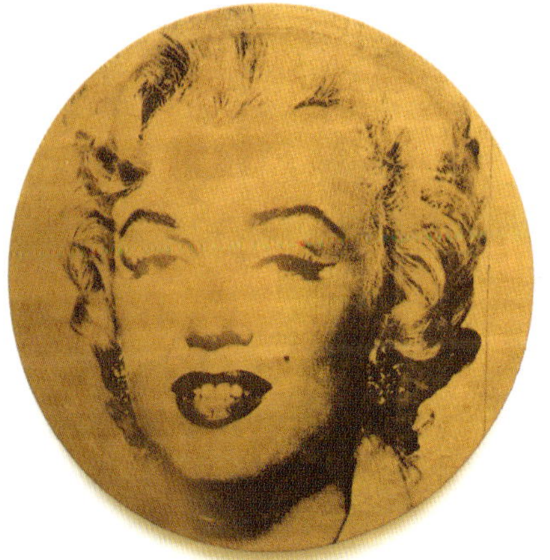

20 Andy Warhol, *Gold Marilyn*, 1962, silkscreen ink and gold paint on canvas, two tondi, each 45.3 cm in diameter.

me years to find out what they really meant by this strange constant request for a value judgment. It's a Protestant sort of fixation, this "Is it a good or bad thing?"', this judgment – and did not allow the world to speak for itself.[29] This began to change with modernism:

> The simple discovery that was made in all the arts around 1860–1870 was that things have formal character and are quite able to speak for themselves. The artist's role is not to stress himself or his own point of view but to let things sing and talk, to release the forms within them.[30]

In other words, the role of modern art was really the same as that of the neo-Scholasticism that arose alongside it at the end of the nineteenth century: to slowly regain the sense, lost since the Middle Ages, that the truth existed out there in the world rather than within the individual human capacity for understanding. As modern art began to close off access to the Renaissance's illusionistic trickery and draw the beholder out of the clutches of perspectival vision and back to the surface, the realm of distant truth not immediately accessible to the beholder's power of reason was reconstituted, producing a measure of the same Wizard-of-Oz effect, the same apophasis, as icons and the iconostasis, the same unapproachable distance as the work of Andy Warhol, even as it held trenchantly to the intimacy of its interaction with the world through its deeply modern powers of judgment.

Distancing, it can be said without controversy, was the single most effective trick in Warhol's kit and, more than anything else, has come to characterize the larger post-Kantian, post-Enlightenment, postmodern sensibility that he helped to define – more than new media and materials, for example, or more than the turn from craft production to industrial and intellectual production methods; more, even, than renewed efforts at the internationalization and collectivization of artistic labour. Some of that distance was simple irony, mockery and camp, or, generally, a critical style born of sensitive souls defending their desires against the judgment of others, of course, and it would surely be a mistake to suggest otherwise. But another part of it – at least for Warhol himself – was inspired by a different desire, one that is not so readily psychologized, sexualized or gendered, or understood to be a function of race, ethnicity or social class. This universalist remainder in Warhol's distinctive affective sensibility is the religious part, and it is best understood to reside in the devotional structure or comportment of the particular form of vision represented in his work, a form not comprehensible without being thought through the influence of the Byzantine and Catholic, modernist models of visuality outlined here.

There are many ways to think about the impact of a particular religious upbringing on a mature sensibility that do not reduce it exclusively to a cultural tag – rightly or wrongly, we talk easily of Catholic guilt or a Protestant work ethic, for example, without demoting either to a simple 'subject position'. Terry Eagleton has provided a rich account of such a sensibility, cultivated by the Catholicism of his own upbringing, particularly as understood in a larger cultural context dominated by Protestantism. For him, Catholicism provides 'a world of compulsive rituals, not of agonized inwardness' and a 'soundly anti-Cartesian spirit' in which institutionalized habits, actions and deeds determined one's salvation, not good intentions, appropriate desires and the like.[31] Its emphasis is on 'material practice, on the public, collective, symbolic dimensions of self-hood' that come from showing up for Mass and confession, not the interiorized sense of good or evil that is born reading the Bible to oneself and establishing a personal relationship to God. As such, according to Eagleton, Catholicism is 'entwined with a callous impersonality which could make even Stalinism seem sentimental', sets itself 'against all phoney subjectivism' and is 'as indifferent to individual feelings as a psychopath'.[32] Catholics, writes Eagleton, 'understand that human life is inherently institutional' – it is not about authenticity but instead about going through the motions, not about the subjective but about the objective – and that is what is most important about their faith, what makes it universal.[33] Lou Reed and John Cale would sum up this ethic in one of their tribute songs, with a lyric testifying that all that mattered to Warhol was work.[34] Work is not who one is or what one feels, as the Protestant tradition would have it and as will be discussed in the following chapter, it is what you do if you are a machine or the Nothingness himself.

Warhol's characteristic distance had all of these trappings and more above and beyond the much celebrated camp attributes that have been detailed by many and will be taken up here in chapters to come. The two forms of distance – the queer one, stepping back from social norms and making a style out of protecting itself by performing itself, and the other, religious one reaching forward without hesitation to realize itself in institutional form, in giving itself over to the non-identity of the sacred body of Christ, the sacred space of Church belonging – are not necessarily at odds or as irreconcilable as they may first seem. There is a significant history of the one overlapping with, and becoming, the other, a history that, as we shall see in chapter Four, would have significant if convoluted influence on the young Warhol. In the words of one insightful scholar of the Decadents, 'Catholicism was the odd disruption, the hysterical symptom, the mystical effusion, the medieval spectacle, the last hope of paganism, in an age of Victorian puritanism, enlightenment rationalism, and bourgeois materialism.' And so it was for figures like Oscar Wilde, J.-K. Huysmans and, particularly important for our purposes, Aubrey Beardsley, who regarded faith 'as a beautiful possibility curiously out of place in a modern context' and as 'a theatre for the articulation of homosexual desire and identity'.[35]

Warhol had little truck with Catholic guilt or the sort of spectacular identity it could spawn. John Richardson phrased it this way: 'It was not soppy social consciousness or guilt that prompted Andy's self-possessed churchliness; it was atavism as personified by his adored and adoring mother, the pious Julia.'[36] Indeed atavism, or the reversion to an ancestral or primordial type or form – this, for our purposes, being something like the reversion to the Byzantine, the medieval, the pre-modern – as a way of countering the modern, may be the single most defining characteristic of Warhol's extraordinary contribution to the history of art and, more importantly, to the historic sense of self that has emerged for us, his heirs, as a result.

2

ANDREW CARNEGIE

What is in a name? Andy received his from his father Ondrej but the link between the anglicized immigrant's version of his name and the 'Two Andrews', Andrew Mellon (1855–1937) and Andrew Carnegie (1835–1919), the great robber barons of Pittsburgh, would likely not have gone unnoticed by his family and certainly would not have been lost on the young Warhol himself. The shift from 'Ondrej' to 'Andrew', from self-image as manual labourer to wannabe-image as robber baron, from struggling immigrant to pillar of the American economy, was the epitome of the nineteenth century's American Dream. As we will see, the shift from 'Andrew' to 'Andy', from producer to consumer, from institution-builder to dodger of institutional authority in the free play of the market, will be the epitome of the twentieth century's. If the meaning of 'Ondrej' for Andy Warhol was tied to the Church in the old, not-yet-modern world, and the adoption of 'Andrew' reached for the factory as the nucleus of its modernity, 'Andy' marked a postmodern world that would be defined first and foremost by shopping and an understanding of oneself as something that can be purchased and consumed.

Even though Carnegie died in 1919, nine years before Warhol was born, and Mellon left Pittsburgh for Washington, DC, in 1921, it is hard to overestimate the place of Mellon's legacy and more particularly that of Carnegie in the civic, business and cultural imagination of Pittsburgh, especially that associated with the visual arts (illus. 21). Mellon made his money as a financier for the steel industry, his political career as a tax-cutter was in the manner later adopted by Ronald Reagan and Margaret Thatcher, and then went on to found the National Gallery of Art in 1938, when Warhol was ten years old, jump-starting its accessioning and establishing a quality threshold for its future acquisitions with his personal art collection. The steel magnate Carnegie completely dominated the cultural landscape of Pittsburgh with his university, museum, libraries, free art classes and the like, amenities that Warhol benefited from extensively (illus. 22). Carnegie was also a prolific philosophizer of all things social, political and cultural, and his ideas had a particular degree of dominance over the understanding of art and its social role in Pittsburgh and beyond. That dominance endured through the period of Warhol's life in Pittsburgh and deeply structured his relationship to both art and labour. In order to understand Warhol's mature artistic sensibility and its meaning for us today, we therefore need to come to terms with what art meant for Andrew Carnegie.

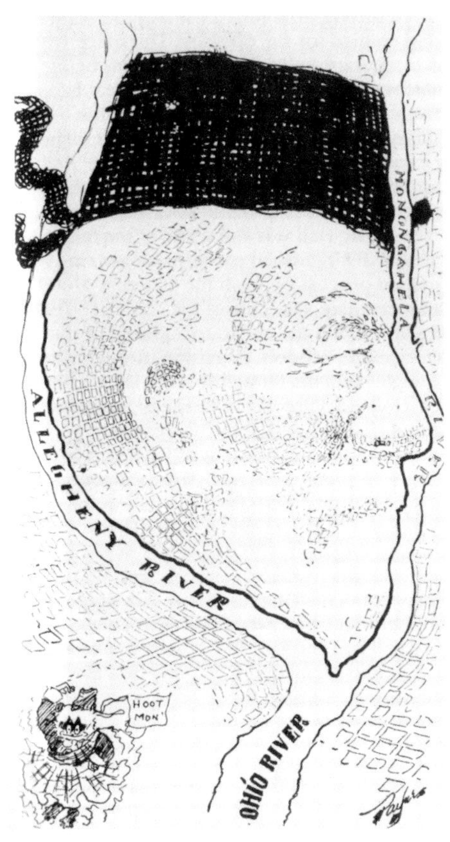

21 Cartoon of Andrew Carnegie from the *Pittsburgh Gazette Times* (10 April 1907).

Carnegie's social and artistic philosophy was grounded in the work of Herbert Spencer, someone he routinely characterized as the 'great thinker of our age' and regularly fawned over when he had the opportunity.[1] In a kinder, gentler version of the

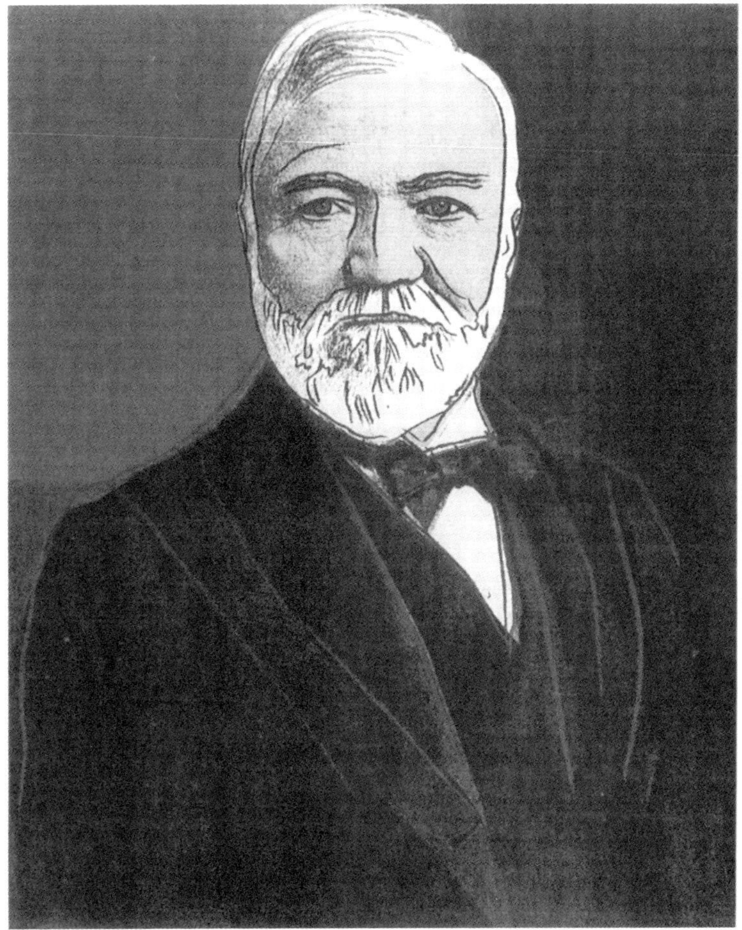

22 Andy Warhol, *Andrew Carnegie*, 1981, acrylic and silkscreen on canvas, 249 × 201 cm.

(neo)liberalism of our own day, this meant that he adopted both Spencer's well-known 'survival of the fittest' doctrine but also his sense that those who rose to the top did so by elevating the standing of those around them and driving social progress generally. Carnegie was full of this mission throughout his voluminous writings and habitually took credit for being among 'the strongest mentally' and of 'the exceptional members of our race' who lifted it 'to its present position, infinitely higher than it was only a few hundreds of years ago'.[2] This was the natural order of things, he thought, and, adopting a Spencerian aphorism while reflecting back on the progress of his life, he once remarked: '"All is well since all grows better" became my motto, my true source of comfort.' There was no 'conceivable end' to man's 'march to perfection'. Elevating his rhetorical tone further still in high nineteenth-century fashion and redirecting the great, horizontal, inward/outward dialectic of the eighteenth century's principle of enlightenment back to the verticality of gods, kings and leviathans, Carnegie concluded that the state of modern man under the guardianship and patronage of his ilk was that 'His face is turned to the light; he stands in the sun and looks upward.'[3] As we will see, the young Warhol was powerfully interpellated by this vision of value and progress and would both carry it forward and react against it as an adolescent and an adult.

This general philosophical outlook was the engine driving Carnegie's philanthropic programme. In 1897, assessing his accomplishment to the president and trustees of his instantly venerable Carnegie Institute (later renamed the Carnegie Museum of Art), he noted with some amazement that the 'mass of latent desire for the things of the spirit which lay inert in the hearts of our fellow citizens of the industrial hive . . . needed only the awakening touch'.[4] Much like the touch of life or spirit commemorated by Michelangelo in the central image of the Sistine Chapel ceiling fresco, the touch that Carnegie had in mind was a kind of gift or endowment from a superior power to a dependent, labouring humanity. This endowment came first and foremost in the Institute itself, of course, and in his public library programme and the free art classes Warhol attended as a child as well as the college education he would later earn from the Carnegie Institute, but it was also there in the gift of Carnegie's high-nineteenth-century transformation of Enlightenment social philosophy,

with its powerful thesis about the renewed, upward march
to perfection. That thesis, together with its accompanying
set of aesthetic values, was institutionalized in every part of
his philanthropic programme and it structured every part of
Warhol's artistic education. Indeed, more than any other it is
Carnegie's vision for the future of art and society that we can
see inverted in Warhol's best-known maxims – the one about
everyone being famous for fifteen minutes, for example, or
this one:

> What's great about this country is that America started the
> tradition where the richest consumers buy essentially the
> same things as the poorest. You can be watching TV and
> see Coca-Cola, and you know that the President drinks
> Coke, Liz Taylor drinks Coke, and just think, you can
> drink Coke too. A Coke is a Coke and no amount of
> money can get you a better Coke than the one the bum
> on the corner is drinking.[5]

As we will see, Warhol flipped Carnegie's high-minded principles
by seeing them realized in his base, workaday world – in the
factory and the marketplace – and not in the rarefied after-
hours world of elite leisure, of social and cultural philanthropy,
museums and education.

Carnegie's aesthetic theory was, like his political philosophy,
based on a similar concept of reconciliation between classes that
could be achieved through great works of art and great institutions. At the dedication ceremony for the Carnegie Institute in
1895, for example, he said that money spent on such higher
purposes is 'put to better and nobler ends than if it had been
distributed from week to week in driblets among the masses
of people'.[6] Rather than being doled out in the form of higher
wages and then frittered away on baser needs or pleasures, such
an investment in educating the masses 'ministers to the divine

in man, his reason and his conscience, and thus lifts him higher
and higher in the scale of being; he becomes less and less the
brute, and more of the man'.[7] Equally so the importance of his
investment in museums and art galleries, Carnegie said, because
it is 'better to reach and touch the sentiment for beauty in the
naturally bright minds of this [working] class than to pander'
to more common taste.[8] Understood in this way, art was a gift
from rich to poor that helped to elevate the humanity of both,
contributing to the larger civilizing process through a manner
of exchange that created a deep and enduring human bond
between employer and employee.

'What has produced this reciprocal affection' between me
and my labourers, Carnegie asked rhetorically in a moment of
wishful thinking:

> Not the mere payment of stipulated wages on the one
> part and the bare performance of stipulated duties on the
> other – far from this. It is the something more done upon
> both sides, and the knowledge each has had opportunity
> to gather of the other, their virtues, kindness – in short,
> their characters.

Indeed, the 'strict terms of the contract', the mere business
aspects of the employment relationship, he argued, presumably
trying to convince both himself and others, 'are drowned in
the deep well of mutual regard'. His conclusion: 'Labour is
never fully paid by money alone.'[9] Instead, the inadequacy
of the money payment was to be supplemented with libraries,
universities and museums – that is, paid for with the civilizing
benefit of culture, and labourers were to reciprocate this
bonus with their loyalty to, and affection for, their employers.[10]
As he put it in 1895, his part was to contribute 'to the enlightenment and the joys of the mind, to the things of the spirit, to
all that tends to bring into the lives of the toilers of Pittsburgh

sweetness and light'.[11] And if those 'toilers' did not reciprocate with their affection, as was the case during the great
Homestead Strike of 1892, for example, three years after the
opening of his first American public library, there was always
Allan Pinkerton's private militia available to bring the rabble-
rousers in line and remind them how to properly show their
appreciation (illus. 23).

Warhol, as we have noted, was a beneficiary of the great,
paternalistic, fringe-benefit economy that Carnegie had endowed,
a beneficiary of the sweetness and light it promised, and he
was well-schooled in the attendant body of social and aesthetic
theory – indeed, the whole of his art education was drawn
from the school of Carnegie and its model for the amelioration
of class conflict. Like the trickle-down training and aesthetic
programme that was an integral part of the even greater Medici
art economy through its academy and other forms of influence,
for example, Carnegie was Warhol's patron, even if their lives

23 'Drunken
Orgies and
Pillages',
illustration for
Allan Pinkerton,
*Communists,
Tramps and
Detectives* (1878).

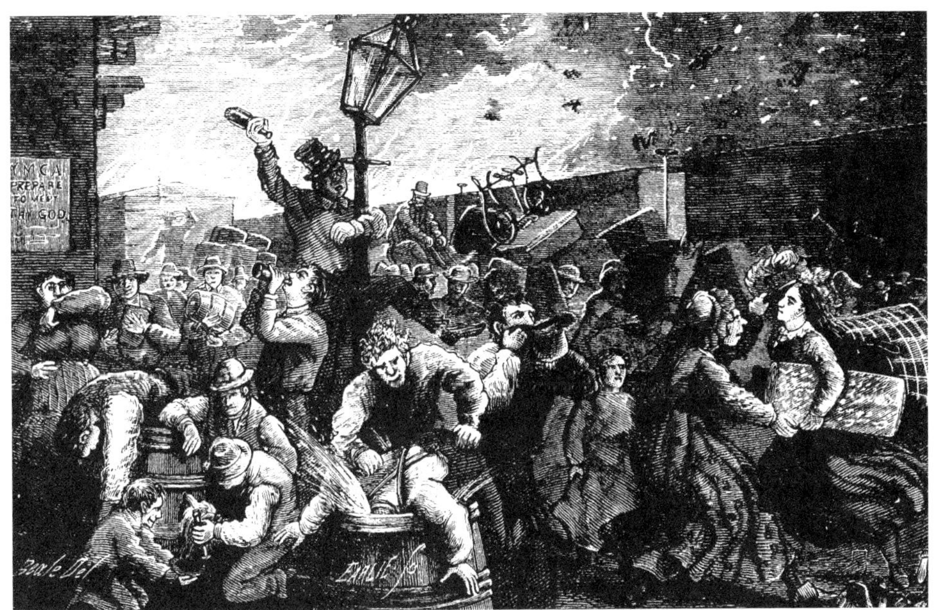

did not overlap, and Warhol in turn was an artist in the style
and sensibility that Carnegie had called for, carrying forward
his socio-aesthetic vision of a better world.

Of course, patronage in Carnegie's Pittsburgh generally
meant something quite different than patronage in Medici
Florence. As one scholar has described the dynamics of influence in the Florentine example, the 'patron's conception of his
oeuvre was the framework within which the artist created the
elements of his'.[12] This was not so much a matter of the individual taste of either patron or artist; rather it was individual
taste that was determined in significant measure by social,
political and economic need. In this sense, art played an
important and worldly role for the Medici and Carnegie
alike, they were just different roles. Put schematically, the
Medici's oeuvre was that of Catholic bankers while Carnegie's
was that of a Protestant industrialist. This meant, above all,
that each had a different audience in mind for the art that it
supported: one audience was made up mostly of bank customers
and competitors – let's call them the Renaissance business class
– and the other made up mostly of Carnegie employees and
their families and friends – we might call them the Industrial
Age working class. One promoted art that served an extravagant,
courtly, pre-industrial finance capitalism at the moment of its
first full flowering, while the other imagined art and aesthetic
values that served a machine-age, factory-based industrial
capitalism at the moment of its coming of age. One aimed to
bring in business and generate influence among an emerging
elite through a broad system of political patronage, social ties,
status negotiations and business relations, while the other sought
to ameliorate dissatisfaction and focus the attention of an
audience of 'human resources' – that is, wage labourers –
assumed to be made up of atomized and dependent future
art appreciators.[13] One dislodged and renegotiated existing
social relations through a process of abstraction, while the

other served as a balm or salve, dressing (and often obscuring) the dislodgement of Industrial Age proletarianization in high-minded social principles. As we will see, serving as such a balm was the role that Warhol was trained for. His great value to us today – the extent to which he lives on as our Leonardo – is the degree to which he made his relationship to that ameliorative role self-reflexive.

'Much of what we call taste', wrote the art historian Michael Baxandall in the context of a study of the cultural affinities of the Medici era, lies in 'the conformity between discriminations demanded by a painting and skills of discrimination possessed by the beholder'.[14] Those skills, he goes on to say, were essentially accounting skills, the skills of bankers and merchants, and the art in question provided opportunity for those skills to be exercised, not so much in the buying and selling of art but in patterns of looking or ways of making sense of the world visually. So too we might view taste in the age of Carnegie. There is a longer history of the kind of social ambitions Carnegie held out for aesthetic experience, of course, and he was certainly not alone in his beliefs (just as the Medici were not), but the gist of it was a way of seeing that did not excite, engage or distract the passions or the intellect but instead oriented them towards the righteousness of labour itself.[15]

Homer Saint-Gaudens, the director of the Carnegie Institute throughout Warhol's years in Pittsburgh and heir of Carnegie's social and aesthetic programme, described that purpose somewhat vaguely as producing a 'rich emotional response'. More tellingly, however, he situated it between two negative poles: 'the high function of art is neither to tickle the eye of the man in the street with coloured magazine covers of pulchritudinous come-hither maidens', he insisted, nor was it 'to bolster the complicated egos of those whose chief source of distraction is not to enjoy the visual aspect of painting but to get loquacious about it'.[16] Saint-Gaudens' taste, like Carnegie's before him, was what would subsequently be called 'middlebrow'. It came with a deep-seated moral calling, a mission of work and ascetic self-constraint that had been the revolutionary ideal of what Max Weber had labelled the Protestant work ethic and assessed to be the foundation for the triumph of industrial capitalism.[17] Put differently, his was a conviction that 'aesthetics should be divorced and remain divorced from all the turmoil of the rest of the world', that art should be a function of isolated individual desire, not of public debate and political contest.[18] It is that middlebrow position – the great means to realizing the American Dream – that Warhol would come to represent with unfailing perspicacity and to pursue unreservedly with all the gusto of an immigrant, even as he rebelled against it from within its own logic and cultivation of desires.

This aim of a culturally enabled upgrade for the industrial working class from lowbrow to middlebrow – from the taste of those who work because they have to and seek the distraction of pleasure in their cultural pursuits, to that of those who work because they want to and go to museums to seek affirmation of their innate sense of purpose – was summed up in the pediment inscription that Carnegie required of all his libraries: 'There should be placed over the entrance to the Libraries I build a representation of the rays of a rising sun, and above "LET THERE BE LIGHT".'[19] This was a version of the old Enlightenment dream, of course, of 'man's release from his self-incurred tutelage', but the release from the tutelage of the rule of law levied by priestly and princely authorities had now been reconceived as an internal rule, an internalized ethic of work bequeathed from on high. 'The contrast between Shakespeare and the ordinary specimen of humanity is as great as that between the average civilized man and the barbarian', Carnegie liked to say, fancying himself and his class of robber barons generally to be of a rank with Shakespeare.[20]

That difference in the measure of humanity had specific and instrumental criteria, of course, just as it always does: it was a taste for something higher, something transcendent, something that 'ministers to the divine in man'. 'I am not content', he insisted, 'to pass down in the history of Pittsburgh as one who only helped the masses to obtain greater enjoyment of those appetites which we share equally with the brutes – more to eat, more to drink, and richer raiment' (no explanation was provided regarding his unexpected claim for the brutishness of the desire for better raiment).[21] That transcendence was to be found in Carnegie's own philosophy of work, which he made every effort to convey through the bully pulpit of his wealth. As he put it in his much-discussed 'Gospel of Wealth' (1889), the riches accumulated by the wealthy take society towards an 'ideal state, in which the surplus wealth of the few will become, in the best sense, the property of the many, because administered [by the wealthy few] for the common good'.[22] As self-proclaimed governor of the commonwealth of good taste – a proclamation he could rightly make because of his role as funder of museums, libraries, schools and the like – Carnegie could orient its meaning and consequence towards hard work as a satisfaction unto itself.

Raised in the context of this powerful and pervasive understanding of art as an expression of human self-realization through labour, of art as an expression of the Protestant work ethic, Warhol essentially rebelled. We will detail some of the forms that rebellion took in chapters to come, but in general terms it was a rejection of interiority *tout court*, a rejection of the premise of an inner purpose or inner ethic that defined and determined the right way to live. And that rebellion was less a matter of turning Carnegie's middlebrow world view upside down (by simply embracing either the highbrow or lowbrow alternatives) but instead a matter of turning inside out and outside in. 'Pop comes from the outside', is how he

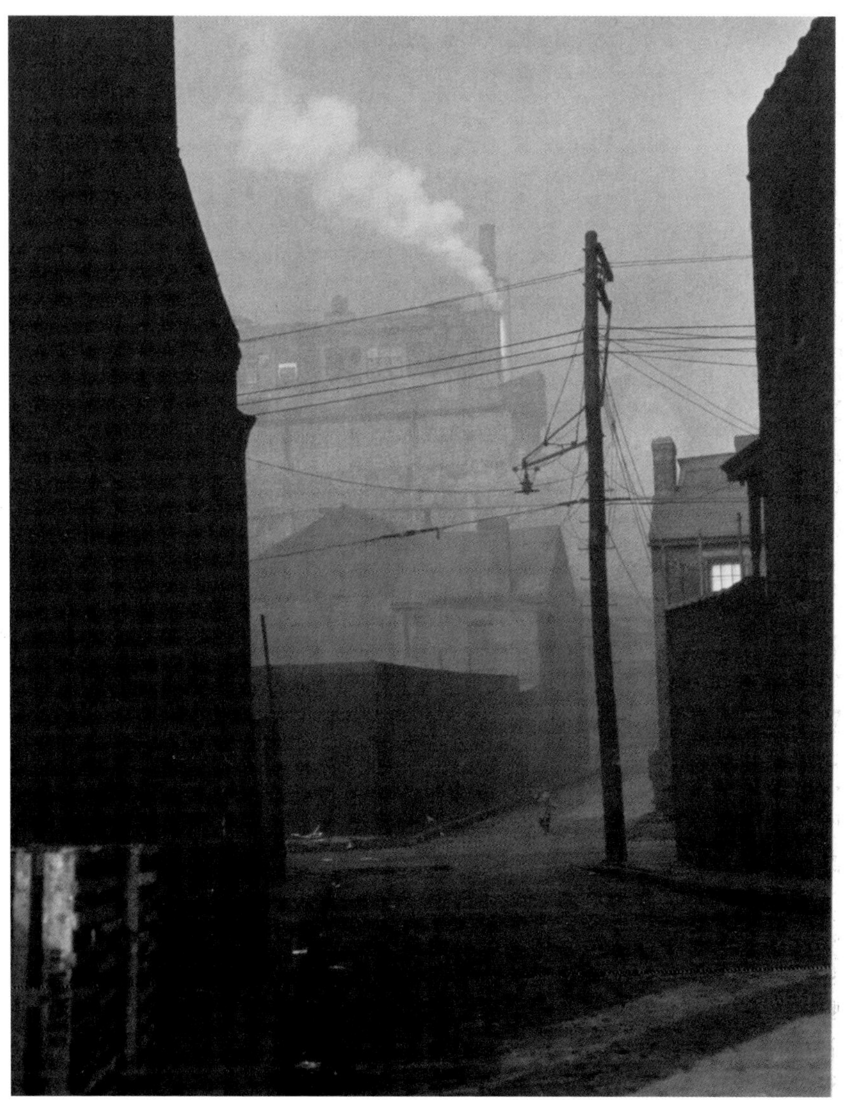

24 Luke Swank, *December Day, c.* 1939, gelatin silver print, 20 × 15 cm.

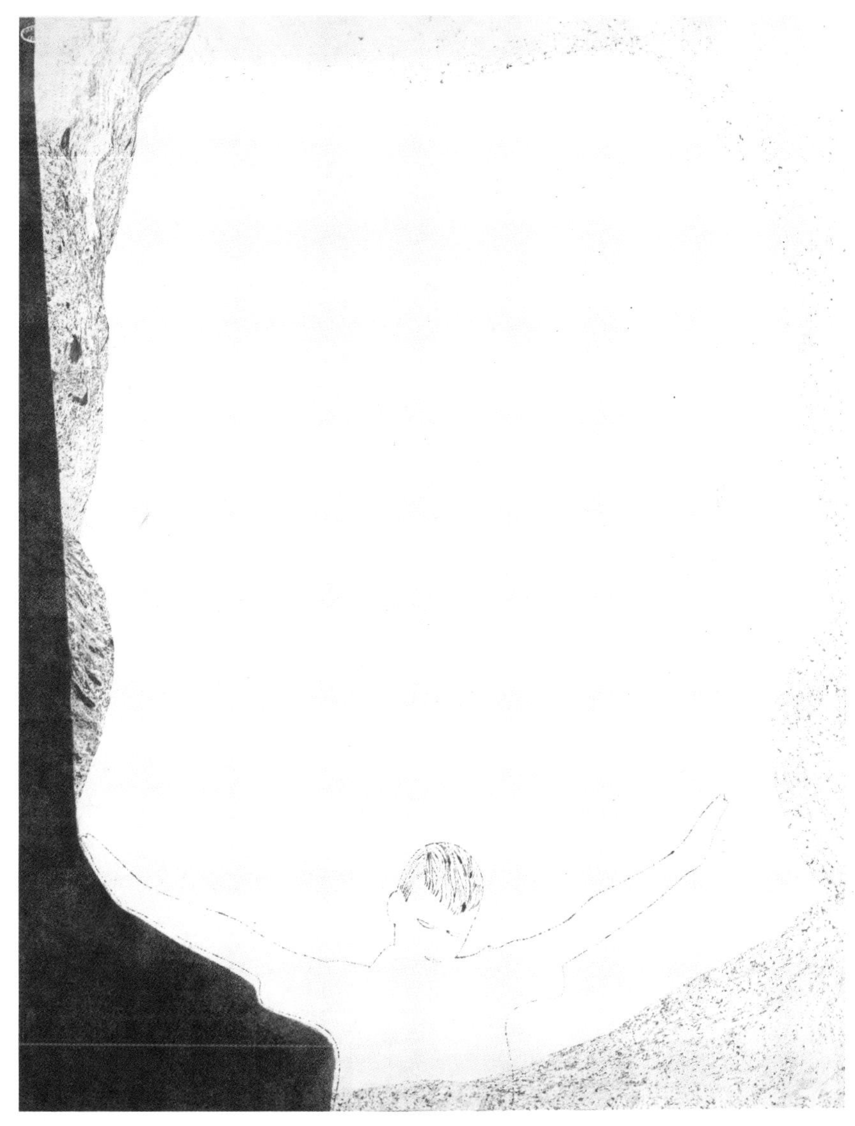

25 Andy Warhol, *Male Child*, *c.* 1952, ink and tempera on paper, 72.4 × 57.2 cm.

would later describe that alternative aesthetic sensibility.[23] Or again, like so: 'What is art? Does it really come out of you or is it a product? It's complicated.'[24] And, of course, in Warhol's case more than any other this was never just about art but about all aspects of being in and experiencing the world: 'I always feel that my words are coming from behind me, not from me.'[25] The fact that he could make such programmatic statements, which radically exteriorized his sense of the authority that gave him purpose, shows that he was very conscious of the prevailing middlebrow reduction and redirection of the Enlightenment's aesthetic ideal. Put simply, we might imagine that his rebellion was born of a sense that Carnegie's work ethic was not in his best interests. Warhol liked to say 'it's just work', as discussed above, meaning that it is just an institution, a social process, a way of surviving in the world; it is not one's identity or being. The same thing, of course, applied to art.

There are many factors that allowed Warhol this distance from the hegemony of the Protestant middlebrow aesthetic values that he was raised with – his immigrant's outsider status, for example, or his strong, Eastern Rite religiosity, or his complex sexual status, or maybe the fact that he was a mama's boy – but there was certainly also a meaningful experience that came simply from growing up working class in Pittsburgh. The photographer Duane Michals, who was raised nearby and in similar circumstances, described the experience:

Because our rivers were orange I thought all rivers were orange. At night the steel mills lit up the sky; it was always this incredible kind of inferno. The mills made a lot of noise; you could hear the cranes dropping enormous things and booming all the time. There was a certain drama about it, kind of scary, too.[26]

The visceral reality of that drama – the intensely artificial light, colour and noise – were in direct opposition to the identification with sweetness and light necessary for the sense of purpose and belonging so central to Carnegie's socio-aesthetic philosophy (illus. 24).

Put most simply, Warhol can be said to have seen the contradiction in Carnegie's position and, in so doing, turned away from the 'rich emotional response' that his art school training championed, back towards the cheap veneer of the 'pulchritudinous come-hither maidens' that Carnegie and his heirs had worked so hard to exorcize from the culture of working-class Pittsburgh. On one level, after all, such would not be a bad description of the Marilyn Monroe images that Warhol latched on to and made even more pulchritudinous in a distinctively come-hither manner by isolating features and flattening out colours with the industrial effects of his silkscreen technique. This was, after all, a period sensibility for Monroe herself, together with a host of other figures from her era – for Elvis Presley, say, or Hugh Hefner and *Playboy*, or for the affected, tramp sensibility of the Beats or, of course, for Warhol himself – all successfully working the ends towards a collapse of subjectivity, a collapse of humanity, in the middle. Benjamin Buchloh summed up this meeting point brilliantly in 1989: Warhol, he concluded,

> unified within his constructs the views of both the victors and victims of the late twentieth century: the entrepreneurial world view, its ruthless diffidence and strategically calculated air of detachment that allows it to continue its operations without ever being challenged in terms of its sociopolitical or ecological responsibility; and the phlegmatic vision of the victims of that world view, the consumers, the 'all-round reduced personality,' who can celebrate in Warhol's work their proper status of having been erased as subjects.[27]

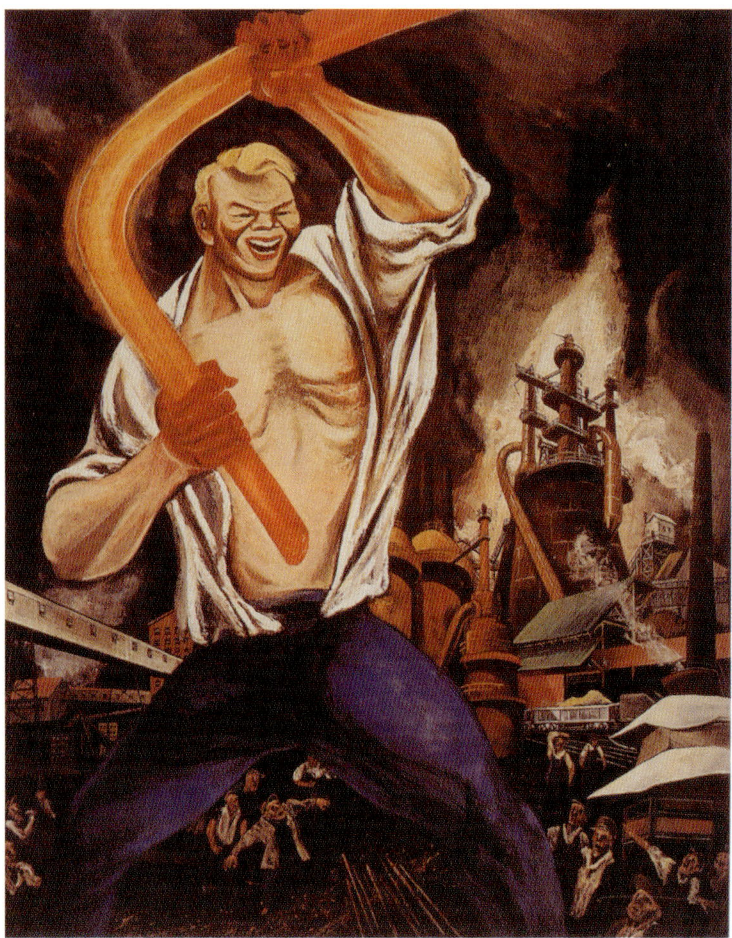

26 William Gropper, *Joe Magarac*, 1946, lithograph.

That said, there was more to Warhol's working-class identity than its foreclosure in period class confusion. We already have a sense of the way it produced a split in him between the promises of industrial labour and fine art, but we do not yet have a sense of the ways in which it cast him in ethnic terms. 'Since the 1870s the Carnegie steel company in Pittsburgh' engaged in 'the systematic hiring of immigrants',

Matthew Josephson wrote in his classic book of 1934, *The Robber Barons*, citing a study done for the pioneering 1907–8 Pittsburgh Survey, which reported that 'It is a common opinion in the district that some employers of labour give the Slavs and Italians preference because of their docility, their habit of silent submission . . . and their willingness to work long hours and overtime without a murmur.'[28] Warhol's immigrant upbringing carried with it not only the distinctively rich relation to the visual imagination of his Eastern Rite Catholic background, it also carried with it the baggage of being a 'Hunky', of the Central European immigrant industrial labouring class. Part of that stock-in-trade was the expected docility, silent submission and hard work without complaint – all traits that Warhol would come to excel at. But they were also qualities he would characteristically learn to flip, to turn from passivity into aggression, with the greatest efficiency and with only the slightest twist in demeanour.

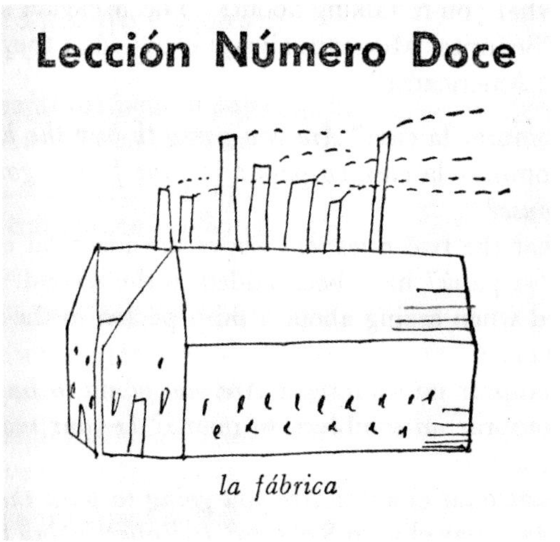

There are many ways to think about that passive aggression, of course. It might well be understood as an innate and idiosyncratic quality of Warhol's personality, or a defensive reaction to his sickliness or sensitivity as a child, or to be born in response to the homophobia of the world at large. All of these are undoubtedly at least partially true but, for our purposes here, we might also imagine it to be a function of Hunky resentment or Hunky rage, of being raised in an environment that was full of cultural cues about his expected docility, silent submission and work without complaint. The

27 Andy Warhol, 'Lección Número Doce', from Margarita Madrigal's *Madrigal's Magic Key to Spanish* (1951).

prevailing ideas about art's social role drawn from Andrew Carnegie – that art should cultivate in its worker-beholders what ultimately amounted to passivity and submissiveness towards their employer – was not the least of these cues.

In the larger picture, this is exactly the sort of emasculating bias that helped to cultivate other kinds of aggression and rage through the twentieth century, much of it directed at the pretence of high culture as a substitute for social welfare of a more immediate, material kind. For example, the comparison between the plight of African Americans and that of the immigrant working class recruited by the steel and railroad industries was clear to one German critic who, in an open letter addressed to the American people written in full baron-like bombast, called for 'some modern Harriet Beecher Stowe' to write an *Uncle Tom's Cabin* about the lot of the 'white negroes of Ellis Island', and for Carnegie and his fellow plutocrat John D. Rockefeller to establish a fund aiding immigrants rather than wasting their millions on libraries and universities.[29] He did not mention museums, but he might as well have.

Indeed, the peculiar passive aggression of Warhol's Hunky hipsterism, which would not fully flower until the 1960s, might well be said to draw on a similar set of desires as those explored in Norman Mailer's much-discussed essay 'The White Negro: Superficial Reflections on the Hipster', published in 1957: 'Generally, we are obliged to act with a nervous system which has been formed from infancy, and which carries in the style of its circuits the very contradictions of our parents and our early milieu', wrote Mailer. The white hipsters he was concerned with had adopted the style and métier of black culture not only to take on 'the "dead weight of the institutions of the past" but indeed the inefficient and often antiquated nervous circuits of the past which strangle our potentiality for responding to new possibilities'.[30] That is, Warhol was trying to work his way out of the habituated, embodied experience of

Slav Industrial Age oppression, to articulate an alternative way of being in the world than that of the passivity that Andrew Carnegie had, more than any other, imbued in the artistic values of his youth.[31]

The most obvious of those flips or reversals of the soft oppression he was raised with turned on the idea or image of the factory and, correspondingly, the worker within. We will explore Warhol's version of factory life in greater detail in chapters to come, but for the moment we can simply note that it felt nothing like the superhuman strength and subhuman sense of purpose celebrated by the great folklore-cum-fakelore figure of Joe Magarac, 'the Paul Bunyan of Steel', who may or may not have been born of Hunky worker pride (even though celebrated as such by social realists like William Gropper: illus. 26) but would subsequently be championed in propaganda by the steel industry itself.[32] Instead, it would be an image of the factory turned from a site of political and economic conflict and cooperation into the palatable fare of consumable experience, into Warhol's rendering of the factory as a childlike fairytale and a playground for childlike adults (illus. 27).

3
SHIRLEY TEMPLE

From the early years of his childhood, Warhol was particularly fond of making art inspired by various contemporary, mass culture sources, and he developed a special and long-lasting obsession with the child star Shirley Temple (*b.* 1928).[1] Temple, it turned out, provided Warhol with something that would serve him well throughout his life: she modelled a manner of operating in the world – a style or role or comportment – that mixed both child and adult functions and attributes, both innocence and *savoir faire*. If anything, Warhol's deadpan demeanour ran to the other extreme from Temple's delightfully bubbly persona, but he nonetheless developed a deep-seated identification with and appreciation for her role as a child or childlike figure operating in an adult world. As one characteristic description of that role has it, 'Little Shirley Temple dispensed sweetness and light, beguiling her adult audiences and upstaging her adult co-stars.'[2] Little Andy Warhola, and, later, successful commercial artist, and later still, Pop Art superstar Andy Warhol, succeeded at playing his own version of the same.

As a star, Shirley Temple was readily available for Warhol's childhood attentions. According to *Time* magazine, in 1936, the year both Warhol and Temple turned eight and the year in which Warhol became obsessed with her, she was the 'world's most photographed person', appearing in an average of twenty mass media celebrity photographs daily and competing evenly

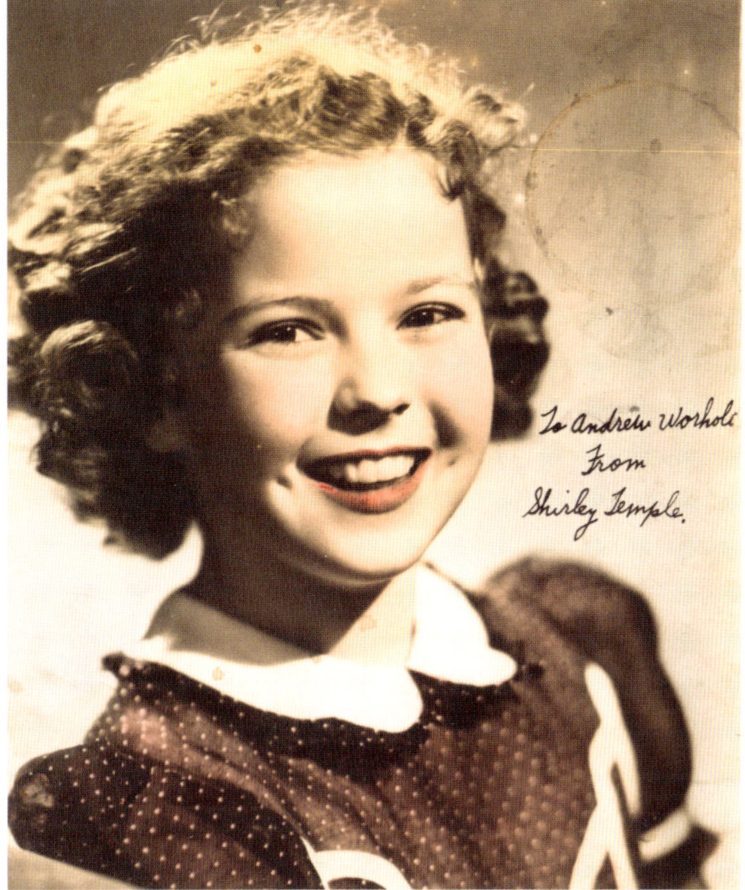

28 Andy Warhol's hand-coloured photograph of Shirley Temple, autographed to Warhol in 1941.

with President Roosevelt for name recognition. She had been made an honorary officer of various children's clubs and other organizations around the world (including, for example, the Kiddies Club of England, whose 165,000 members pledged themselves to 'imitate' her 'character, conduct and manners'), a captain of the Texas Rangers, and mascot to the Chilean Navy.[3] Her films regularly broke revenue records and she set a standard of success that has still not been surpassed when, for the four years running from 1935 through 1938, she led all other stars at the box office. The tremendous sales of the coats, hats, shoes, dolls, books, toys, dresses, underwear, soap, hair ribbons and tableware produced in her name, together with her films, which grossed \$1–\$1.5 million each, made for a boom industry during the later years of the Great Depression.[4]

The young Warhol was an active and enthusiastic participant in this mass cultural economy, regularly attending Shirley Temple screenings, joining the Shirley Temple fan club, collecting Shirley Temple merchandise and promotional materials and contributing his share to the 4,000 fan letters that deluged the child star each week.[5] His role as fan was honoured by his family when what was reportedly his single most cherished possession, a publicity still signed 'To Andrew Warhola from Shirley Temple', was displayed on the living room mantlepiece next to the crucifix that commemorated his father's death (illus. 28). This active interest continued even after Temple's star began to fade in 1939 and was not fully displaced until the autumn of 1948, when Warhol redirected his attentions (and his fan letters) to Truman Capote. 'When he was a child, Andy Warhol had this obsession about me and used to write me from Pittsburgh', Capote reported. 'When he came to New York, he used to stand outside my house, just stand out there all day waiting for me to come out. He wanted to become a friend of mine, wanted to speak to me, to talk to me. He nearly drove me crazy.'[6] In the end, as Capote would later describe Warhol's adolescent transition, 'I became Andy's Shirley Temple (illus. 29).'[7]

According to his biographers, much of the artwork produced by Warhol throughout his childhood bore the signs of obsession and devotion characteristic of the fan's peculiar form of appreciation. Picking up techniques as a child he would use all his life, he made artworks by collaging, tracing, transferring and otherwise appropriating images from various

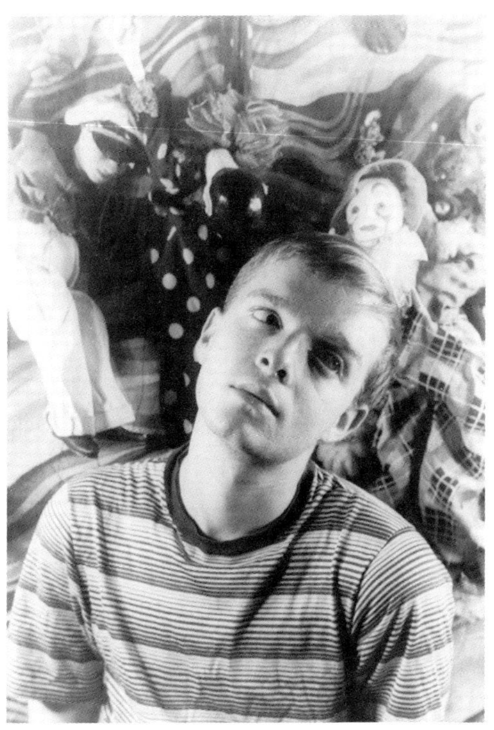

29 Carl Van Vechten, *Truman Capote*, 1948, photograph.

mass cultural sources. On the whole, his artistic imagination was captivated by movie magazines rather than baseball cards and by displays of grace rather than demonstrations of vigour. Among his childhood and adolescent boy peers, such enthusiasms were probably distinctive. Not only did Warhol display a general disregard for sports stars or action heroes such as Flash Gordon, Superman or gangster-cum-G-man James Cagney, but he was particularly drawn to child-size figures like Mickey Mouse, Little Orphan Annie and Shirley Temple, who functioned successfully in the worlds they inhabited through the exercise of impish charm and cleverness rather than through feats of bodily strength and bravura.

Warhol would continue to occupy such a position as an enthusiast during his art school days and after. He was, his art school colleagues have reported, 'innocent and naïve' and just 'like an angel'. He was 'the damndest mixture of a six-year-old child and a well-trained artist', one remembers, 'He put them both together totally without inhibition.'[8] At art school, Warhol came to be particularly drawn to imagery that confirmed his position as the innocent or 'class baby', if often in a mischievous manner. Images of cherubs and putti were recurrent motifs, for example, and his drawings and paintings of little boys masturbating and urinating, numerous images of himself as a young boy picking his nose, images of haloed figures and others vomiting, an image of a woman sitting on a toilet titled *Constipated Woman* and an image of a woman breastfeeding a puppy (about which he confided to a friend that he had always 'felt like a puppy' as a child) all received special attention and consolidated his distinctive position among his peers.[9] As his early art teacher and mentor Joseph Fitzpatrick described him, Andy 'knew exactly what to do to get the attention he outwardly seemed to avoid', and he achieved this again and again by playing the role of the child operating in an adult world.[10]

Temple's immense star appeal and reception in the 1930s reached well beyond mere novelty effect or an audience of children.[11] The leading film critic Gilbert Seldes referred to her in 1935, for example, as 'one of the few interesting actresses of the present screen', ultimately on a par only with Mae West, the box office leader of 1933. There was, Seldes wrote, 'something rude and rowdy in [Temple's] characteristic expression [that] is positively boisterous, a sort of hoot at the pomposity of the entire grown-up world'.[12] In all her films of the 1930s, Temple's characters assumed a precocious masquerade of adulthood, enabling them to intervene in adult situations and address adult themes without risking adult repercussions. The licence granted her as a child-innocent-cum-adult authorized her special powers: 'precisely *because* she was young – and not yet a sexual being to control or fear,' one film historian has noted, 'she could dictate her needs, act on her whims, and meddle in the business of all concerned.'[13]

Beyond her general appeal, however, such affecting boisterousness and uncommon mode of authority, with its implicit critique of adult norms and pretences, probably had a distinct appeal for the young Warhol. By all accounts he felt isolated as a child and did his best to keep to himself. 'Little, queer, mommy's boy', as Simon Watney has described the child Warhol, 'Spotty', as the kids in his Pittsburgh neighbourhood nicknamed him after his uneven complexion, or 'Andy the Red-nosed Warhola', as his own family called him, was 'predictably teased, bullied, hurt and humiliated'.[14] Feeling like an outsider in his home town because of his shyness, his complexion, his various childhood traumas and his sexuality, Warhol found comfort, community and a shared sense of exceptionalism through his spectatorial relationships with mass-mediated personalities.

Such a special relationship with the cinema is not unusual for homosexual children growing up in a heterosexist society.[15] Feeling isolated and out of sync with the sexual culture surrounding him, the surplus glamour, personality and excitement of cinema may well have provided Warhol, as for many others, with a corollary for the manner in which his own sexuality exceeded local norms. In particular, the roles played by leading female film stars have been important for this identification with cinema by gay boys and men.[16] Michael Moon, for example, describing the 'impulse to "scream with joy"' as a homosexual boy at the movies, raises the following question about gay male fan response to Hollywood leading women:

> For how many gay men of my own and the previous generation were our earliest intimations that there might be a gap between our received gender identity and our subjective or 'felt' one the consequence not of noticing our own erotic attraction to another boy or man but of enthusiastically enjoying and identifying with the performative excesses of Maria Montez rather than John Hall, or Lana Turner rather than Burt Lancaster, or Jayne Mansfield rather than Mickey Hargitay?[17]

Warhol, according to his biographers, identified with Temple in a manner similar to the experience described by Moon. He would bear that early identification throughout the rest of his life in, among other things, several characteristic hand gestures. His appropriation was not yet aestheticist and ironic in tone, or even overtly theatrical and boisterous, but it did provide something related to the critical cultural foothold often associated with camp. Shirley Temple's magical silver screen ability to play a double role, claiming and exploiting both child status and adult status in her negotiations with the adult worlds she moved in, provided Warhol with a dynamic structural model for his own social relations. The position Temple occupied both inside and outside 'the pomposity of the entire grown-up world' offered Warhol a means for negotiating a place for himself in the sexual culture of his youth and in the professional art cultures of his adulthood.

In order to get a full sense of the peculiar 'performative excess' of the Shirley Temple that Warhol responded to, we need to understand her appeal in the context of the star type of the period, which first emerged with the gangster genre in 1930–31 and developed with the rise to dominance of Mae West in 1933 and with Temple's own emergence as a star in 1934. For our purposes, the determining historical factor linking the development of the idea of the star across this series of very different figures was the institution of a clearly defined line delimiting acceptable from unacceptable film content, formalized by the 1934 Production Code. In each of the three moments, the prohibitions made law by the Code functioned as a boundary that each of the three star types – tragic gangster, ironic vamp and delightful imp – transgressed. While the three approaches to the Code's limits of propriety differed dramatically, it was the transgression itself that generated appeal and success for each of the genres. As we will see, Warhol adapted his distinctive, and distinctively appealing, approach to the transgression of societal norms from these predecessors.

The Production Code, instituted when Warhol was six years old and thus at the onset of his movie-going career, was a film industry capitulation to demands generated by a nation-wide campaign led by Church groups, politicians, newspaper publishers and others seeking content restrictions. This campaign was incited by a series of academic and popular studies assessing the ill effects of cinematic violence on children in particular and on social values generally.[18] Beginning in 1933, explicit representations of and allusions to sexuality would also be targeted by the reformers and incorporated into the Code's restrictions, but initially the principal concern was violence. The catalyst for this campaign was the gangster genre that came to drive the industry in 1930 and '31, keeping it viable in the period just following the stock market crash. After the significant box office success of Warner Brothers's graphic drama *Little Caesar*, the industry stepped up production, bringing some 50 gangster films to the screen in 1931.

With increased production and increased audience interest there came increased criticism by a wide variety of reformers. The threat posed by gangster films, it was argued, far exceeded the threat of gangland crimes themselves or the threat of reports about such crimes in the media because of the cinema's unique and powerful capacity to create internal 'states of excitement' and a 'loss of self-control'.[19] The glamorization and melodramatization of violence and crime in gangster films, it was claimed, was having a strong psychosocial impact and negatively affecting public morality. What the reformers achieved, regardless of their intentions, was a sublimation and thus redirection of violent and sexual energies in the movies. That redirection would later become the hallmark of the diffuse sexuality and violence in Warhol's mature artwork.

The gangland genre was only the beginning of a much larger transformation in Hollywood-manufactured mass culture during the 1930s. Robert Warshow described that change broadly in his still useful essay of 1948, 'The Gangster as Tragic Hero': 'At a time when the normal condition of the citizen is a state of anxiety, euphoria spreads over our culture like the broad smile of an idiot.' Gangster films played a central role in the cultural expression of that euphoria but they also marked an important difference from its purest expression in, for example, the large-scale production values, exaggerated glamour, overwrought sentiment and preposterous imagery of too-easily realized social harmony that characterized the work of directors such as Busby Berkeley and Frank Capra. The euphoria generated by Hollywood's Golden Age was thin and never fully satisfying to its participants, Warshow argued, and as a result there also existed 'a current of opposition seeking to express by whatever means are available to it that sense of desperation and inevitable failure which optimism itself helps to create'.[20] This was the other side of the gangster genre's saleable excess. Its double valence – euphoria and despair – registered aesthetically in the gritty, fast-paced urban realism and in the mix of isolation and autonomy of the gangster-hero (illus. 30).

With a mass appeal corresponding to the degree to which he registered as outside community and outside the law, both autonomous and alone, the 1930s figure of the gangster was an abstraction. Dissociated from existing social institutions, he was defined only negatively, as threatening to, rather than productive of, social value. Attempting to pre-empt criticisms from reformers that would exploit that appeal, Warner Brothers provided a concise summary of this abstract position in a textual moral at the conclusion to *The Public Enemy* (1931): '"The Public Enemy" is not a man nor is it a character – it is a problem that sooner or later WE, the public must solve.' 'It' – the gangster – drew its appeal and its threat from a form of free-market purity separate from political concepts of value. 'WE, the public', on the other hand, were assumed to be a strictly

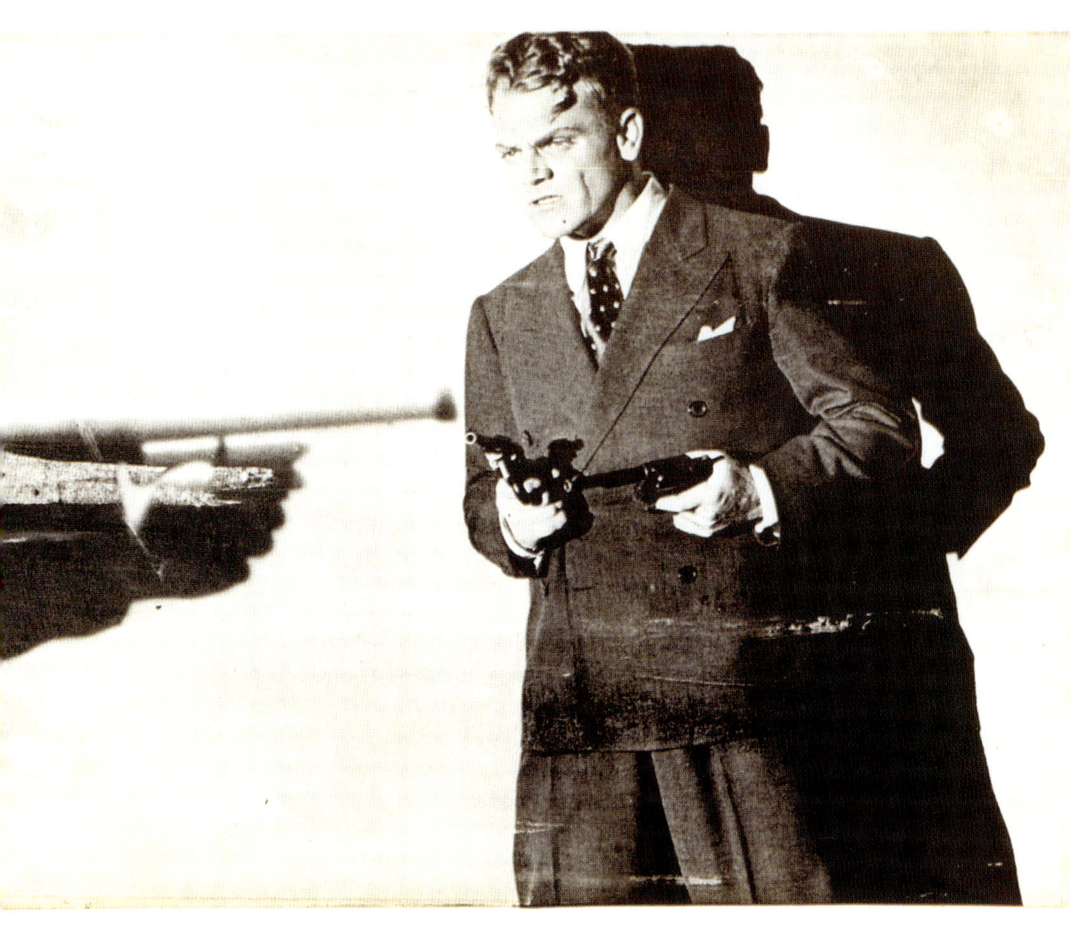

30 Andy Warhol, *Cagney*, 1962–4, silkscreen ink on paper, mounted on canvas, 76.2 × 101.6 cm.

political body faced only with issues of collective welfare and threatened by the gangster's disregard of such issues. The idea of public value was both the source of appeal and the source of condemnation of the gangster as star.

The '30s gangster, thus, was both the full realization of and antidote to the businessman as the leading cultural icon of the 1920s. Insofar as he was successful in portraying a position fully removed from the rule of law, he functioned as the sign of uninhibited free-market exchange. Insofar as he succeeded in embodying that role, he was reduced to a sign of pure market relations. The gangster's star status and function were based on a phantasmatic position outside the law not subject to the political mediation of social relations governed by the state. However, by focusing attention on the desperation structural to the place of the beholder in the marketplace during the Depression and highlighting the newly conflicted relations of political and economic forces, the gangster film also functioned as pastiche and the gangster-as-star registered as pathos: he served as an exaggerated representation of the critical condition of capitalism, and of the primary subjects of capitalism – that is, the capitalists themselves – in the 1930s. By allegory and by exaggeration, the gangster genre melodramatized the social Darwinism of the marketplace, rendering it for popular consumption. The gangster's bigger-than-life star status drew its affective charge from both its profit-motivated transgression of civic norms defining the limits of marketplace competition and its pathos-ridden burlesque of the free-market purity of the businessman-transgressor.[21]

I will pause here briefly to indicate the main implication of this sidebar on film history for the larger story about Warhol. The structure of the complex role I have been describing – the gangster as exception and pastiche, as an outsider that surpasses and an insider that symptomatizes the social ambitions available in the world around him – would serve Warhol well as a model for his own practice as an artist and as a recurrent theme in his art. That theme would be developed across a whole host of exceptional public figures that stood in to illustrate the central conceit of his portraiture: the interloper-cum-notable-cum-buffoon. James Cagney, Marilyn Monroe, Elvis Presley, Huey Long, Mao Zedong, Vladimir Lenin and many more would all serve in that role for Warhol's art, each having made his or her name as a manner of outsider, only to have that name hollowed out by notoriety inside the larger celebrity system. The problem that Warhol adopted as his project was how to forestall the final, (tragic) moment of buffoonery in this narrative scheme by effectively preserving the critical foothold of the outsider within the position of the notable insider as a stable duality. I turn now to a discussion of how this double role of the outsider as insider came to be readily available as a model and an ideal to the young Warhol.

Up to and through 1932, the Hollywood reform movement had focussed primarily on gangster films and the effects of their glamorization of crime. Beginning in 1933, however, Hollywood would respond to the criticism by starting to play down the gangster and initiating his conversion from underworld mobster into a voice of the law itself, as the G-man (or Government-man), modelled after J. Edgar Hoover and his suddenly popular FBI. At the same time, the reform campaign took on new purpose and vigour in response to the Mae West phenomenon.[22] West had already earned a national reputation from her arrest in 1927 on obscenity charges for producing two plays: *Sex*, a story about prostitution, and *The Drag*, 'a comedy-drama of homosexuality'. In 1933, however, with her first two starring pictures, *She Done Him Wrong* and *I'm No Angel*, she attained a new level of popular notoriety. In the words of the trade journal *Variety*, she was 'the biggest conversation-provoker, free space grabber and all-around box office bet in the country', and was even 'as hot an issue as Hitler'.[23] At the centre of the new moralism driving the development and enforcement of the Production Code now was the threat posed by the unbridled sexuality of West's characters.[24]

West represented a very different idea of sexuality from her screen-temptress predecessors, Greta Garbo and Marlene Dietrich. One contemporary critic referred to her as 'the first real Waterloo of the Garbo and Dietrich schools of sultry, languorous, erotic emotions'. West made the earlier stars appear 'slightly foolish – as if they didn't know how to get a "kick" out of life'; her 'healthy Amazonian, audacious presentation of the ancient appeal known as sex' made 'the world-weary, secretive charm of Greta and Marlene appear feeble by comparison' (illus. 31).[25] West herself played this card as well: 'I think that the pictures are all wrong in the way that they feature starved ingénues. You know the flat-chested girls you see on the screen. Pained faces, sharp shoulders, knobby knees, terrible spaces between their legs So flat you can't tell which way they are going.'[26] The 'audacity' or sexual surplus of West surpassed the deep, throaty, feminist sexuality of Dietrich and Garbo in a specific sense. Leo McCarey, who directed West in *Belle of the Nineties* (1934), put it this way:

> I wonder how many people realize that Mae West satirizes sex? She has made our old-fashioned vampires, those

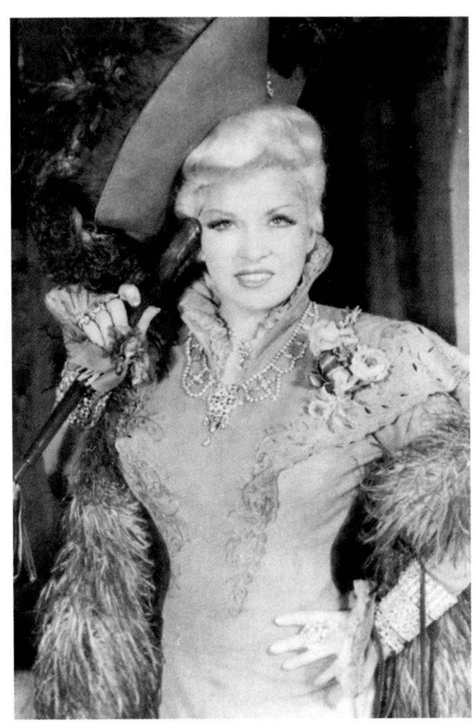

31 Mae West as 'Diamond Lil', c. 1928.

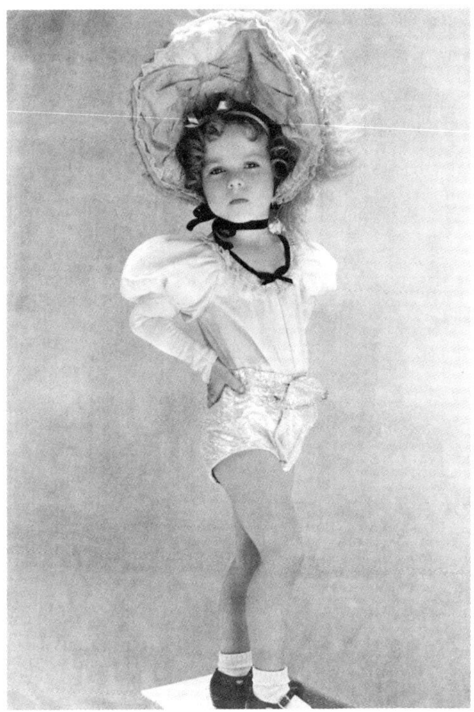

32 Promotional photograph of Shirley Temple as 'La Belle Diaperina', modelled on Mae West's 'Diamond Lil', for the film *Glad Rags to Riches* (1933).

mysterious, pallid, emaciated, smoky-eyed females appear as futile as they usually are in real life.[27]

She was, as George Davis put it to *Vanity Fair* readers in 1934, 'the greatest female impersonator of all time'.[28] In the words of one feminist film historian, 'She had balls.'[29] West's audacity and her power were to make sex and sexual identity casual, and the social role of sex fun, fluid and impermanent. She engaged directly and frankly with sexuality without the burden of love or worry about commitment, without the peril of loss of virtue or the threat of castration. She 'divests sex of everything that is dark, dangerous, primeval', writes one commentator on West as camp, 'under her aegis, it becomes a children's romp.'[30]

Proposed in West's work, and central to what she described as her career ambition to educate 'the masses to certain sex truths', was an image of a libidinal economy unrestrained by moral strictures.[31] Her role as actress-educator was to occupy the position of the ever-unattached sexual impulse or abstract desire, circulating freely and undermining the social boundaries that cloistered women, isolated homosexuals and repressed everyone. As her contemporary, the French novelist Colette, put it, 'She alone, out of an enormous and dull catalogue of heroines, does not get married at the end of the film . . . She alone has no parents, no children, no husband.'[32] Alone and autonomous like the gangster, the West character used abstract sexuality – sexuality separate from its role in social organization – against society's strictures while at the same time lampooning or camping on her own role as the harlot degrading social mores. Representing both sexual autonomy and social isolation, she functioned as both agent and burlesque of sexual liberation. This, in a nutshell, would be the trick that Warhol would take from Mae West and her subsequent sublimation in the child star Shirley Temple: he would take the 'dark, dangerous, primeval' – the profoundly abrasive, industrial setting of Pittsburgh, the powerfully conflicted desires of a homosexual boy growing up in a sometimes brutally heterosexual world, the ritual mysteries of his deeply felt Byzantine Catholic faith – and make it over into a burlesque of the unrestricted play of 'a children's romp'.

By the end of 1934, after an ineffective first effort, the reformers at the Production Code Administration had succeeded in suppressing West's sexuality and personality to their satisfaction.[33] In her place, Shirley Temple emerged as the premier Hollywood figure celebrated for spunk and candour. This substitution was noted in 1935 by Gilbert Seldes in an *Esquire* article titled 'Two Great Women', in which he asked the reader to 'relish the similarity between Shirley Temple and Mae West'.[34] Temple's appeal, Seldes argued, was like that 'which you find in every movement of Mae West across the screen'. It was not only the six-year-old's childlike qualities that were compelling, in other words: 'I am thoroughly convinced, not only by herself, but by her audiences', Seldes wrote, 'that the celebrated dimpling and cuteness have very little to do with her real power, because at her good moments something like a growl of satisfaction arises from the men in the audience.'[35]

Such a growl was audible in several of the reviews by the film critic and soon-to-be-novelist Graham Greene, the last of which resulting in a successful libel suit brought by Temple and her benefactors. On his first viewing of her in *The Littlest Rebel*

(1935), he described his response by saying that he had not expected her 'tremendous energy' which he found 'a little too enervating' and which he included in the category of 'disreputable enjoyments'.[36] In his review of *Captain January* (1936), Greene described the picture as being 'a little depraved, with an appeal interestingly decadent' and concluded by saying that Temple's 'popularity seems to rest on a coquetry quite as mature as Miss [Claudette] Colbert's and on an oddly precocious body as voluptuous in grey flannel trousers as Miss Dietrich's'.[37] Finally, in the review for which he was found to be libellous and which effectively ended his career as a film reviewer, he wrote: 'infancy is her disguise, her appeal is more secret and more adult.' Referring to his earlier review but now in more explicit terms, he added,

> In *Captain January* she wore trousers with the mature suggestiveness of a Dietrich: her neat and well-developed rump twisted in the tap-dance: her naked eyes had a sidelong searching coquetry. Now in *Wee Willie Winkie* [1937], wearing short kilts, she is completely totsy . . . Watch the way she measures a man with agile studio eyes, with dimpled depravity [using] her well-shaped and desirable little body.[38]

With language like this, it is tempting to make assumptions about Seldes's and Greene's individual sexual predilections and 'imaginary or displaced' projections on to the screen image of Shirley Temple. Such assumptions on their own, however, may not be completely fair or historically adequate. Both reviewers claimed to be observing a response consistent among male audiences. Seldes invoked the 'growl of satisfaction' from men in the audience and Greene called on his reader to 'hear the gasp of excited expectation from her antique audience' of 'middle-aged men and clergymen'.[39]

In the just-born era of the Production Code and in the years just following the low point of the Great Depression and the greatest losses the industry had ever seen, Hollywood producers needed to develop new ways to use the old formulas. Sex and violence that exceeded social norms, it had been proven in 1930 and 1933, would sell, even in the depths of the Depression. The burden faced by industry strategists in search of greater market share was to subsume the aesthetic charge of transgressive social types like Mae West and James Cagney into new, Code-passable forms. The violence problem was overcome with relative ease, by shifting from one side of the law to the other, from gangsters to G-men as the agents of male power and authority.[40] The sex problem, however, was more difficult. It was not possible, for example, to simply switch from extramarital sex to that bound by marriage, or from promiscuity to single-partner sexuality, because sexual subject-matter and direct allusions of all varieties were explicitly prohibited.[41]

The formula role played by Shirley Temple in nearly all of her early Hollywood hits was that of an orphan taken care of by an unmarried man.[42] The male lead is depicted as noble and generous, looking after the welfare of little orphan Shirley, and she is depicted as the source of some essential human bond that had been missing in his life prior to their relationship. That relationship is typically filled with emotional and physical intimacy, as man and child forge their bond. Typically as well, those scenes are most tender at moments when the relationship is threatened by a moralizing outsider who assumes that these relations between a young girl and an unmarried, adult man are inappropriate. Frequently a love triangle develops, with the male lead refusing the attentions of an available adult woman and devoting himself instead to Temple. By the end there is a rapprochement, with Temple returned to child status and the two adults paired off, but that is only a formality and is superfluous to the central narrative dynamic.

The primary narrative agency of her characters is unguarded and innocent intimacy, and the distinctive charge Temple generated resulted in large part from the way her characters worked the boundary between child and adult sexuality.

Such play across levels of maturity was explicit (and intended as the punchline) in the pre-Production Code, one-reel 'Baby Burlesks' of 1932–3, in which she played roles modelled after Marlene Dietrich in the character of Morelegs Sweet-trick and after Mae West as prostitute in the character of Gold Digger, as well as other memorable personalities such as Girlfriend, La Belle Diaperina (illus. 32) and Madame Cradlebait. The juxtaposition of child and adult qualities was more nuanced and less slapstick in Temple's blockbuster films of 1934 to 1938 but nonetheless governed their narratives and the provocation that helped generate their audience appeal.[43]

Temple's sexuality and its place in film history have been observed by many film historians and critics. Molly Haskell, for example, has argued that Shirley Temple functioned as a 'deviant in disguise' and as the 'ideal post-Production Code sex kitten', while another commentator labelled her 'a stunted figure of feminine sexuality in an era of economy and restriction'.[44] In this regard, Temple did to Mae West exactly what the G-man did to the gangster: she sublated an image of transgressive excess into a socially acceptable form. However, such accounts, which focus on the repression of sexuality by housing it in the more protected, more regulated body of a child, only explain part of her appeal.

The best study on this question is Charles Eckert's essay 'Shirley Temple and the House of Rockefeller' (1974). In Eckert's analysis, Temple's appeal as a character served specific narrative functions that we can also compare to West and her gangster predecessors: 'to soften hard hearts (especially of the wealthy), to intercede on behalf of others, [and] to effect liaisons between members of opposed social classes'. More than simply a toned-down, Code-passable form of sexual surplus, Temple's characters used that sublimated surplus as a medium for social change, breaking down the boundaries between existing social groups. As Eckert describes her new mode of being in the world without conforming to its categories, 'The solution Shirley offers is natural: one opens one's heart.' Like the appeal of the gangster and Mae West, Temple offered her audiences an image of autonomy and escape from the strictures of existing social institutions. No longer able to sell tickets with graphic images of violence and explicit references to sex, Shirley Temple raised the bar by sublimating the mobile sexuality of West and invoking an alternate ideal of abstract, disinterested, non-institutional love – the love of an orphan – love without enduring ties to any single individual or social group but instead equally available to all.[45] As Warhol would put it in 1962, expressing his dissatisfaction with the normative rapprochement that concluded Temple films,

> I was so disappointed when Shirley found her father [or, we might add, when her male co-star found his mate]. It ruined everything. She had been having such a good time, tap dancing with the local Kiwanis Club or the newspaper men in the city room.[46]

Or, as he had it a few years later about his own idea of a good time: 'I never wanted to be a painter; I wanted to be a tap-dancer.'[47]

Thus, Temple's special powers as a child-adult made her different from the G-man, and in a manner similar to Warhol's adult-child workaround of social norms in the decades that followed. Where the G-man fully institutionalized violence in the service of the law, shoring up the boundaries that delineated acceptable from unacceptable social forms, Temple retained the abstract, boundary-crossing imperative of her transgressive antecedent, Mae West. Neither Temple nor West represented group interests: their characters were typically free of stable relations with friends, lovers, families, neighbourhoods or any larger social institutions, and their affective bonds with others were grounded on the universal principles of love and desire rather than on family histories or community mores. Temple's appeal as a child was her unguarded, seemingly unmediated affection; her appeal as an orphan was her availability. Like West, her characters circulate freely in her films without responsibility or attachment to family or other traditional social unit. She was in this way *alone* like West and the gangster before her, and her ebullient personality – her capacity to radiate love outwards towards all those around her – was rendered as an abstract social principle: fluid, mobile, unattached. Temple's great appeal, therefore, the way in which she contributed to the spectacular 'idiotic euphoria' of the 1930s, was that she made love casual and occasional, free from the rule of family, community or state, divorced from the rule of governing social institutions. Warhol, as we will see, did something similar for the 'idiotic euphoria' of the 1960s and, by extension, for that of our own day.

This ideal of an unattached and mobile affect running askew to socially accepted forms of civic participation and adult sexuality was the model for relating to the world that Warhol would adopt and develop as his artistic medium. Among other gains that this provided, it made him emotionally invulnerable.[48] It is important, however, to also be clear about what such an ideal is *not* in Warhol's case: it is not a normative, heterosexual relationship to the world or that of a naturalized gender role, of course, but neither is it really a form of gender-bending or the adopting of a transgender, inter-gender or pointedly queer persona, a persona that revels in its status as a third sex in the manner of a fabulous and flamboyant drag queen, for example (illus. 34). Instead,

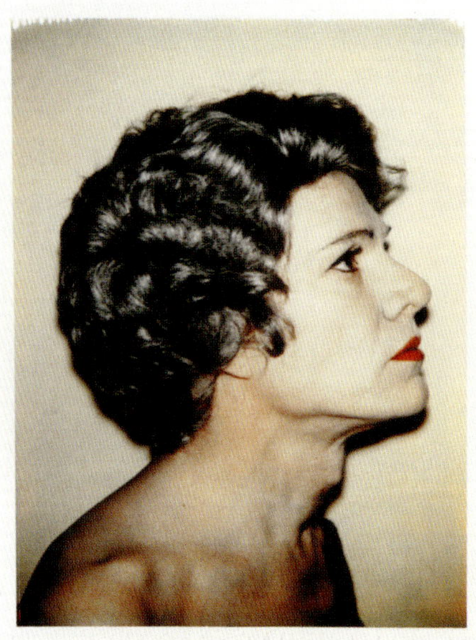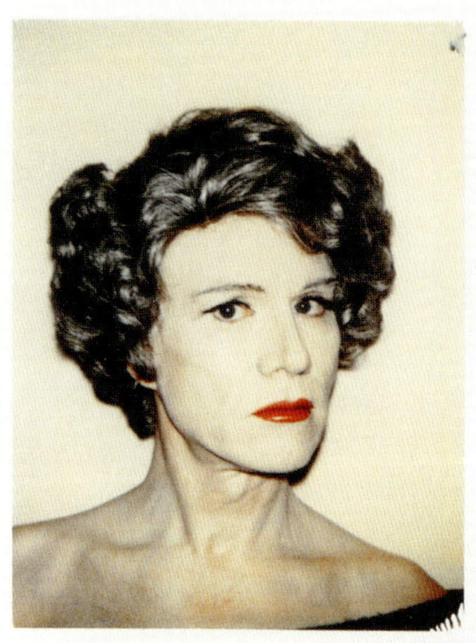

Warhol's sexual ideal was really asexual, or omnisexual, or maybe something like infrasexual (illus. 33). Like Mae West's, his was really a satire of sex – it was sexuality without love or commitment or reproduction, of course, but also sexuality without intense, exceptional pleasure, without the targeted surge of libido that makes mature sexual beings shine with the thrill of feeling alive.

    This, it might be said, was the cost and the gain of maintaining childlike status as an adult. The gain for Warhol born of sidestepping 'normal' adult sexuality was, as the film historian said of Shirley Temple, that 'she could dictate her needs, act on her whims, and meddle in the business of all concerned'. This allowed him his status as abstract, untethered social principle, as fluid, mobile, unattached sexuality, as the 'idiotic euphoria' of sexual satire. The cost, however, was to live a life of negation or denial, a life of being other to himself. This had its own pleasure too, no doubt, but ultimately it

33 Andy Warhol, *Self-portrait in Drag*, 1980, polaroid photograph, 10.8 × 8.5 cm.

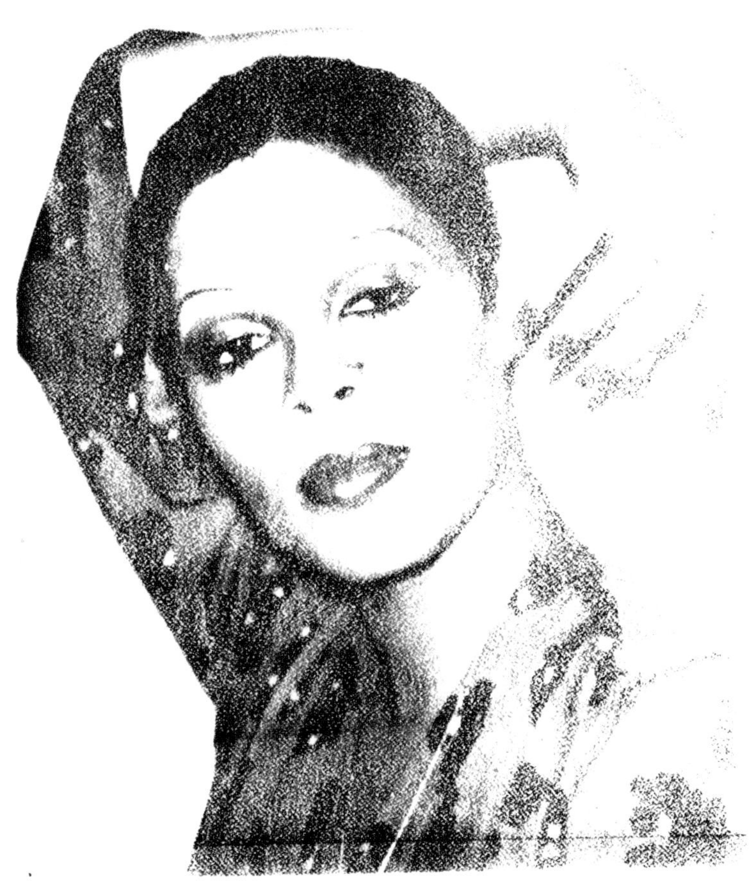

34 Andy Warhol, *Ladies and Gentlemen: One Plate*, 1975, screenprint, 102.2 × 64.8 cm.

might be best understood as the pleasure of discipline, the pleasure of labour, the pleasure of realizing his own, transformed version of the passive Hunky work ethos, and not the ecstatic, life-affirming pleasure of release.

4

AUBREY BEARDSLEY

According to his art school colleagues, Warhol went through
a brief period of fascination and identification with the tragi-
comic artistic master of the British Decadence movement,
Aubrey Beardsley (1872–1898), during his first year at Carnegie
Tech (illus. 36). His classmate and later roommate Philip
Pearlstein described this period:

> He was doing these eccentric drawings that the faculty
> didn't like – Aubrey Beardsley-type things . . . only wavy
> lines. It wasn't that he refused to conform; like any young
> kid, he was just doing what he did naturally.[1]

Indeed, as we will see in the next chapter, there were consid-
erable period justifications for the faculty to reject Warhol's
youthful and, at the time, idiosyncratic artistic inclinations that
are not easily reducible to simple normative criteria – homophobia, for example, or academic conservatism, or priggish,
heartland conventions and taste. Nonetheless, Warhol's
Beardsley phase was important in its own right too, even if
in the end it was so negatively, as something that would help
him come to terms with not only what worked and what didn't
with his audience – he would not have become the mature artist
that he eventually did had it not been for the rejection he faced
as an art student – but also what was and was not suited to his

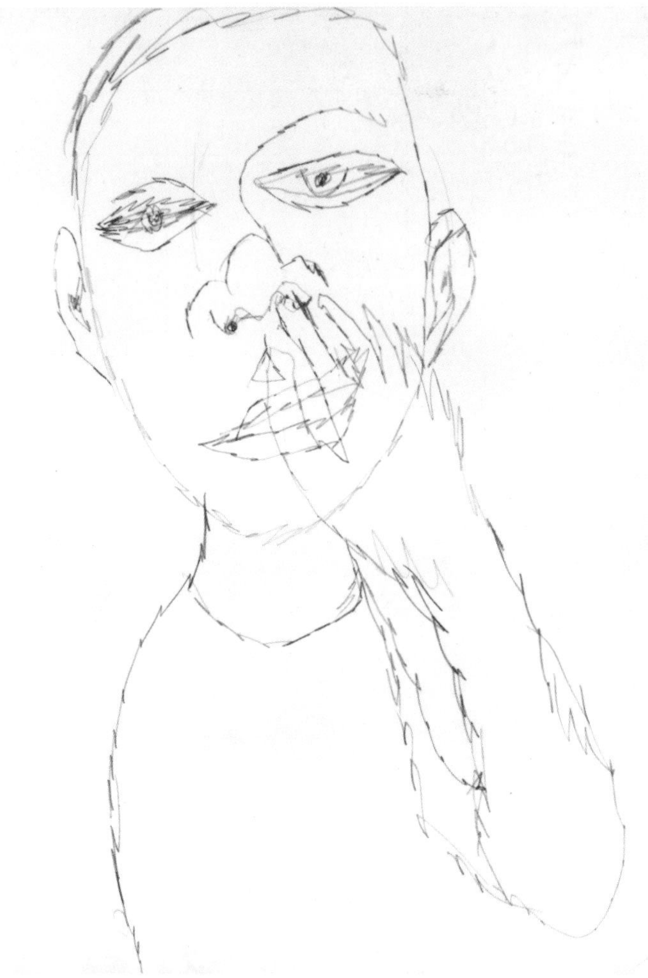

35 Andy Warhol, *Boy Picking His Nose*, 1948–9, pencil on paper, 48.3 × 34 cm.

personality, his upbringing and the community that gathered around him during the heyday of his career in New York.

Like a number of his fellow Decadents, Aubrey Beardsley converted from Protestantism to Catholicism as an adult, and his life as a whole was filled with fervour – fantastic, erotic, religious – and the different facets of that fervour are not so easy to extricate from one another. What the Church offered

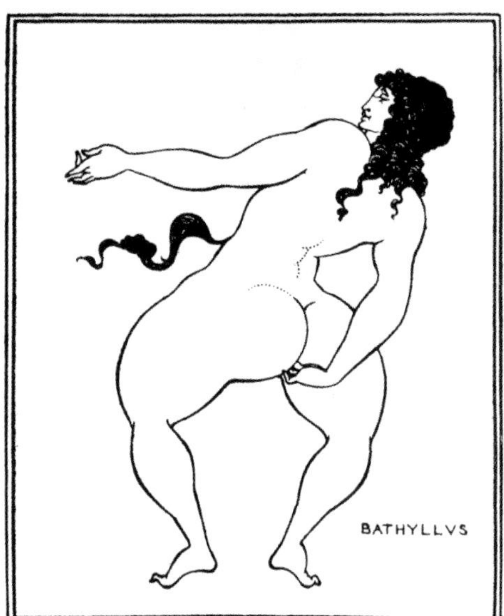

36 Aubrey
Beardsley,
*Bathyllus
Posturing*, 1896.

him, like any modern, was complex; what it did as a Decadent, even more so. As Ellis Hanson's thoughtful and well-researched study has it about the art and literature of Decadent Catholicism as a whole, the move to Catholicism and religiosity more generally was part of a larger 'border war that the Church has lost in modern times – that is the battle to maintain the paradox as such, to maintain the distinction between the spirit and the flesh, the Word and mere words'.[2] This effort to preserve 'paradox as such', as we saw in chapter One, was not so different from Warhol's own impulses and would certainly have been a point of identification for him. Maintaining that paradox was inextricable from the 'callous impersonality which could make even Stalinism seem sentimental', the mode of being in the world 'as indifferent to individual feelings as a psychopath', the Catholic understanding of human life as 'inherently institutional', which we have seen in Terry Eagleton's account of his own religious upbringing.[3]

There is a fundamental difference between Catholicism and Eastern Rite religious traditions like Warhol's, however, that goes back to the first millennium and carries on in the present. This difference helps explain a lot – a lot about Warhol's difference from Beardsley (or Eagleton, for that matter), for starters, but also much about his complex relations with the largely Catholic cohort who would later gather around him at the Factory. At the centre of that difference are two competing views of sin and salvation: the Orthodox doctrine of theosis, or the ever-present possibility of human divinization, on the one hand, and the

Augustinian doctrine of original sin, which holds that all of humanity is forever burdened with the guilt of Adam's transgressions. As Fr. Michael Azkoul plainly puts this distinction on behalf of the Orthodox faithful, 'We do not inherit the "guilt" of Adam. Human beings are victims of Adam's sin, not the bearers of it.'[4] One way to understand Warhol's social genius, the capacity that he would develop so effectively in the 1960s to inspire and direct others to a degree that often seemed cult-like, is to see it through this rudimentary distinction between the Byzantine and Roman traditions. Warhol learned how to work that distinction – and thereby work his largely Catholic colleagues, followers and hangers-on in the social swirl that became the Factory – by discovering his difference during a youthful foray into Beardsley's distinctively Catholic sensibility.

The Augustinian sense of endemic guilt and its corresponding experience of shame for Beardsley and his colleagues was the central engine of their distinctive sensibility. Shame, as Hanson puts it, was perceived as 'an artistic opportunity for self-fashioning' and 'the founding gesture of decadent style, a gesture appropriated from an earlier art form that we might call Christian penitence'.[5] Shame provided a kind of grace, a humanity or self-realization for a rationalized, instrumentalized and commercialized world that had lost its religious bearings. It represented a 'spiritualization of desire, a rebellion against nature and the instincts, and a polymorphous redistribution of pleasure'.[6] It was pleasure imagined, experienced and understood not through knowing the biomechanical system of desire developed by Darwin or the shrewd socio-mechanical calculus of Herbert Spencer, or through the guilt-free economy of petty bourgeois consumption being championed by the magnificent new department stores, shopping arcades and commercial postings, but instead in the affective register of the penitent, subordinate believer deeply entangled in the clerical and courtly traditions of the past.

The ritual exercise of that shame in Beardsley's stiff, formal, confessional drawings produced the pleasure of self-recognition, the pleasure of recognition of one's feelings despite their social unacceptability. The shame of wealth, of cruelty, of servitude, of greed and sloth and corpulence, of art and leisure, of luxury and finery, of fluid and elaborate gender and sexual identifications, are all pleasingly and painfully, tragically and comically represented in the refined line, sumptuous texture, extravagant posturing and indulgent theatrics of Beardsley's oeuvre. Shame was made the bearer of self-recognition by being given dispassionate, institutional form: the form of the confessional booth, of ritualized ceremony, elaborate doctrine and spectacular collective iconogenesis rather than the form of self-doubt. This was the pleasure of self-imagining, of identity glorying in the experience of its own self-elaboration in doctrine, ceremony, image and taste, all drawn from the wellspring of shame setting itself off against the judgment of law and the law of judgment. It was the pleasure of knowing oneself and being known.

Warhol, by contrast, was shameless. Everything about his personal and aesthetic sensibility bore the mark of that difference, of that disregard for the judgment of law. Even his most seemingly Beardsleyesque work, which flaunted its transgression and thereby conjured the boundary of moral judgment – such as the *Nosepicker* series and other mildly naughty drawings he did in art school, or the various sexualized drawings he produced during his stint as a commercial artist in the 1950s, or any of his sexually provocative films from the 1960s such as *Blow Job* or *Taylor Mead's Ass*, or his *Madonna and Child* photographs and silkscreen paintings of women breastfeeding in the 1970s – draws back from any acknowledgement of guilt or shame and from any acknowledgement of institutionally authorized boundaries of appropriate behaviour. Shame and taste, Warhol suggests, are inextricable concepts, inextricable feelings, because both rely on judgment. In the *Nosepicker* and

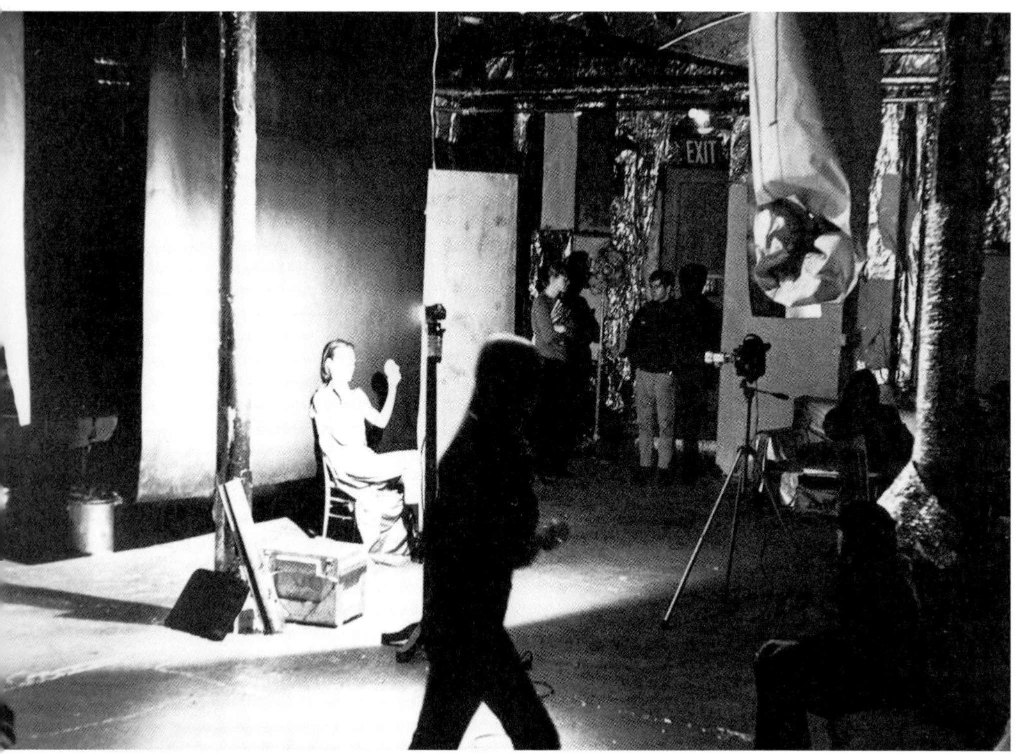

related drawings, for example, his means for sidestepping the
authority of judgment is simple: instead of adopting the refined
stylistic means of the adult sinner and indulging in the shame that
goes with it, he developed the sensibility and drawing style of the
precocious child, the child who works back and forth across the
boundary of adulthood (illus. 35). The great benefit of being a
child, Warhol learned early on from Shirley Temple, is the freedom
it offers from shame, the way in which it allows one to do or say
anything without the burden of normal adult self-censorship.

So it is that both Warhol's Orthodox upbringing and his
Shirley Temple-like child-adult persona served a common cause
in freeing him from reigning normative strictures – from the
burden of original sin to the would-be elevated form of docility,

37 Billy Name,
*Ivy Nicholson
Prepares for the
Shooting of her
Screen Test*, 1965,
photograph taken
at the Factory.

submission and work without complaint that Andrew Carnegie cultivated in the Hunky-cum-leisure-class artistic sensibility for his labourers in Pittsburgh, and to the great bourgeois imperative of progress, self-improvement or enlightenment more generally. No doubt such freedom was a powerful counter-incentive to the pleasures of adult sexuality and adult identity defined by moral authority, even if its cost was high. There was another benefit for Warhol born of suppressing his identity and sexuality, however, one that had more practical application.

Many in Warhol's circle of regular associates, assistants and collaborators were Catholics and their bond as a group and their attachment to Warhol can be understood in Catholic terms. Factory habitué and star of several of Warhol's films, Viva, explained it this way: 'The Factory was a way for a group of Catholics to purge themselves of Catholic repression' (illus. 37).[7] Christopher Makos had a related but different explanation for why the circle around Warhol was so consistently Catholic: 'He may have related better to us Catholics because we all had the same background: mass, priests, nuns, Catholic school, a sense of guilt.'[8] Makos's intimation that Warhol shared in this background is not correct, of course, since his background was not Roman Catholic at all but instead Eastern or Byzantine Catholic and thus did not share the Augustinian sense of guilt, but that does not mean that it was unimportant to him. Warhol's relationship to his Catholic retinue can be understood not as one of identification with their Catholic school education and deep-seated sense of guilt but instead as one of knowing how to work with that upbringing as an outsider to it. It is hard to know what he took from his brief period of interest in the tragic figure of Beardsley, but it seems likely enough that he would have developed an operative understanding of Beardsley's sensibility as a kind of trap – a trap of adulthood, perhaps, or a trap of morality, or the trap of identity – that was born of being too much in thrall to the guilt and shame of the Catholicism he turned to as

an adult. Warhol learned from his brief adolescent foray into
Beardsley's sensibility that guilt and shame were as much
indulgences as anything else and as such amounted to a form
of vulnerability. As a result his own relationship to the Catholics
that came to surround him in the 1960s and their need to 'purge
themselves of Catholic repression' was much more measured.
It might even be understood as opportunistic.

Beardsley and Warhol shared much, for sure, not the least
being their amorphous and complex sexuality, and the evident
desire of each to work the boundary between fine and commercial art. 'May not our hoardings claim kinship with the galleries,
and the designers of affiches pose as proudly in the public eye as
the masters of Holland Road or Bond Street Barbizon', Beardsley
could propose in 1894, for example, while savouring the
imagined affront that 'London will soon be resplendent with
advertisements.'[9] Warhol put it more simply when asked in
1962 if billboards influenced him: 'I think they're beautiful',
he replied.[10] Despite this commonality, however, the affront
posed by this common taste was different for each.

In Beardsley's case, we might understand it to be in keeping
with the class resentment that structured his *oeuvre* as a whole
and was developed in his best-known poem, about a barber whom
'nobody had seen . . . show / A preference for either sex', who
'cut, and coiffed, and shaved so well, / That all the world was at
his feet', until he encountered a thirteen-year-old princess whose
beauty was already so 'joyous and . . . lyrical and sweet', so
perfect, that the only service he could render and thereby be
recognized in his capacity as a razor-wielding barber was to slice
her neck.[11] The resplendence of the service class can only finally
and fully realize itself at a cost to that of its rulers, we are to
understand from Beardsley; it can only arrive as an inevitable
transgression of the law. 'That is the beauty of original sin',
Hanson puts it about the Catholicism of the Decadents generally,
'Sin attains the status of shame, an originary affect as inevitable

as desire.'[12] Beardsley's hoardings found their splendour in the shame that came from their transgression of a class-bound definition of good taste, in the beauty of exercising their original sin.

Warhol, on the other hand, found a different form of satisfaction in his transgression of the margin between fine and commercial art. What mass reproduction and consumer culture represented for him was not the emotional indulgence and self-absorption of shame but rather the formal authority of emotional distance and self-denial. Put differently, the boundary between 'the designers of affiches' and 'the masters of Holland Road or Bond Street Barbizon' mattered greatly to Beardsley, and his work is full of the frisson that results from transgressing that boundary. Warhol's genius, by contrast, was to not care, to not acknowledge the difference between one side of the boundary and the other, to pretend or believe that they were the same thing. Where Beardsley amplified the experience of judgment, in other words, Warhol rendered it insignificant, even non-existent.

Mirroring the world rather than carrying its weight on his shoulders was Warhol's manner, something that Truman Capote was able to summarize well when asked to explain Warhol's relationship to those that gathered around him:

I'll give you an interesting analogy here. Have you ever read Carson McCullers' *The Heart is a Lonely Hunter*? All right. Now, in that book you'll remember that this deaf mute, Mr Singer, this person who doesn't communicate at all, is finally revealed in a subtle way to be a completely empty, heartless person. And yet, because he's a deaf mute, he symbolizes things to desperate people. They come to him and tell him all their troubles. They cling to him as a source of strength, as a kind of semi-religious figure in their lives. Andy is kind of like Mr Singer. Desperate, lost people find their way to him, looking for some sort of salvation, and Andy sort of sits back like a deaf mute with very little to offer.[13]

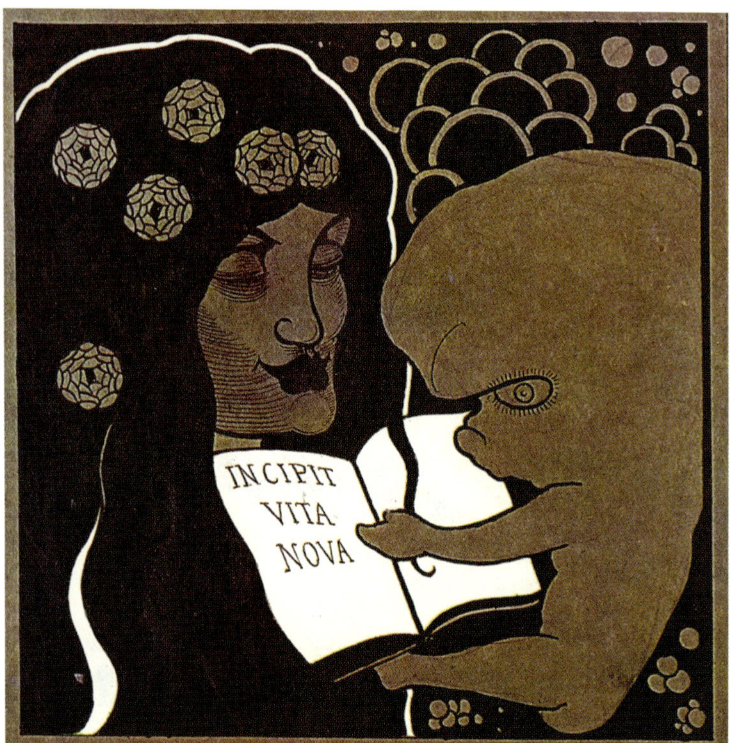

38 Aubrey Beardsley, *Incipit Vita Nova*, *c.* 1893, water-colour drawing.

Warhol's role was that of the deaf mute, the mirror, the icon or iconostasis, the blank screen that reflected back the desires of those around him and, in so doing, he constituted himself in the imaginary projections of others. As Wayne Koestenbaum has put it, 'into the unsafe space' of interpersonal relations '[Warhol] inserted not his own, vulnerable, actual body, but a replacement body, a mannequin, a dummy. *It looks like me, but it's not. I'm elsewhere.*'[14] The cost of this role was to lose out on the experience of his own desire and his own identity, but the gain was, as Capote termed it, a 'semi-religious' authority over those around him and the accompanying freedom from the burden of shame and resentment.

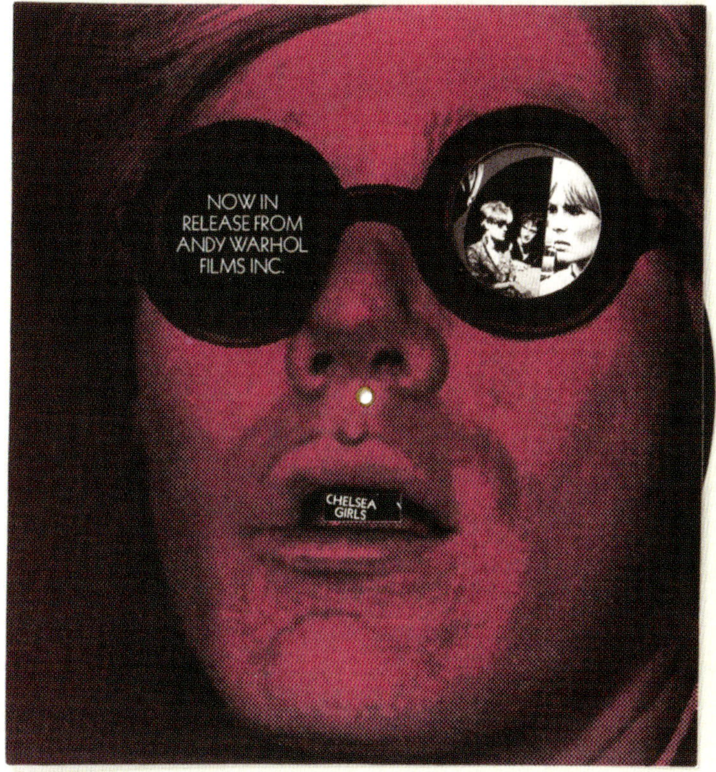

39 Andy Warhol, film leader for *Chelsea Girls*, 1966.

Warhol's relationship with Beardsley, like his relationship with the Catholic retinue that gathered around him, was therefore never one of bonding or identification or comradeship, never one of sharing in a group project of Catholics purging 'themselves of Catholic repression', as Viva had it, but instead more like the relationship of cleric to congregation or, better, idol to idolaters or icon to iconophiles. Such a formulation does not suggest that Beardsley, who died in 1898, had some prescient knowledge of the Warhol of the 1960s, of course, but instead that he represented to Warhol one side of the idol/idolater or icon/iconophile divide, which Warhol used to develop his own position on the other side. 'I have one aim

– the grotesque', Beardsley famously once said, 'If I am not grotesque I am nothing': if I do not experience shame, I am nothing, if I cannot grovel in my guilt, I am nothing (illus. 38). Conversely, Warhol wanted to be the 'nothing' that Beardsley fended off, and had no interest in the grotesque for its own sake or, really, anything for its own sake. He wanted to be 'The Nothingness Himself' (illus. 39).

As one of Beardsley's contemporaries, Arthur Symons, put it, 'Beardsley is the satirist of an age without convictions.'[15] He generated an unseemly religiosity, an unseemly sense of shame, in an age that had given it up, an age that did not want to acknowledge that there was anything that a modern might feel shameful about. Warhol, by contrast, made his name as the apostle of that same age-without-convictions. The novelist, occasional art critic and arch-modern, John Updike, summed up the central contradiction of Warhol's position nicely in 1989 in a review of his first comprehensive post-mortem exhibition:

> There was an efficient churchly atmosphere to his show, of duty discharged and superstition placated. Visitors, I noticed, kept glancing slyly at one another, as if to ask, 'How foolish do *you* feel?' One woman, with a seemly irreverence, combed her hair in front of a Warhol self-portrait whose framing glass reflected back from that dead opaque face. It might have been an act of oblation. Andy has become – what he must have wanted all along – an icon.[16]

Reportedly, Beardsley spent hours on end reading about the lives of Catholic saints towards the end of his short life. What he wanted from these readings, presumably – as any avid follower of the lives of saints certainly wants – must have been a touchstone for his faith, a way to shore up belief in the face of doubt. 'Decadent Catholicism is the assertion of faith as a

work of art in an age when one ought to know better', Hanson
tells us, 'Catholicism is embraced even as it falls to pieces.'[17]
Faith, shame, art: all came together in the ritual, formal offering
of the Decadent's own sinfulness, now rendered as a form of
desperate extremism for the age of science, industry and budding
consumer capitalism. 'Aubrey Beardsley did not shirk a diffi-
culty by leaving lines to the imagination of critics', is how one
fan phrased it.[18] The 'paradox as such' of faith, art, self, in all
its depth, complexity and contradiction – the truth of another
reality hidden from view – was pinned down again and again in
Beardsley's work by desire, belief, longing and ritual, by willing
it into being, by asserting it with an overly certain drawing style.

Warhol, on the other hand, had nothing of that desperate,
last-ditch voluntarism, nothing of Beardsley's obsessive, guilt-
burdened confessionalism. Instead of bringing into being the
otherness of God, art and self through the power of his own
longing, through the summoning of conviction, Warhol did so
by casting himself as the point of oracularity, of indeterminacy
and caliginosity – as the paradox itself, the divide between sacred
and secular realms, between the artistic and commercial, between
the interiority of subjectivity and the exteriority of the world.
Rather than conjuring the figure of otherness in the curtain,
or casting himself in the role of the wizard behind it, Warhol
made himself into the curtain itself. 'I always feel that my words
are coming from behind me, not from me', he liked to say, and
indeed, without exception, his art gives us the same message.[19]
He would free himself from both desire and shame, from both
enlightenment and judgment, by becoming the boundary or
screen that stood between the truth of God, art and self, and
the reception of that truth in the world outside.

5
BEN SHAHN

In an interview conducted early in Warhol's career as a fine artist, the young and thoughtful critic David Bourdon branded him 'a social realist in reverse', suggesting that he was a satirist of commercial art and critic of consumer culture generally.[1] Warhol set him straight immediately:

> You sound like that man on the *Times* who considers my paintings to be sociological commentary. I just happen to like ordinary things. When I paint them, I don't try to make them extraordinary. I just try to paint them ordinary-ordinary. Sociological critics are waste-makers.[2]

Warhol, of course, was right about his own work: it was 'ordinary-ordinary' and that quality of self-reflexive ordinariness, or ordinariness emphasizing or staging itself, was always its strength, its single most compelling quality, its claim to art historical innovation and to truth and value more broadly. That said, however, the critical insight of Bourdon, the unspecified man from the *Times* and the legions of others since who have responded to Warhol's work as if it were critical were not really wrong either – their interpretations were not simply symptomatic critical impositions, as Warhol suggested, nor were their sociological interpretations merely excessive 'waste'.

As most of his contemporaries assumed, Warhol's claim that he just happened 'to like ordinary things' was, at least in part, disingenuous. Gregory Battcock, for example, put it this way:

> Because he was always sort of quiet and wide-eyed, you'd think, 'Oh, this is a little bushy tailed boy from Pittsburgh.' But it was just this performance that Mid-Westerners always try to calculate: the little lost boy in the city of business. He wasn't.[3]

Indeed, 'sociological criticism' was a central part of Warhol's art school training and played a seminal role in forming his mature artistic sensibility in both his capacity as a commercial artist in the 1950s and his function as a fine artist from the 1960s onward. This perspective came from several of his instructors in art school who had formed their careers in the crucible of 1930s Social Realism and the legacy of Constructivism, particularly Robert Lepper and Balcomb Greene. The primary influence on Warhol, however, was the work of Ben Shahn (1898–1969). His turn to Shahn was not unrelated to the sway that his art school teachers had over him, of course. Indeed, Warhol nearly flunked his first year, according to his colleagues, for working in a Beardsley style. As one classmate had it, 'Andy painted the way he wanted and they flunked him. So he went to summer school and painted the way they wanted.'[4] Downplaying the mixed bearing and resplendent sheen he drew from Beardsley and his other early influences, he responded to faculty criticism by turning first to the Social Realist themes of the 1930s and later to the coarse and flatly earnest, ragged-line, blotted-ink drawing style of Ben Shahn.

In the late 1940s, Ben Shahn was a likely candidate for an art student in search of a new influence. His socially committed and emotionally transparent style would be celebrated in a major retrospective at the Museum of Modern Art in New York in autumn 1947, earning him an unusual degree of scorn from Clement Greenberg in *The Nation* but kudos from many other sources, including a poll of leading museum directors, curators and art critics published in *Look* magazine.[5] According to Robert Lepper, Warhol's primary instructor during his junior and senior years in art school, Shahn was 'a prevailing hero of the period'.[6]

The Shahn style served Warhol well as a student and would serve him even better as a commercial artist after his move to New York in 1949. Shahn was a leading figure not only in fine art but in commercial art as well, and New York art directors knew of Warhol and regularly hired him in the early 1950s as 'a cheaper Ben Shahn'.[7] In an event that secured his career in commercial art, in 1952 the influential Art Directors Club honoured Warhol with its prestigious and coveted design award for an assignment he did in the Shahn style, working with a Shahn-like social documentary theme, for a large and lucrative account that he had won away from Shahn.[8]

A big part of Shahn's prestige at Carnegie Tech had to do with his principled commitment to an artistic style and sensibility that was fast becoming obsolete in the late 1940s but had shaped the professional identities of many of the faculty. In a talk titled 'If I Had to Begin My Art Career Today', presented in 1949 to a symposium at another art school, for example, Shahn attempted to warn his young audience about the changes that were to come by distinguishing between two goals for art. 'If I were a young artist beginning to paint today,' he said, 'I would want to be

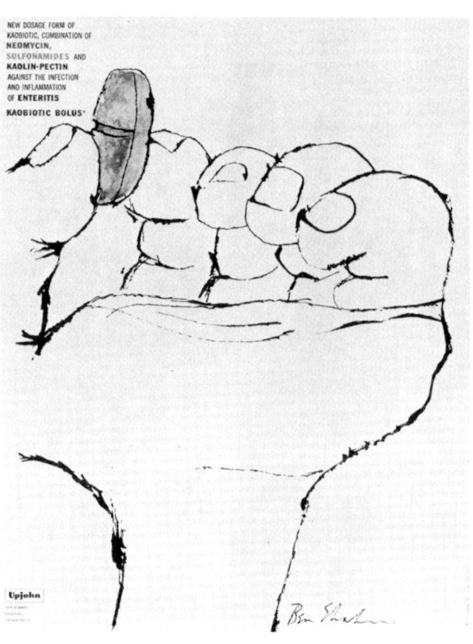

40 Ben Shahn, *Kaobiotic Bolus*, 1959, drawing for an advertisement.

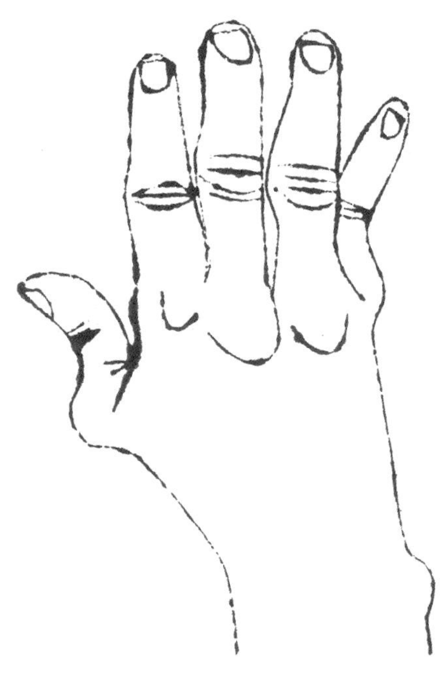

41 Andy Warhol,
Male Hand,
c. 1952,
ink on paper,
33.3 × 18.4 cm.

clear as to whether my own need were to communicate, or whether, on the other hand, the paramount desire in me were to express – to crystallize – the moods of my innermost self; to explore the subjective part of me; to make permanent some of the transitory vistas of my own imagination.' Such a distinction was a set-up, of course. The second position was a 'crusade' for 'abstruse', 'self-revealing' form and was not 'produced for the public', he argued, but only for the isolated artist himself and, if lucky, for 'dogmatic' critics and decadent, art-buying connoisseurs.[9]

As Warhol was finishing up his art schooling, the residual call for an 'art for the masses', barely concealed in Shahn's criteria, still harboured substantial influence. Shahn's work had evolved over the previous fifteen years but he had not yet made the shift to the 'personal realism' for which he would become known in the 1950s and '60s.[10] In his MOMA retrospective of 1947, for example, he could still be celebrated by the curator James Thrall Soby as a 'propagandist' focussed on 'mass appeal on the far flung scale peculiar to our times' and be linked with Honoré Daumier and George Grosz as his most significant forebears.[11] The 1930s fellow traveller principles at work in Shahn's art – once described by Diego Rivera as 'the struggle of the proletarianized American petit-bourgeois intellectual against the degeneration of the European bourgeoisie translated on this continent' – could still be

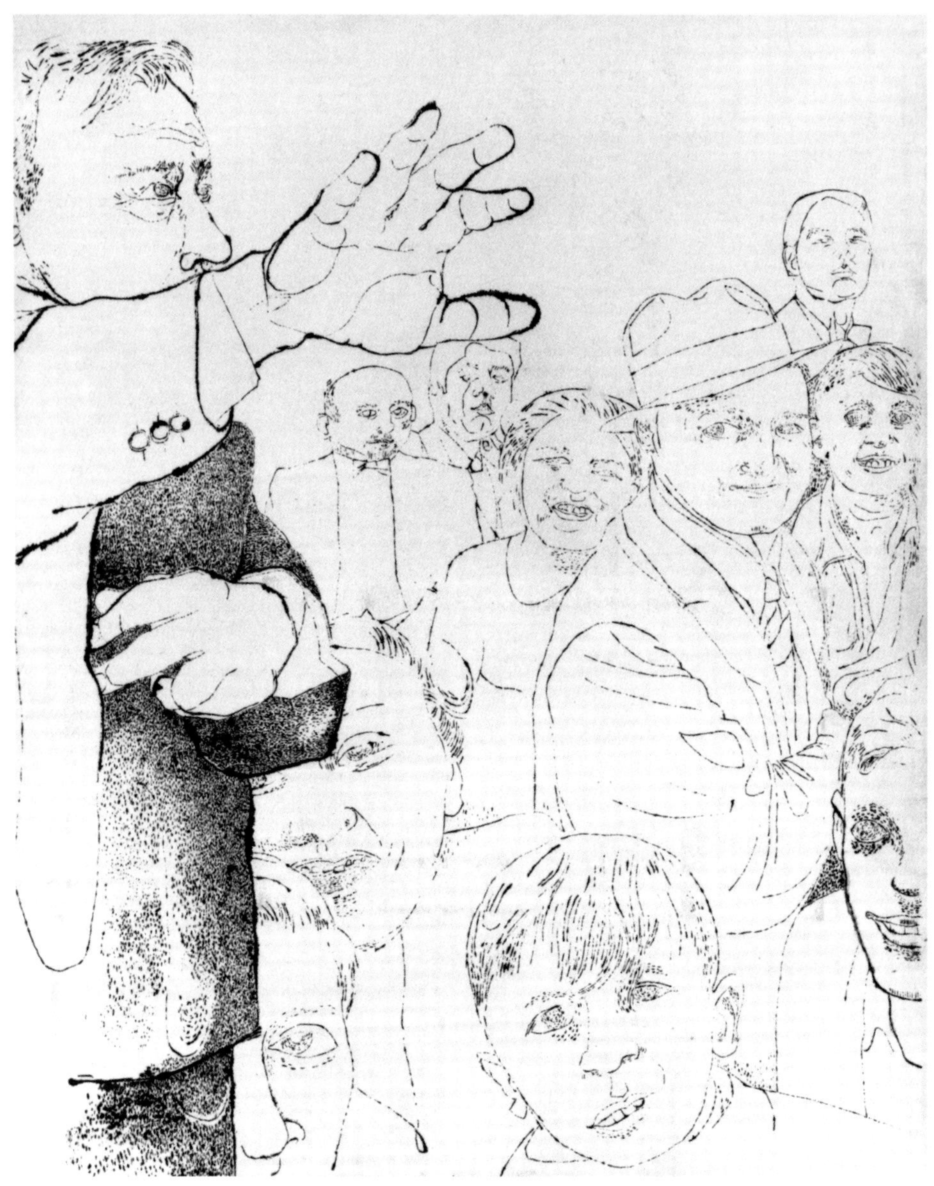

42 Andy Warhol, *Untitled (Huey Long)*, 1948–9, pen and ink on paper, 73.8 × 58.6 cm.

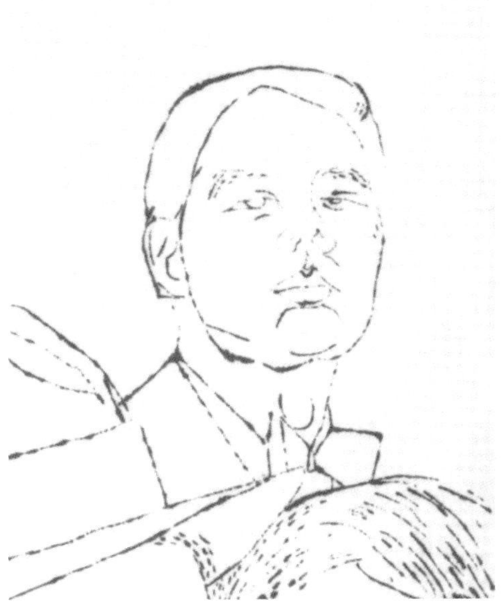

43 Detail of Warhol's *Untitled (Huey Long)*.

compelling in the mid- and late 1940s when Warhol came under their influence.[12] The stridency of the 1930s ideals that Rivera and Shahn represented had been tempered under attack from critics like Clement Greenberg and under strain from the horrors of Stalinism, but still dominated much thinking about the role of contemporary art, if only from habit or inertia. The emphases on the social and political functions of the artist, on addressing working-class audiences rather than the traditional class of collectors, on a critical refusal of bohemianism and, perhaps foremost, on the moral innocence of the labourer, had not yet been displaced, or even significantly challenged, in the art culture at Carnegie Tech. The existentialisms of Abstract Expressionism had not yet made their way into art schools; at least not in Pittsburgh.

The values that Shahn championed as an artist were present not only in his heartfelt rhetoric, his rough-hewn drawing style and in the subject-matter he chose to depict but also in his un-wavering predilection for depicting big, beefy, labourer's hands as the primary locus of activity in his compositions. Warhol adopted this as well, and we see it again and again in studies and commissioned works from the period.

There is one drawing from Warhol's final year at art school that best shows his stylistic switch, or at least shows both influ-ences together in the same composition (illus. 42). The drawing uses a heavy, rough, Shahn line to depict the commanding hand gesture of a public orator that serves as the primary focal point for the image, and a fine, intermittent-line technique similar to that used by Beardsley to depict the crowd in attendance. There is some crossover in this division of stylistic responsibility but, on the whole, line weight and expressive emphasis are being used in a conventional manner to distinguish between two categories of subject: that which is primary and at the centre of both narrative structure and composition, and that which is secondary and subordinate. This formal distinction between styles, between primary and secondary figures and between foreground and background all served to distinguish between performer and audience, between a public figure and his public.

The drawing was done as part of an assignment while Warhol was a student in Lepper's course in Pictorial Design at the Carnegie Institute of Technology.[13] The course spanned the junior and senior years of the curriculum for Warhol's academic major and was designed around seven coordinated problems or projects. In a report from 1948 on the teaching techniques used in this course, Lepper introduced his pedagogical ambition as follows:

> The pictorial artist is concerned with the perception and projection of meaningful experience. A great portion of meaningful experience stems from the social flux by which is meant the ever-changing relation of the individual to the community of which he is a member. A formal study of this flux and of its components is important to him in its potential for broadening his field for pictorial expression.[14]

The first year of the two-year course was devoted to problems One to Six and was split in two, the first half of the year spent collecting and analysing 'objective data' and cultivating the 'general viewpoint of a cultural anthropologist', with the second half devoted to 'subjective data', including gathering information about the 'moulding influences' of the student's own personality in order to 'achieve an understanding of why he is as he is'.[15] The second year of the course was divided between 'commission' issues and problem Seven, the final in the sequence, in which the student was asked to interpret a recent novel in pictorial form.

'The complexity and scope of this final problem', Lepper wrote, 'demand of the student his full power of mature independent thought.'[16] Indeed, as his allocation of a full half-year to this portion of the project indicates, this seventh project was intended by Lepper to serve as a vehicle for summarizing and synthesizing the objective and subjective data gathered and analysed in the first year. This is borne out in the curricular diagram Lepper included in his report. The course as a whole was to have both the general 'effect of increasing sharpness of observation and retention of data' and, ultimately, to produce a single work of art that was socially and historically conscious and personally meaningful.[17] This final project at its best, therefore, would summarize a significant portion of the student's education and demonstrate artistic maturity and depth of investigation in a single work.[18] The novel that Warhol and his colleagues were asked to work with for this final project was Robert Penn Warren's *All the King's Men* (1946).

Since its publication, *All the King's Men* has been interpreted to make specific allusions to the populist leader, founder of the influential Share Our Wealth society, 1930s Louisiana governor and u.s. senator, Huey Long.[19] The focus of the story, however, is not on the Huey Long character (Willie Stark) but instead on the complex psychological identification of an upper-middle-class intellectual with the populism and mass politics of the period. As such, the novel served as a general allegory of the intellectual culture of the 1930s and the support given to leaders of popular insurrections such as Lenin, Hitler and Mussolini by its fellow travelling artists and intellectuals.[20] Published just seven years after the Nazi–Soviet Pact of non-aggression and just one year after the end of the war, when the horrors of the

Holocaust were beginning to be revealed, Warren's troubled ethical inquiry into the complicity of fellow travellers with the suffering caused by mass political movements was tremendously powerful to a generation that had witnessed first-hand the transformation of art and intellectual work into propaganda in the service of Stalinism and Fascism.[21]

Warhol, however, was really not part of that generation – he was only eleven in 1939 and only seventeen in 1945 when the war ended – and despite the two years of work leading up to his drawing of this ready-made dramatic theme, the result is tentative and confused. It is very much a student effort and, perhaps, betrays the lack of lustre or enthusiasm that comes when a youth is asked to speak meaningfully about something that was important to the generation before him but not his own. The drawing is nevertheless also ambitious and complex, with a number of different aesthetic and narrative themes vying to determine its overall impact.

The story would have been meaningful for Warhol's teachers, however, many of whom came of age with the emphasis on proletarian labour and industrial production developed by the Social Realists, Mexican muralists and Bauhaus-influenced industrial designers of the 1930s. Like many other American art schools at the time, the teaching methods, social ambitions and artist-cum-engineer professional ethos of the Bauhaus, particularly as it had been transplanted to Chicago by László Moholy-Nagy and his Institute of Design, still dominated the pedagogical theory operating at Carnegie.[22] So too the experience of Works Progress Administration patronage (which began to taper off at the end of the 1930s but did not fully dry up until the early 1940s), with its mandate for public art projects and public themes, continued to influence the institutionally sanctioned expectations for art's social function.[23]

Robert Lepper had contributed significantly to reframing Carnegie Tech's mission as the training of students in industrial

design and 'pictorial design' (Warhol's major) in the 1930s.[24]
In an article of 1940, for example, he explained his beliefs
and interests in a 'vulgar art' as follows:

> Our common art is really common . . . indeed so much
> a part of life that the scholarly critic might easily miss
> it. It is composed of works which are our parallel to the
> handsome commonplaces of the Greeks and Medieval
> Europeans . . . the paraphernalia of the railroads and of
> the building industry, aviation and the automobile, all of
> these mobile sculpture. Add the highway system and all
> the thousands of utensils, tools, instruments and appliances
> that are the common equipment of the farmer, craftsman
> and housewife . . . It is submitted that the vast majority
> of these structures are genuine, earnest and obviously
> vulgar (common); that they possess an honest dignity,
> are democratic, constructive, experimental . . . developed
> out of life . . . and supported by popular approval.[25]

In search of a standardized vocabulary for such populist artistic
values, Lepper developed a system of associations between the
formal properties that were the stock-in-trade of the visual
artist and their 'industrial equivalents' (illus. 45). The elements
of visual perception in Lepper's thinking were much like the
elements of industrial production: the artist was understood
to construct a work of art out of line, area and volume much
in the same manner that a labourer would construct a machine
out of wire, sheet metal and casings.

Such were the formal and social values that Warhol was
asked to reach for as a student. The measure of art's success,
for those who evaluated his progress and potential as an artist,
was to be realized by escaping from its bohemian ghetto. Art's
redemption was to be found to the extent that it achieved
functional value on a par with 'the paraphernalia of the rail-

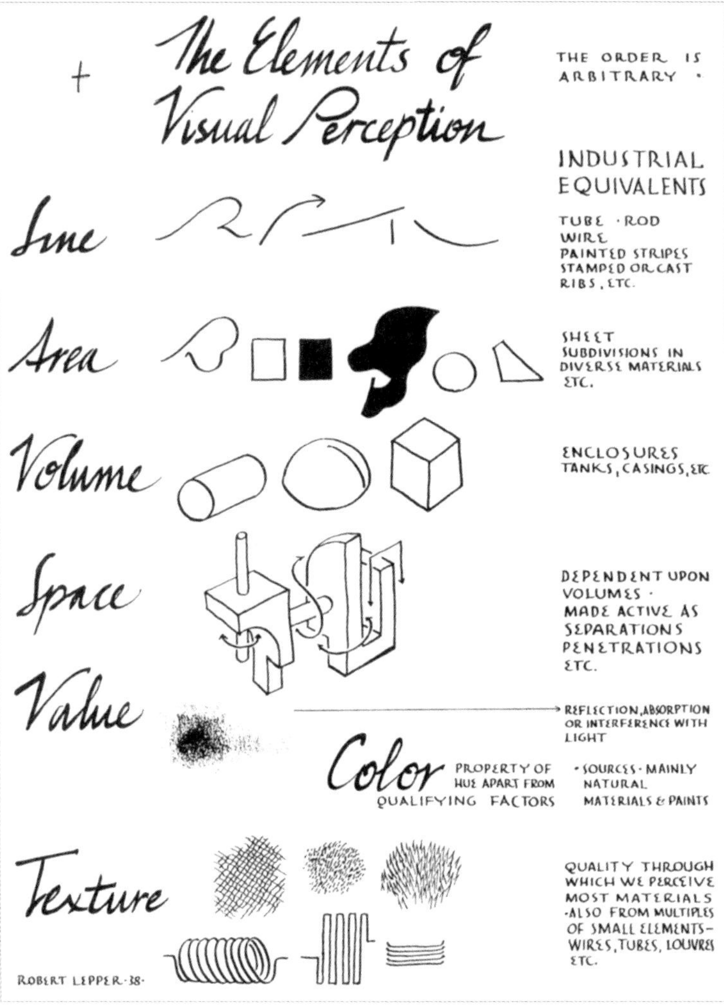

44 Robert Lepper, 'The Elements of Visual Perception', from *Art Instruction* (October 1938).

roads and of the building industry, aviation and the automobile'. If students at Carnegie Tech did not at least aspire to live up to the great public works projects and industrial design innovations of the 1930s, if their artworks could not reach the standard of 'the common equipment of the housewife', the spectre of insignificance would weigh heavy.

When Warhol entered Carnegie Tech in 1945, however, he came equipped with a very different set of assumptions about art, about its public function and about its sources of legitimation. Art in Warhol's experience was, as Lepper had said about bridges and the like, 'so much a part of life that the scholarly critic might easily miss it', but it had nothing to do with 'industrial equivalents' or artist-cum-workers. High art, for the young Warhol, was nearly indistinct from its lower, mass cultural forms. Both the mature Lepper and the young Warhol subscribed to a common form of populism – neither seemed to believe in the old bohemian ideal of art as a rarefied or even exceptional practice – but they had very different models governing their thinking about art's role. For Warhol art was a matter of adopting something like the idealized innocence of a child, whereas for Lepper it was a matter of adopting the idealized innocence of the industrial labourer.

Young Andy the Red-nosed Warhola – 'Spotty' – was an outsider who found a niche for himself in the role of child-artist and pop culture enthusiast. As a youth, this allowed him to occupy the social position of someone who plays their part and makes their contribution by mastering the production of, and obsessively consuming, visual entertainment. This position was reportedly both odd and acceptable in the context of his immigrant, working-class Pittsburgh neighbourhood. In the late 1940s, Warhol faced a similar social task in the community of other artists at Carnegie Tech. Instead of finding like-minded commonality and alliance within this new group, he once again found himself, or made himself to be, exceptional. His niche was no longer that of artist but that of the impish innocent, the loveably naughty 'class baby', the child-adult who could speak about adult themes and manipulate adult situations without bearing adult responsibility or taking on the stability of conventional adult identity. In his new role as innocent, Warhol was able to work effectively both inside and outside the various codes available to him at Carnegie Tech, to paint both 'the way he wanted' and 'the way they wanted', as his classmate worded it. This manoeuvring between the expectations placed on him by his art school environment and ambitions drawn from childhood interests and enthusiasms, and between adult and child personas, can be seen in Warhol's drawing of *All the King's Men*.

In the foreground and on the left of Warhol's drawing we see the figure of Willie Stark – the 'King' of the book's title, the 'Boss' as he is known by his 'Men' – with his hand raised in a gesture used to control and appeal to crowds that is repeated throughout the novel.[26] His body and hands are drawn in the Ben Shahn blotted-line technique, while his face is mostly rendered in a cross between the Shahn style and a sketchy version of the Aubrey Beardsley, dashed-and-dotted-line technique. There is a strong contrast set up between the force and determination of his raised hand and the equivocation and indirection of his facial expression, with his gaze looking slightly upwards away from both us and the crowd; the circular dot pattern in his eyes which makes no distinction between iris and pupil and thus gives a sense of lack of focus, even madness; the wrinkled brow and raised, questioning or confused eyebrows; and the fact that our view of his mouth, the locus of power for any orator and particularly so for the character of Willie Stark, is obscured by his arm.

The audience is broken into two groupings: a crowd in front which stares at us with the same psychotic eyes and with broad smiles betraying full involvement in the moment – this is Warhol's art student rendering of the crowd psychology that dominated the story – and a tier of three men behind them, who stand back from the group with more distant, observant expressions on their faces and without the crazy eyes. Two figures can be readily identified from the novel in addition to Willie Stark: in the centre, the man with the fedora cocked to one side is the narrator, fellow traveller Jack Burden. The other, just below Stark's thumb, is the pivotal character Tiny Duffy, who is described as 'a city-hall slob [with a] face . . . creamed and curded like a cow patty in a spring pasture, only . . . the colour of biscuit dough'.[27] The others in the front all share the crazed eyes and are more or less indistinct, with no telltale features or attributes (like Burden's fedora or Duffy's cow-pat face), and collectively are probably meant to represent any of the rural Louisiana crowds Stark addresses during the course of the story.

The two remaining men in the back are more curious: they also have the singular or distinctive features of specific rather than generic figures but do not correspond to any character in Warren's narrative. Like the figure of Duffy who turns out to be more shrewd and calculating than any of the other characters in the story, these two stand back from the group with more reserved body language and without the maddened stare of the others. The figure on the right appears to have been an after-thought (or else is very tall), rising up as he does above the rest of the crowd (illus. 43). The most striking thing about him, given the enthusiasm of the crowd, is the laconic and seemingly disinterested quality of his gaze as he stands there high above the others looking down through half-closed, heavy-lidded eyes. Different, too, are some of his facial characteristics when compared with the broad and bland peasant features of the people in front. The square jaw and full lips, for example, the thick eyebrows that build up in the middle, the bulbous nose and chin, the long neck, all allude to a particular rather than generic person. My conclusion is that it is a drawing of the young Warhol himself (illus. 44). It looks like him before he had a nose job and before he began taking amphetamines to keep his weight down. Including himself in the drawing would have been one easy way, as per Lepper's assignment, to incorporate 'subjective data' into the project.[28]

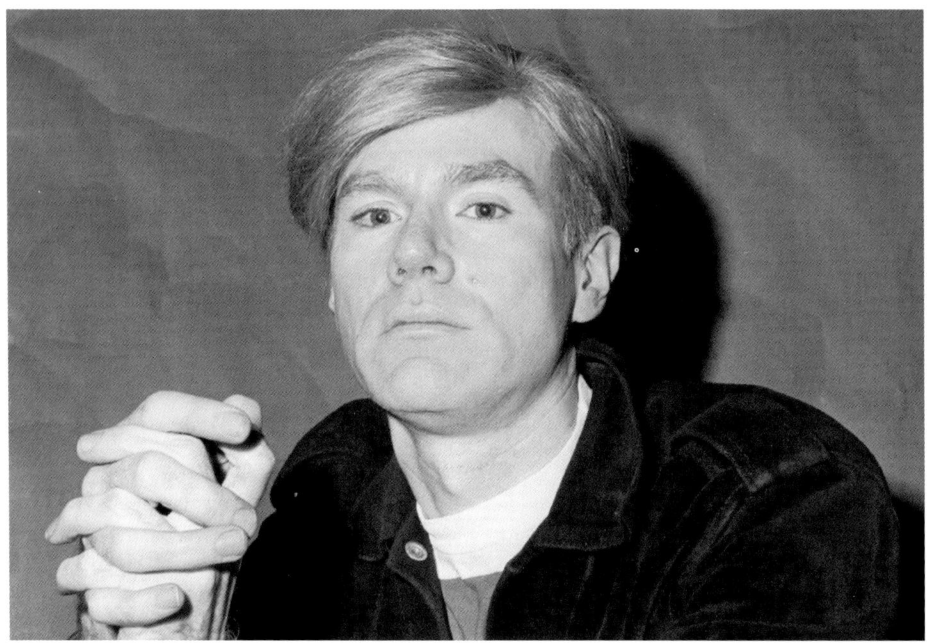

45 *Portrait of Andy Warhol,* 1966, photographer unknown.

This leaves the other figure, to the left of Tiny Duffy and just under Stark's palm, who is more mysterious still: the thinness of his features and the moustache and goatee seem improbable for 1930s Louisiana, or 1948 Pittsburgh for that manner. He seems, rather, to be striking a pose of cultivation and learning and perhaps a European identification in what is a distinctly un-intellectual, un-European environment. And his gaze is different too. He has neither the crazed absorption of Willie Stark and the crowd – there is no spiral pattern in his eyes – nor the cool, knowing distance of Tiny Duffy, nor the uncommitted, wait-and-see distance of Warhol. Instead, with head tilted forward attentively, eyes wide open and strongly defined, headlamp pupils, his vision seems sharply focused and energized. He does not seem to be sharing in the frenzy of the others – he does not have their sense of unguarded relaxedness and slightly deranged distraction – but instead seems to be drawing something from them as an outside observer. Like the image of Warhol, this figure seems very specific and yet does not correspond to any character in the novel. There is nobody of his size or presentation, for example, and all the characters are represented as either cynical and self-serving, like Tiny Duffy, or naive and deluded, like Jack Burden – none have anything approaching a clear-eyed appreciation for the political culture stirred up by the Huey Long character that Warhol seems to be illustrating.

All the King's Men was a fictional interpretation of the life of Huey Long and his appeal to a troubled intellectual, but it also had grander ambitions. Diana Trilling, for example, described the book as 'a fictional demonstration of Hegel's philosophy of history'.[29] The story is not about the 'King' in the end but the ways his followers ('all the king's men') respond to the mass political leadership he represented. It is Hegelian, according to Trilling, because it attempts to synthesize a 'system of political morality' for a generation from the lesson provided by Jack Burden's ill-fated relationship to the 1930s populism of Willie Stark. Through Burden, Warren tells the story of the moral struggle of fellow travellers as a type – bourgeois intellectuals who aligned themselves with working-class social movements out of a guilt-born emotional investment in the justness of the cause rather than clear-cut, material self-interest – as they confront the ethical complications that arise in actual political practice. In 1946, when the novel was first published, Nazism and Fascism no longer loomed as pressing threats. Soviet world domination, however, did. The central subtext of the novel, one that would have been paramount in the minds of its original audience as anxiety about the Soviet Union was mounting and an easy parallel for readers of *All the King's Men*, was the legacy of the Red Decade intellectuals and their identification with Lenin's realization of what was then called 'actually existing socialism'.[30]

By late 1948 or early 1949, on the eve of the McCarthy era, communism and anti-communism had become mainstays of the popular media. The major weeklies regularly indulged in red-baiting, with debates that extended over several weeks on such topics as whether communism should be outlawed or whether communists should be permitted to teach (in *Time*, *Newsweek* and *The New York Times Magazine*, for example). Caricatures of 'typical' communists, fellow travellers and prominent communist leaders were also popular, with articles like 'What is a Communist? How Can You Spot Him?' in *The New York Times Magazine* and *Life*'s hugely popular 'Portrait of an American Communist'.[31] In this climate, the myth of Lenin as engineer of the evil communist regime was renewed with a vengeance. His bald head, hollow cheeks, piercing gaze, moustache, goatee and tie were all components of his popular iconography. In an unsigned report on the 'Foreign News', for example, *Time* described him in late 1947 as 'a stooped man with hollow cheeks and a potbelly who ['always' wore 'neckties' and] came out from behind the book stacks where he had spent most of his life, and kidnapped a state'.[32]

There was also a tremendously successful mass-circulation biography of Lenin published in early 1948 that raised the spectre of Lenin's political afterlife by being promoted as 'A fascinating biography of the man who, from his grave, directs the strategy of the Kremlin today' (illus. 46).[33] This was a time, immediately after the war and on the cusp of McCarthyism, when mass politics was being repudiated on all fronts and populists like Huey Long and Father Coughlin, fascists like Hitler and Mussolini, and Bolsheviks such as Stalin and Lenin were all being lumped together. Despite the tremendous differences in their political outlooks and agendas, the ongoing development of Lenin's communism was a readily available parallel to Huey Long's Share Our Wealth platform for the audience of the time. So too, the character of Jack Burden would have been a ready-made model

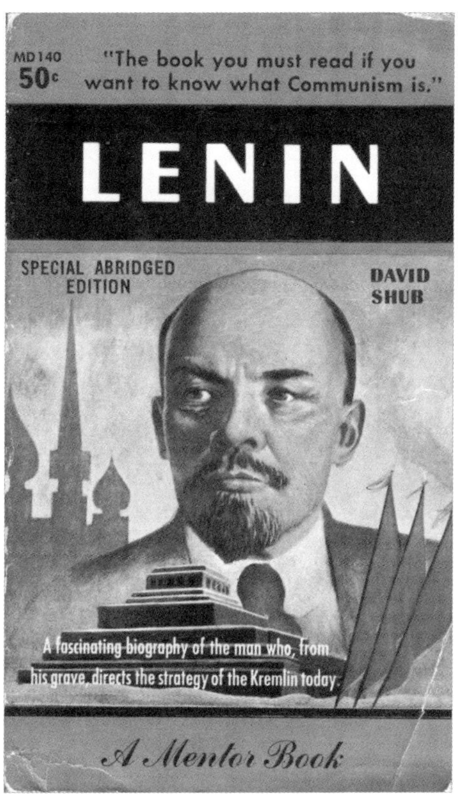

46 Front cover of David Shub's *Lenin* (1948).

of the fellow travelling artists and intellectuals of the 1930s.

Throughout his career, Robert Lepper repeatedly insisted, 'We must expect the arts of our time to sense and reflect the present social order.'[34] To do so, however, is never a matter of simply commenting on current events: instead, he specified in 1948, the student artists are 'asked to examine a "total environment"' in order to become 'more conscious of the intricate interrelations of its components'.[35] The artist's goal is to articulate his work in such a way that it demonstrates complex understanding of historical and social forces – 'geographic location, economic resources, occupations, cultural interests, traditional ties . . . social, group and sectional prejudices and the like'.[36] Robert Penn Warren's depiction of Huey Long and the character of Jack Burden in the context of Lenin's communism and the artists and intellectuals of the 1930s would have been a likely – really, inevitable – topic of conversation for Lepper's classroom during the half-year that Warhol and his classmates worked on the novel. Whether he did so on his own initiative or under the influence of Lepper and/or his classmates, Warhol seems to have drawn that parallel between Lenin's class-based populism and Huey Long's by incorporating a caricature of Lenin into his drawing. At the very least, such a parallel would have been an appropriate and convenient solution to the demand for historical consciousness that was the driving force behind Lepper's assignment. From our

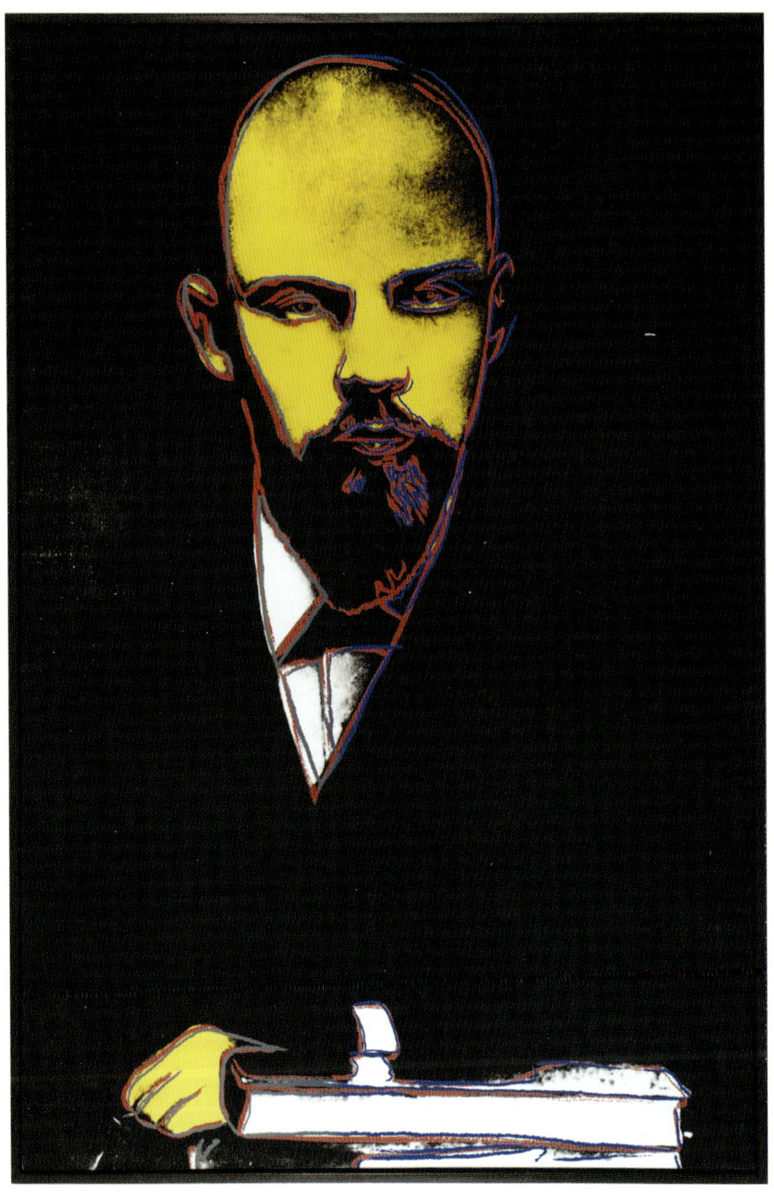

47 Andy Warhol, *Lenin*, 1986.

perspective now looking back on Warhol's career as a whole, this parallel is also consistent with his recurring and long-standing interest in communist themes, manifest in many of his works, not the least of which being his *Lenin* series and exhibition of 1986 (illus. 47).[37]

This interest was not drawn solely from his role as a latter-day observer of the political passions of the prior generation. Sometime in late 1947 or early 1948, Warhol and many of the other students in his class reportedly signed a petition supporting Henry A. Wallace's third-party bid for candidacy in the upcoming presidential election. Warhol was undoubtedly influenced by peers like Philip Pearlstein and he may have been swayed by the examples set by prominent artists such as Ben Shahn, who had made public displays of their support for Wallace. He may have signed the petition following Wallace's speech at Carnegie Tech in November 1947 or following a pro-Wallace rally on 1 March 1948 at Carnegie, which was upended by several hundred anti-Wallace protesters from neighbouring Duquesne University and the University of Pittsburgh who were dressed in red or red-and-white underwear, with some sporting Stalin-like moustaches, shouting 'Comrades! On to Helsinki!'[38] In any case, the decision to sign the petition was charged with the suspicion of communist sympathy by many in Pittsburgh. In one of the most notorious examples of pre-McCarthy era red-baiting, the *Pittsburgh Press* published the names of all those in western Pennsylvania who had signed the petition to put Wallace on the ballot in April 1948. When Warhol's name showed up in the *Press*, it reportedly came as a shock to his family.[39]

One likely response to *All the King's Men* in the wake of the war would have been to identify with its disaffected fellow traveller Jack Burden. This is the response that the book calls for as we learn at the end that Burden, the narrator and the author are all one and the same. Disaffection of this sort, however, is a class-bound response, a privilege for those who have faith that, regardless of what they do and what decisions they make, they will be able to make it in the world one way or another. Andy Warhol came from a Pittsburgh, immigrant, working-class family, was raised during the Depression and war years and, in all likelihood, did not share that confidence. Jack Burden, with his privileged, 1920s Southern-genteel upbringing and failed bourgeois illusions, would thus be an unlikely character for Warhol to identify with. This is borne out by Warhol's cool, deliberative pose in the drawing – it displays none of the sympathy for Burden and his story that is a central component to Warren's novel.

The core dramatic tension in the novel, the conflict between political idealism and political cynicism, is figured across three different registers in Warhol's drawing: in the ambivalence between the forceful hand and the confused eyes of the Stark character; in the contrast between the stylistic influences of Ben Shahn and Aubrey Beardsley; and in the juxtaposition of the figures of Lenin and Tiny Duffy. While Warhol does illustrate the central theme of Warren's novel, he also alters the experience of the story by shifting the locus of narrative tension. Where the reader of Warren's novel experiences shock, guilt, hope, despair and finally euphoria as he or she identifies with Burden's burden and his release from it, the viewer of Warhol's drawing views Burden with analytical distance, as someone in the thrall of group hysteria, and is therefore held back from such an identification. This shift of focus is accentuated in the drawing by the use of the heavy, more assertive Shahn line to emphasize the three figures in the crowd that surround Burden but not the figure of Burden himself, who seems to dissipate into the background despite his prominent location in the composition. In place of such identification with the protagonist-narrator-author of the novel, we are asked to stand back and observe the scene with a critical detachment on a par with that of the three figures in the back row.

Warhol's dilemma was different from that of Burden's or the older generation of former fellow travellers who would have identified with him. Confronted with the prospect of entering the world and the need to decide on a way to negotiate it (this was his senior year at Carnegie Tech and he had already resolved to go to New York), he too was given a choice by the narrative, but not between bourgeois propriety and working-class populism. The bourgeois paths were unavailable – Warhol did not have the option of going back to the security of Burden's Landing (Jack's home town), nor could he abandon his worldly concerns and resolve the conflict between self- and collective-interest by giving up on both sets of beliefs and resorting to existential despair and tortuous self-exploration (in the pro forma, post-war manner of bourgeois intellectuals and artists). He never opted for the existential aesthetics of the Abstract Expressionists, for example. Instead, his options of identification fell somewhere between adopting the utopian promise ('stick it to the fat boys', in the 1930s parlance of the novel, or working for a politically attained redistribution of wealth) and adopting the dystopian threat (corruption and opportunism), represented as the political spectrum available to the working class in Warren's story. That is, Warhol was left with the more limited set of choices, somewhere between an old-fashioned, idealized working-class populism that sought to change the world and a cynical, petty-bourgeois opportunism that sought to exploit it. As his career progressed through the 1950s, he would continue to refer to these two identities but increasingly as alternating and opposing tendencies rather than using one to disguise the other. By the 1960s it would be just this ambivalent juxtaposition of these two tendencies – an art of social and political issues on the one hand and an art of commerce and innocent seduction on the other – that would confound critics accustomed to making evaluations on a scale from avant-garde to kitsch.

PART TWO
EXTERIORS

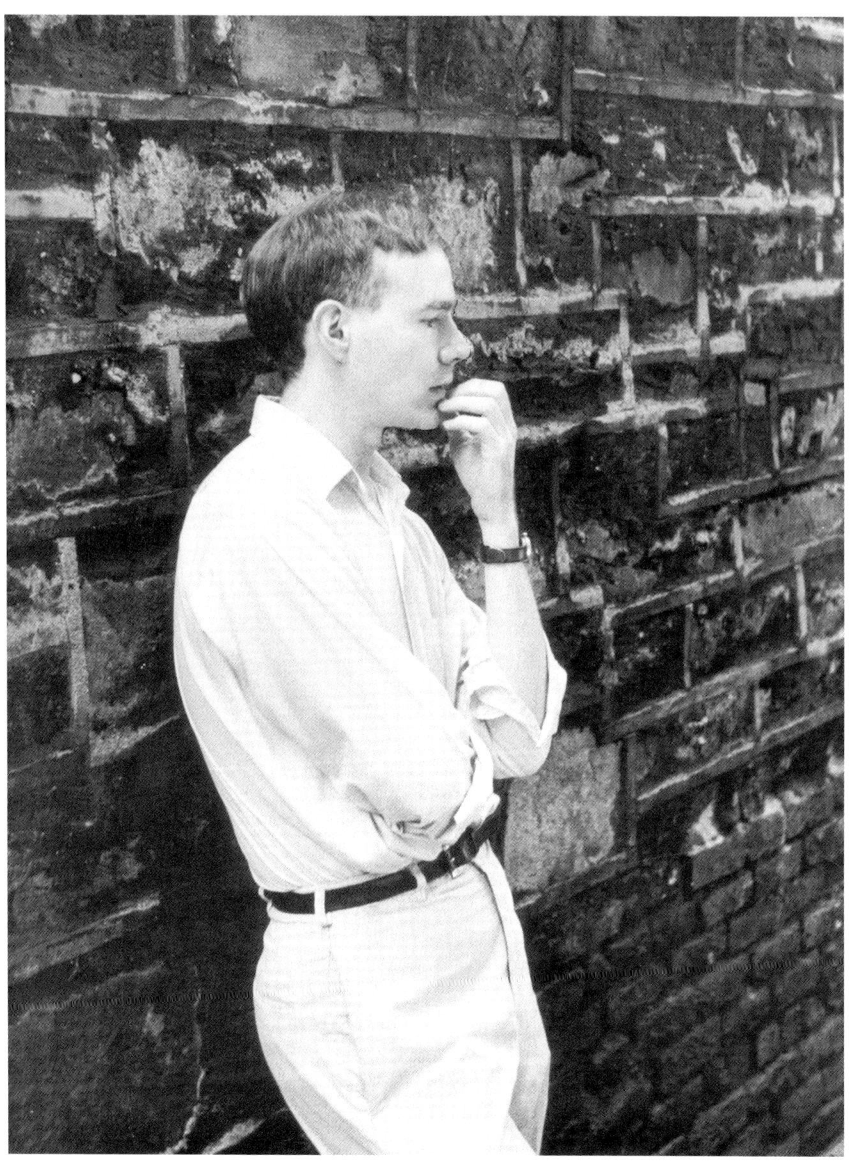

48 Andy Warhol in New York, early 1950s.

6

ANDY PAPERBAG

While Andy was an unusually fervent lover as a child and adolescent – to the point of obsession in his fandom for Shirley Temple and Truman Capote, for example – by the mid- or late 1950s he had become much more sober and more Catholic in his passions and fascinations, and began distributing his attachments more uniformly across his acquaintances and standardizing his expressions of appreciation for everyone and everything. According to the conventional armchair psycho-analysis provided by Warhol himself, his associates and his biographers, his feelings were too strong, too pointed, too overwhelming, so he dispersed them to diffuse their impact, allocating his emotional attachments evenly across the object world in the objective manner of a camera or other recording device. 'I think everybody should be a machine. I think every-body should be like everybody', is how he famously put his older and wiser, more adult and more practical way with desire to Gene Swenson early in the 1960s. 'Is that what Pop Art is all about?' Swenson asked, to which Warhol responded, 'Yes. It's liking things', it's about doing 'the same thing every time', about liking people or things 'over and over again' instead of falling enduringly, passionately, obsessively in love with any single person or thing, any image or idea.[1]

This radicalized form of ordinary adult restraint would serve Warhol well by offsetting and authorizing the polar impulsiveness and wide-eyed naïveté of his childlike persona, 'looking very young and very old at the same time', according to his long-time business manager Fred Hughes.[2] It was a winning couplet – superego and id with little in the way of ego mediating between – and it made him into an endlessly beguiling enigma or contradiction for anyone and everyone who would encounter him. One version or another of the account of his appeal to those around him has been a refrain since the 1960s: 'Warhol creates a vacuum', said one characteristic adaptation of this theme, for example, 'causing the reader to rush in with his own emotional coloration.'[3] He was the 'black hole in space, the vortex that engulfed all', said another.[4]

This distinctive charm came naturally to Warhol, to be sure, but he also worked at maintaining it with impressive discipline, rarely stepping out of character. There were a couple of revealing moments in 1964 and 1965 or '66, however, when his more youthful way with desire broke through his still relatively new adult jurisdiction and suggested that there might indeed be a more conventional adult ego at work. These instances amounted to ego-building, narcissistic attachments – not unlike his childhood and adolescent connections to Temple and Capote – even if, in the end, what they helped erect was the ego-emptying superego–id couplet that would define his adulthood. As such they were anti-objects of a sort, but they were nonetheless bona fide objects of desire, objects he had a special attachment to, that rose above his customary, everyday consumer's fare of commodities, celebrities and 'beauties' (as he liked to call the attractive people he continuously recruited as models or actors or staffers or companions).

Warhol's associates, in many interviews over the years, have regularly been asked if there was ever a particular cultural object or event that stood out because Warhol responded to it, something that would expose a distinctive taste, desire, attachment or identification, something that revealed and oriented his passion. Typically, this is a question that cannot really be answered because of Warhol's policy about liking things generally, but there were two instances when it could, revealing special attachments – special because they were singular – that were surprising to his companions at the time.

The first occurred when Gerard Malanga, his primary assistant through much of the 1960s, was asked about movies. He and Warhol would go to see films all the time, he said, but 'I only knew of one movie in particular that Andy and I enjoyed, and went to at least three times' – quite a startling statement in and of itself about someone who likes everything, particularly so movie stars.[5] The movie was the Paramount production *The Carpetbaggers*, released in 1964 and based on the novel of the same name by Harold Robbins (1961). The lead character, Jonas Cord Jr, is modelled on Howard Hughes and defined by two intertwined qualities born of childhood trauma: unbridled ambition that cannot be contained by a single field of endeavour, and radical emotional indifference that prevents him from maintaining any stable relationships. Warhol himself would later refer to *The Carpetbaggers* as his favourite film, confirm that he had seen it three times when it was first released, and describe it thus:

> Vacant, vacuous Hollywood was everything I ever wanted to mold my life into. Plastic. White-on-white. I wanted to live my life at the level of the script of *The Carpetbaggers*.[6]

And, indeed, it would seem he was largely successful in doing so.

The review in *The New York Times* echoed Warhol's desire in several resonant ways. Describing the film as 'a sickly sour distillation', Cord is characterized as 'grotesque', bulging 'with money instead of muscles' from a 'crude and cruel career', and as a 'contemptible hero, conforming to the myth of the heel'.

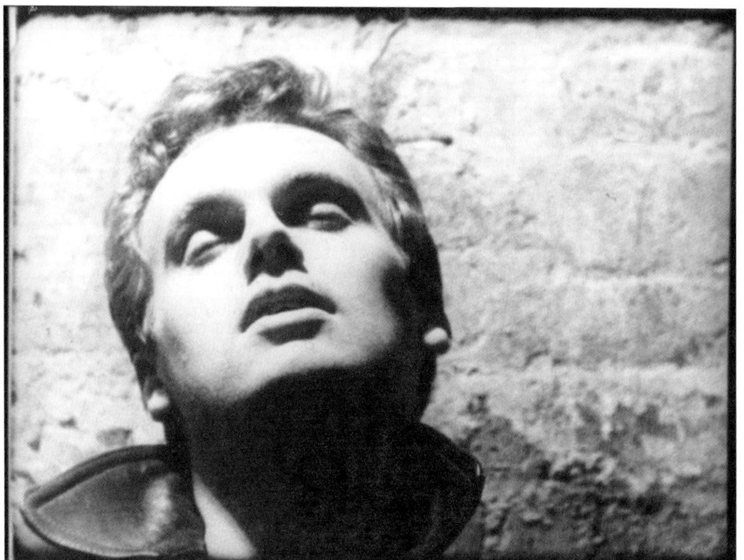

49 Andy Warhol, film still from *Blow Job*, 1964.

Even George Peppard's portrayal of Cord was described as 'expressionless, murky and dull', an 'outright synthetic fabrication of a character' and a 'thoroughly mechanical movie puppet, controlled by a script-writer's strings'. If the reviewer's appeal to the unfeeling machine metaphor were not enough, his assumption about how it pandered to the baser instincts of its audience – 'with as much innuendo (without using the four-letter words and the detailed boudoir descriptions) as the law and the Production Code will allow' – would certainly have struck the id–superego progression of Warhol's chord.[7] All in all, the film was pretty consistent with the Robbins novel it was taken from, at least if we judge from the latter's review in the *Times*: 'an excuse for a collection of monotonous episodes about normal and abnormal sex and violence' made 'boring for the simplest of reasons: the author's caricatures, as presented here, are non-human.'[8] That the novel was a best-seller and the film the top grosser of 1964 would only have only made it resonate all the more with Warhol's own sense of self.

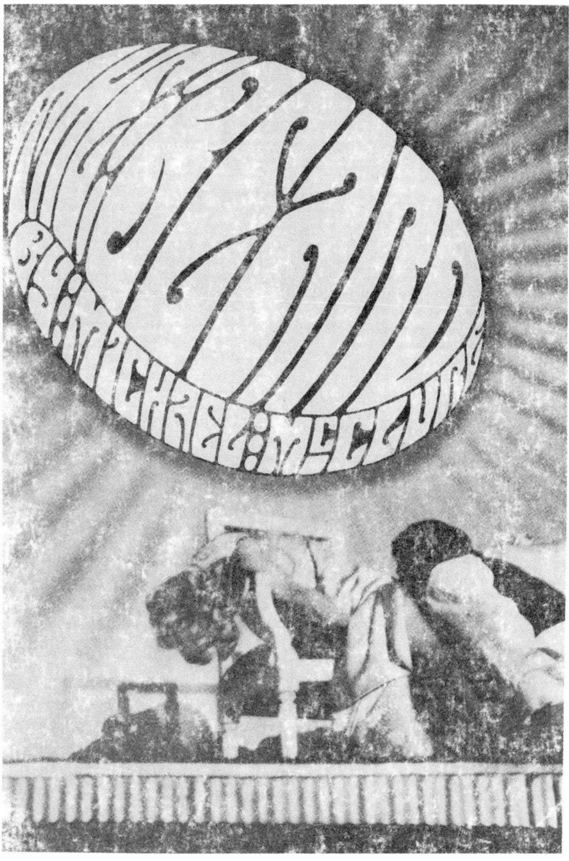

50 Cover of the Coyote Books edition of *The Beard* (1967).

The second cultural event that Warhol responded to with uncharacteristic enthusiasm was Michael McClure's challeng-ing two-person play *The Beard*, first performed in San Francisco in 1965, where Warhol seems to have seen it.[9] A searching review in *The New York Times* characterized it somewhat politely as 'an experimental play about a sexual relationship', although 'not a sexual relationship specifically but the general condition', but *The Wall Street Journal* was more graphic and more definitive in its depiction of the play's decoupling of sexuality from emotional self-imagining and attachment, calling it 'A Reptilian Mating Fugue'.[10] Interviewing Ultra Violet, one of Warhol's Factory superstars, John Wilcox asked a standard question raised by most of Warhol's biographers: 'Can you remember going to any particular thing in public that would throw any insight on Andy's character, by his actions, by what he did, how he reacted to something, whether he enjoyed something, whether he was surprised by it, anything like that?' Was there anything that broke through his indefatigable gee-whiz consumer mould that seemed to like everything equally? There was one such moment that 'really surprised me', she said: his response to *The Beard*. 'Andy said "God it is beautiful", and he really was sincere', Ultra Violet insisted, adding, 'he said, "That's how all my movies should be, my movies should be as beautiful as that play."'[11]

The beauty that Warhol refers to in McClure's play was born of the 'meat politics' philosophy that McClure had been developing since the late 1950s, according to which all human beings are understood to be 'bags of meat'. Influenced by the transcendental effects of peyote and other hallucinogens, he was principally concerned with confronting and reconfiguring the psychosocial boundaries maintained and policed by meta-physical principles such as love, beauty and identity, and undergirding social institutions like family, community and nation. By embracing a form of radical embodiment, McClure sought to reconceive the basis of interpersonal and social bonds. Working through various approaches to self and self-expression in his long list of publications, such as 'Peyote Poem' (1958), 'We're in the Middle of a Deep Cloud' (1959), 'We Are Impervious as the Skin of Our Dreams' (1960), and 'GRAHHR GROOOOOOOOOOOOOO NYARR GARHOOOOOOOSH ROSE' (1963), the process of reimagining that bond is the central drama of *The Beard*. The leitmotif is established by the female character, Jean Harlow, playing her refrain of coy interiority – 'Before you can pry any secrets from me, you must first find the real me!' – again and again against the interiority-refusing, boundary-transgressing rejoinder of her male adversary-lover, Billy the Kid: 'YOU'RE A BAG OF MEAT!'

The same theme plays out in all of McClure's writing from the period, such as in this excerpt from an essay on suicide and death in his volume *Meat Science Essays* (1963):

> The repressed love-energies of the man beat against his tied-up and knotted reactive muscle. They try to push outwards. He is confined by the separateness of his being. He feels the energy pushing outward against his skin and muscles from the interior and he imagines *auras* of that energy in the world. He loses track of the obvious visible truth that his skin is his bounds. He misunderstands himself and his *outlines* and he confuses *self* with outward objects, ideas, and persons. Superstition and degenerate concepts of romantic love, and metaphysics result from the damnation of desires. Reality is blockaded.[12]

The great cunnilingual climax of *The Beard* (illustrated in one way or another in most of its promotional materials: illus. 50) is the moment of skin and self losing their capacity to bound and, therefore, their capacity to prop up the metaphysical ruse of interiority. In so doing, we are to understand, reality is *un*blockaded, being becomes *un*separated and superstitions, metaphysical principles and 'degenerate concepts' like romantic love are sundered by the higher truth of base, animal desire. That moment of word/concept/identity-become-flesh – the great theme that McClure shared with San Francisco psyche-delic poster designers and with the hippy, hallucinogenic drug culture generally – is heralded to great effect on the cover of the 1967 Coyote Books edition of *The Beard*, as a counter-ideal hovering like a radiant new sun or luminous new god in the sky.

The psychosocial imagination of Warhol and his circle was very different from that of Bay Area Beat-cum-hippy culture, of course, and the New Yorkers' memoirs and interviews are full of disparaging comments. 'We had vast objections to the whole San Francisco scene', Lou Reed complained, for example. 'It's just tedious', he added, noting later that the 'whole LSD scene' was 'foreign to our sound'.[13] Similarly, in one memorable instance, the film-maker and Warhol's business manager Paul Morrissey reportedly taunted the famed San Francisco music promoter Bill Graham to the point of outrage by insisting that real musicians used heroin rather than LSD, and then later complained to Warhol about hippies 'retribalizing' around their drug use by thinking of it in the transcendental terms of religion. 'People are always so boring when they band together', he said, 'it's so tedious'.[14] Indeed, the social hub that Warhol and his circle returned to again and again was not any kind of neo-tribal, transcendental ideal but instead some version or another of the universality of the great anti-ideal, death.

This was a recurrent theme in Warhol's work, of course, but it was also central to the drug culture driven by amphetamines, barbiturates and opiates rather than hallucinogenic or quasi-hallucinogenic agents like marijuana, peyote or LSD. This connection is evident enough in what are, perhaps, Lou Reed's two most influential songs, 'Heroin' and 'White Light/White Heat' (1967), with their ecstatic allusions to the heroin- and speed-abetted bodily release of giving in to death-like, drug-addled psychosis. It seems fair enough to say that this drug-assisted dream of death of self and its corollary diffusion of desire beyond the boundaries of one's own body outwards to the entire field of object experience, was the transcendental, psychosocial, aesthetic core of Warhol and the culture that developed around him. In this regard, it shared with *The Beard* and *The Carpetbaggers* the transgressive primacy of the id as a social organizing agent. In all three cases, existing standards of propriety and decorum that govern human interaction by demarcating the boundaries of individual action are dispensed with in the name of desire. It also seems fair to say that this is the meaning of the formal property of repetition that structures all three: the endless string of conquests by Jonas Cord, who is introduced by the film's narrator as a man who gambles 'everything' and 'leaves his personal brand on everything and everyone he touches'; *The Beard*'s numbing duet/duel/*pas de deux* that Norman Mailer characterized as 'simple, repetitive, and obscene', emitting 'an odd but intense field of attention, almost like a magnetic field'; and Warhol's own introduction of a hardened, anaesthetizing repetition without narrative unfolding into the canon of art history.[15]

In keeping with their Freudian pedigree, all three work the boundary between Eros and Thanatos, mourning and melancholia that, according to Freud and his followers, bears the special function of repetition defining the condition of possibility for emotional attachment. While *The Carpetbaggers* joined ego and id against superego in a hyper-capitalist tear of 'creative destruction' through existing business models, professional standards and social mores (with alcohol as the enabling drug), and *The Beard* pits ego against superego, dissolving both in an orgy of boundarylessness so that a new communion of the two can be drawn straight from the id (with peyote and its ilk as the operative agents), Warhol and his cohort pitted id against superego in order to dissolve ego again and again using uppers, downers and opiates.[16] 'Repetition', as Roland Barthes once put it about the Warholian subject-cum-object, 'induces an adulteration of the person (a notion simultaneously civic, moral, psychological, and of course historical).'[17] The Factory was a vacuum, a black hole, a 'desert of destroyed egos', as a one-time Warhol-film superstar put it, and in that sense it was just another variant of the same creative destruction marshalled in *The Carpetbaggers*.[18] As Warhol's early collaborator, adviser and business associate Emile de Antonio would later describe him, 'Andy is to me, essentially, a phenomenon of capitalism: upward and onward and to hell with the people who were there before.'[19]

Warhol arrived in New York from Pittsburgh in the summer of 1949, 'a pale, blotchy boy, diffident almost to the point of disappearance', according to one of his first employers, Tina S. Fredericks at *Glamour* magazine, and seemingly 'all one colour: pale chinos, pale wispy hair, pale eyes, a strange beige birthmark over the side of his face'.[20] As with his self-effacing roles as the 'class baby' in art school and mama's boy as a child, or as 'The Nothingness Himself' that he would later adopt, this pale, blotchy, receding persona served him well. He had various names for this role. He tried out 'André Warhola' briefly and

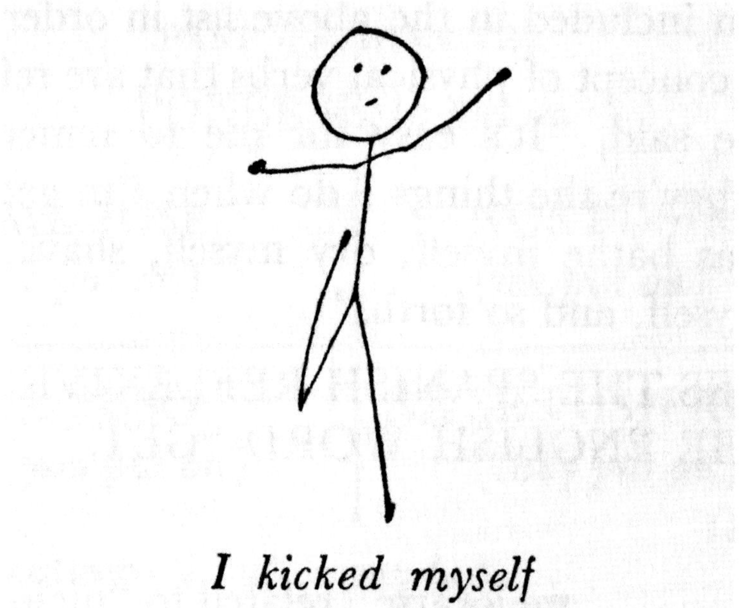

51 Andy Warhol, 'Reflexive verbs', from Margarita Madrigal's *Madrigal's Magic Key to Spanish* (1951).

later 'Andy Morningstar', but was more inclined to 'Raggedy Andy', 'Look at what the cat dragged in' and, particularly, 'Andy Paperbag', which he considered adopting permanently.[21] By all accounts, Warhol was very self-conscious about his skin, his bulging red nose, his rapidly receding hairline and his ethnic heritage, and his tendency to retreat into the background was genuinely born of these insecurities. However, most of those who knew him well perceived his paper-thin-skinned raggedness to be also something of a pose. Gregory Battcock's account is typical enough: 'he was always sort of quiet and wide-eyed', he reported, so

> you'd think, 'Oh, this is a little bushy-tailed boy from Pittsburgh'. But it was just this performance that Mid-Westerners always try to calculate: the little lost boy in the city of business.

He wasn't really that at all, Battcock insisted, 'It was a device.'[22] Charles Lisanby, Warhol's friend from the early 1950s, travelling partner and (apparently unconsummated) love interest, put it more simply: 'He affected being nondescript.'[23]

Even so, Warhol's 'Andy Paperbag' persona was, and continues to be, very effective as site for identification and projection. More than any other, Wayne Koestenbaum's thoughtful and empathetic book of 2001 works through that process. 'In imaginary conversations with him as I try to reconstruct his life', he tells us on the first page, 'I greet him as "Andy Paperbag" – Andy, my bag lady, a sack over his head, concealing the features he disliked; Andy, stuffing a world's refuse into tatty, woebegone containers.'[24] Judging by most of the reports from people who knew Warhol in the 1950s, Koestenbaum's rich and sympathetic description does not overreach – 'the purpose of the "bag" in Andy's life', he writes towards the end of his book, 'was to replace the body, to hide it by wrapping or enclosing it, and also, with shy exhibitionism, to expose (or indecently "flash") his practice of fabricating enclosures' – but instead describes something fundamentally human in every aspect of Warhol's life and work.[25]

'Trauma' is one term that gets used a lot, or we could use Warhol's own term for homosexuality: he called it a 'problem', broadening its meaning to suggest whatever unresolved psycho-social issues might be said to be at the heart of his sensibility. It 'comes from his mother', according to one early intimate. She made him feel 'so, *so unloved*', as if he was 'the ugliest creature that God put on this earth' – or we might even risk the term 'disease'.[26] Warhol was sickly enough as a child and strange enough as an adult, after all, that it is plausible he suffered from one or another mild neuropsychological con-dition disrupting his brain's capacity for emotional recognition – Capgras or Cotard's syndromes, for example, the latter of which being 'when the body image becomes "empty"'.[27]

In the end, such hard and fast diagnoses of the tattered nature of Warhol's bag/body/psyche do not matter much for our purposes because they are too narrowly biographical, telling us little about his place in the world that we find ourselves in today. Our concern, again, is to read Warhol as the mirror he claimed to be, to see his life and work as a Rorschach inkblot in order to reveal something about ourselves. One way to do this is to flip the reading of his tatty paper bag and see it as an opening rather than a wound, as permeable rather than simply weak or vulnerable or hurt, as fluidly social, cultural and historical rather than a positive psychological condition that was confined to Warhol himself. Individual personalities have always affected and influenced collective personalities – politicians, celebrities and, occasionally, artists – and it is the premise of this book that we very much live under the sign of Warhol, that Warholian subjectivity is, in some deep and meaningful way, inextricable from American subjectivity and, more broadly, the conditions of possibility for subjectivity in an American-style, globalizing world. When having coffee at Starbucks, or shopping at IKEA or Wal-Mart, or browsing the Internet, it sometimes seems reasonable enough to say, 'We are all Warholians now': we all share in a common myth of centre-lessness, a common myth of psychosocial existence as an empty, tatty paper bag that we endlessly try to fill with stuff.

Charles Henri Ford, an American heir of the Surrealist tradition and elder statesman in the larger Factory circle, described the permeability of Warhol's boundaries this way: 'everything is sexual to Andy without the sex act actually taking place.' Ford betrayed his modernist pedigree when he associated this quality with artistic genius generally: 'Of course', he said, 'the greatest artists have always been the most highly sexed', adding that their genius was not really born of sublimation or suppression and redirection of sexual impulses but rather of an 'overflow'. We might, however, reverse Ford's genius claim in true post-modern fashion and say instead that it is something like that overflow that makes us all Warholians.[28] Put differently, it may be impossible to dissociate dispersal and diffusion of sexuality from discrete attachments to centralized love objects – lovers, family members, friends, religious figures, politicians, celebrities and the like – outwards into the object world more generally. Indeed, we could simply take this to be a working definition of post-war consumer culture, with its ever-expanding panoply of choices. Put differently again, we might say that Warhol represents for us the flattening, or horizontalization, democratization or universalization, of our own desire.

Sexuality is understandably a much-discussed theme in the many reports and studies of Warhol's life. In part, no doubt, this is a function of his radical adult restraint. 'If one topic was taboo at the Factory', according to long-timer Bob Colacello, 'it was Andy's sex life. He wanted – demanded – to know every detail of ours, but his was strictly off limits.'[29] By nearly all available accounts, he was not only acutely uncomfortable when anyone touched him, he more or less did not have sex, at least not in the conventional sense of interpersonal genital contact. In a recorded dinner conversation with William Burroughs, for example, Warhol reported not having sex until he was 25, and then giving it up a year later at age 26, suggesting that his sexuality had been ill-affected at the tender age of five when, as mentioned earlier, he witnessed a boy being forced by an older group of toughs to perform fellatio on another boy underneath some stairs.[30] But, equally so by every account, Warhol was endlessly, obsessively interested in sex and constantly seemed to want to be experiencing his own sexuality by proxy – by gathering reports from his cohort as Colacello describes, by asking those around him to have sex with partners of his choosing, by creating and attending social or artistic situations where sex was happening without participating himself, and by taking weekly 'sex lessons' where, apparently, he would sit and watch a heterosexual couple having sex, presumably while they gave him pointers and he asked questions.[31] These lessons began just a few years after he reportedly stopped having sex, and when his assistant at the time, Vito Giallo, declined Warhol's request to attend a lesson with him, he became very angry and cut off their relationship.

One way to think about the consequences of Warhol's sexual idiosyncrasy, again, is to say that he socialized or democratized sex, universalized it. That is, he made it corporate or institutional in the manner of Hugh Hefner, say, or *Cosmopolitan* magazine, or Walt Disney, with the Factory or his career or his shopping and collecting practices standing in for a conventional love life. 'It's like his life is a byproduct', Gerard Malanga put it, 'he's like an institution, like Walt Disney.'[32] Another contributor to the institutional life of the Factory, the curator Sam Green, made sense of it this way:

> I think for anybody who doesn't have any kind of love
> life, people who are totally dependent on the world, that's
> always their role. I don't know what Coco Chanel's love life
> is all about but I gather there couldn't be very much of it,
> I mean there could be some sex, but I doubt whether she has
> any interest in anything but dresses and the dress business.
> And so I think it's like the sales lady, the public relations
> people, the head cutter, the designers, the people who are
> studying underneath her, are all like family, children and a
> love life, and I think that's what Andy's got going for him.[33]

In this sense, Warhol's way with his 'family, children and a love
life' was not so unusual. To put another sort of diagnosis on
it, he was a particular kind of workaholic. What makes his art
and life distinctive and particularly revealing, however, was his
desublimation and disaffection of that love, his making it about
sex instead of love.

Perhaps the most telling or symptomatic expression of this
distinctive form of sexuality was Warhol's turn to feet and shoes,
on the one hand, and 'cocks' (as he liked to call them), on the
other, as his primary artistic subjects. This turn occurred in the
year or so after he allegedly gave up sex and coincided with,
or more likely contributed to, his landing of the I. Miller shoe
company account in 1955 that led to his second Art Directors
Club award in 1956 (illus. 53). He had won his first in 1952
working in the Ben Shahn style for an account that had been
Shahn's, illustrating social documentary subject-matter and
highlighting big, beefy, working-class hands. A certain clarity
to this turn was made almost comical when Warhol's mother
Julia tried on the I. Miller shoes that he would bring home:
'She couldn't get into them; she had these huge peasant feet',
Warhol's assistant Vito Giallo reported, adding, 'I think she
used to work in the fields in Czechoslovakia.'[34] This, no doubt,
made Warhol squirm a bit; by this time he was routinely pursuing

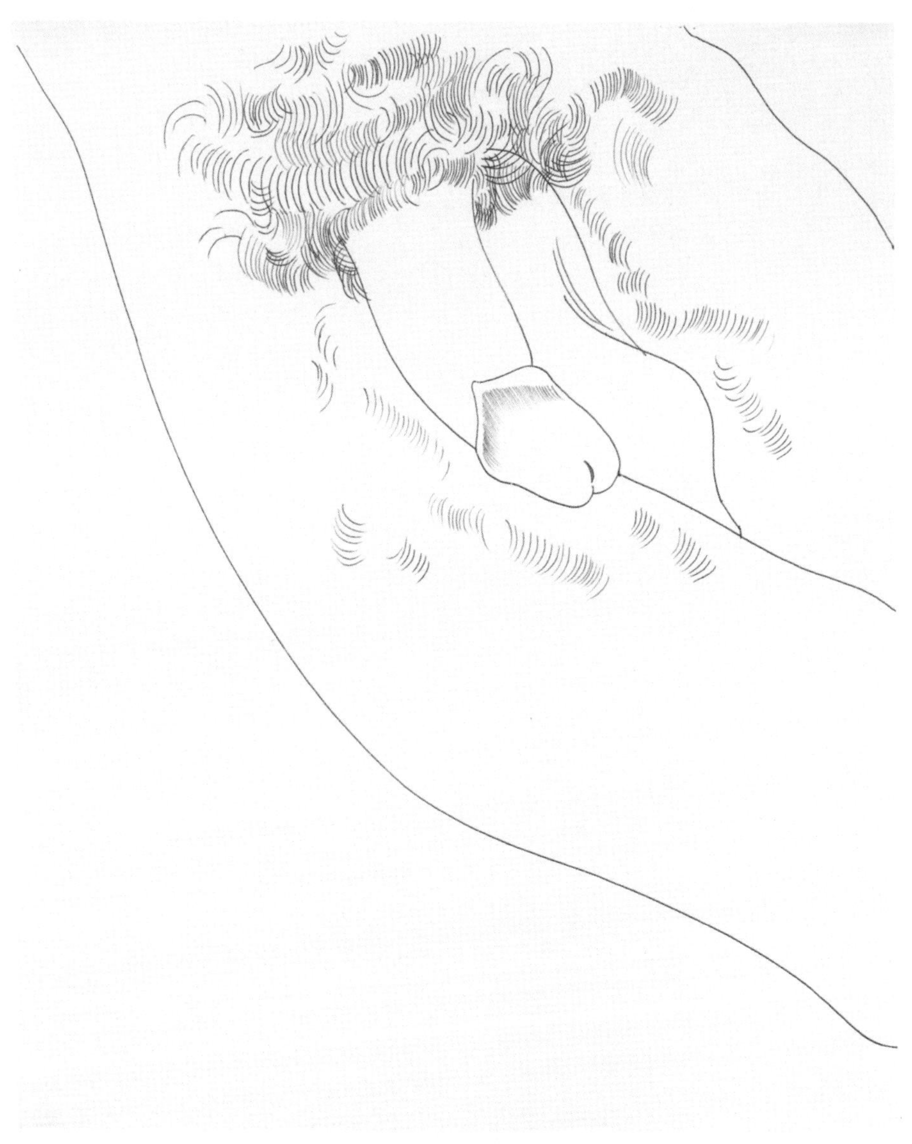

52 Andy Warhol, *Reclining Male Nude Torso*, 1950s, ballpoint pen on paper, 43.5 × 35.6 cm.

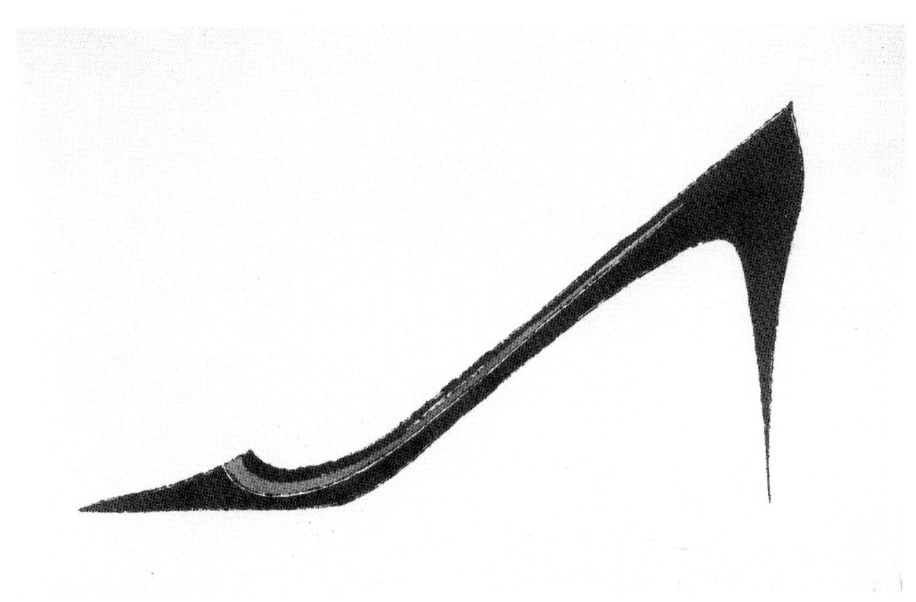

53 Andy Warhol, *High Heel*, 1950s, ink on paper, 37.1 × 58.4 cm.

intimacy with 'beauties', as he took to calling them, by writing to men he did not know but wanted to ('You know,' Lisanby says, 'people who were "known", as it were') and asking if he could draw their feet, and asking those that he did know, or had just met, if he could draw their 'cocks' (illus. 52).[35] By nearly every account of the middle and later 1950s, Warhol made hundreds of these drawings, and pads full of them piled up in his living room studio.

Various commentators have referred to his interests as being overdetermined. The thoughtful art and film critic Parker Tyler saw Warhol's predilections this way:

> Andy Warhol is a very young artist who may be said to be addicted rather than dedicated. Currently, he is addicted to shoes . . . If one doubted they were fetishes, his doubt would be dispelled by noticing that an evening slipper is inscribed to Julie Andrews and a boot to James Dean.[36]

Indeed, the only first-person report about sex with Warhol makes this fetishism its centrepiece. The kiss-and-tell partner was John Giorno, the poet and star of Warhol's *Sleep* (1963), and the sexual encounter took place on the occasion of the first of several shooting sessions for the film:

> I was sitting on a seventeenth-century Spanish chair as he checked out where to put his tripod and lights and suddenly Andy was on the floor with his hands on my feet, and he started kissing and licking my shoes. I had always heard he was a shoe fetishist. 'It's true!' I thought with a rush. 'He's sucking my shoes!' It was hot. And I got some poppers to make it better. I jerked off while he licked my shoes with his little pink tongue and sniffed my crotch. It was great. Although Andy didn't come. When I wanted to finish him off, he said, 'I'll take care of it.'[37]

In its various psychoanalytical, anthropological and political-economic definitions, fetishism always involves some form of narrowing or restricting of experience, typically by substituting part for whole. In foot or shoe fetishism, for example, sexual engagement with the body of another person is abridged and concentrated in the foot or shoe. Such distillations of affect are always forms of desublimation because they render desire less sublime, less magnificent, less metaphysical, and more mundane, material, everyday, vulgar. Sublimation generalizes and abstracts sexuality by making the object of desire into the be-all and end-all, into the horizon of truth and beauty and understanding and desire. It is the kind of magnified or heightened importance attached to the sexual instinct that Nietzsche railed against – the dressing up of libido with culture, progress, morality, truth and so on.[38] Desublimation, on the other hand, cuts to the chase by peeling the mythical moralism and the like away from raw bodily function – a shoe is a shoe, a foot is a foot, a cock is a cock.

Such fetishism is at the heart of Warhol's influence, at the heart of his postmodernism, and in myriad ways. Before moving on, however, it is worth at least noting that its moment of triumphant hegemony is also the moment of emergence for one particularly forceful rival conception, in Herbert Marcuse's *One-Dimensional Man* of 1964 and its central thesis about 'repressive desublimation'. In Marcuse's account, the making worldly or material or everyday of desire – the 'conquest of transcendence', he called it, where your love object is knowable as a great pair of shoes, say, or a great foot or a great cock, rather than a sublime, inexplicable, transcendent other – represents a mythologization of power on the level of the body. 'The environment from which the individual could obtain pleasure – which he could cathect as gratifying almost as an extended zone of the body – has been rigidly reduced', localizing, contracting, desublimating the libido such that 'it loses the greater part of its truth' – that is, its capacity to see outside or beyond the day-to-day business of commerce and the day-to-day subjectivity of the consumer.[39]

Understood in Marcuse's sense, Warhol's emphatic spread of sexuality outwards from one-on-one interpersonal relations also represents a pronounced contraction of the field of desire, by reducing its object from a subjectivity that exceeds one's own being in the world to an object that can be drawn or photographed or filmed, possessed or even owned.

7
THE NOTHINGNESS HIMSELF

The Danish painter and founding member of the Situationist International, Asger Jorn, may have understood the modernist way with form better than any other of his generation – its tortured interiority, of course, but more importantly its wilful lack of grace, or better still its refusal of the day-to-day expediency that comes from having the world line up in the orderly, rational manner that human reason imagines it should (illus. 54). The raggedy and untoward unpleasantness of his work – the way in which its goofy, antisocial, adolescent vulgarity seems to undercut even, say, Willem de Kooning's would-be misogynistic impetuousness, or David Park's churlish or intractable clunkiness, or Francis Bacon's seeming merger of the visions of butcher and painter, or Jean Dubuffet's unseemly and slightly ridiculous cartoon blobs, or even Kazuo Shiraga's abject grovelling in mud – is a kind of triumphant last hurrah for the old school. He has little of the Picassoid or Pollockian childlike posture to redeem his way with imagery, less of an association with A-bombing or firebombing or genocide to justify it, nor even the old standby of Dada-like irony and pastiche to rescue it from charges of simple self-indulgence. In the epoch-old modernist race to the bottom, it seems to this observer at least, Jorn wins hands down.

What is at stake in that race is pretty simple, of course, just as it always was for modernism. Artists, like everyone else, want autonomy; they want to feel as though they are subjects

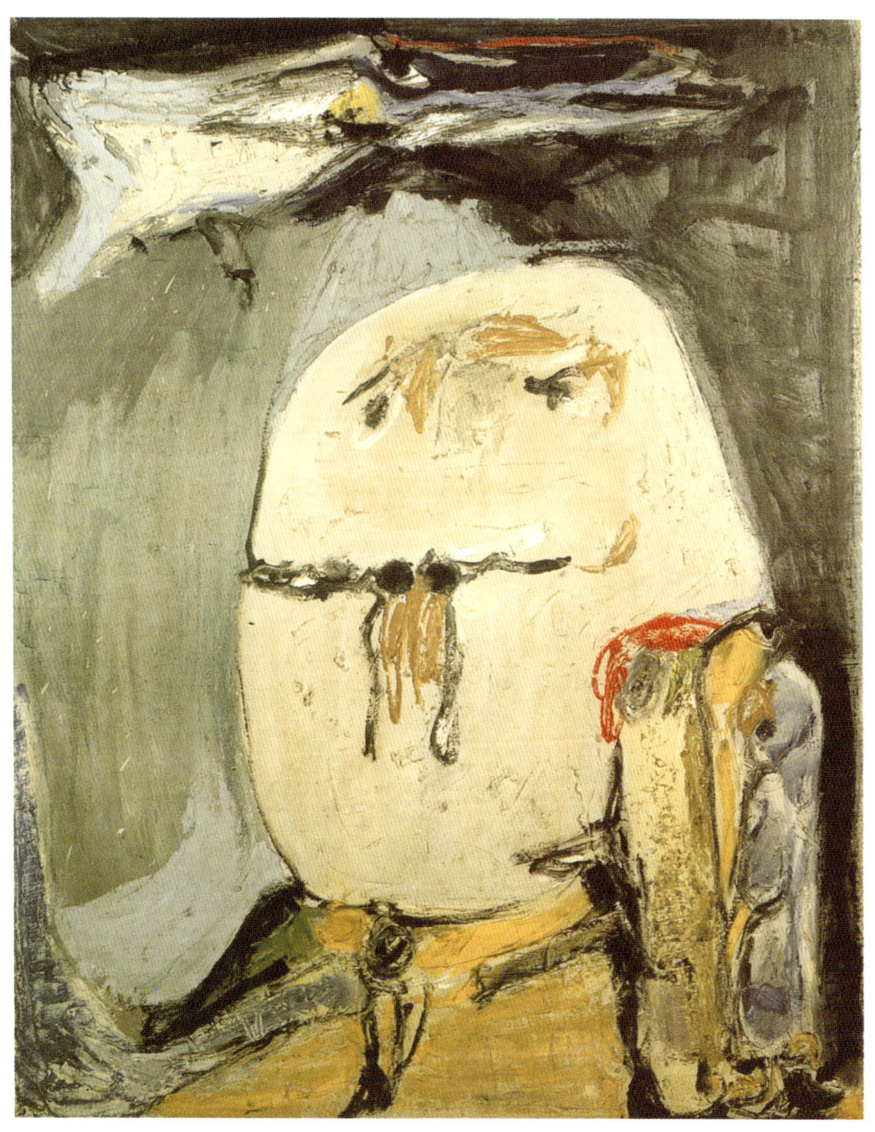

54 Asger Jorn, *The Poet Guillaume Apollinaire*, 1956, oil (mixed media) on canvas, 124.5 × 100.5 cm.

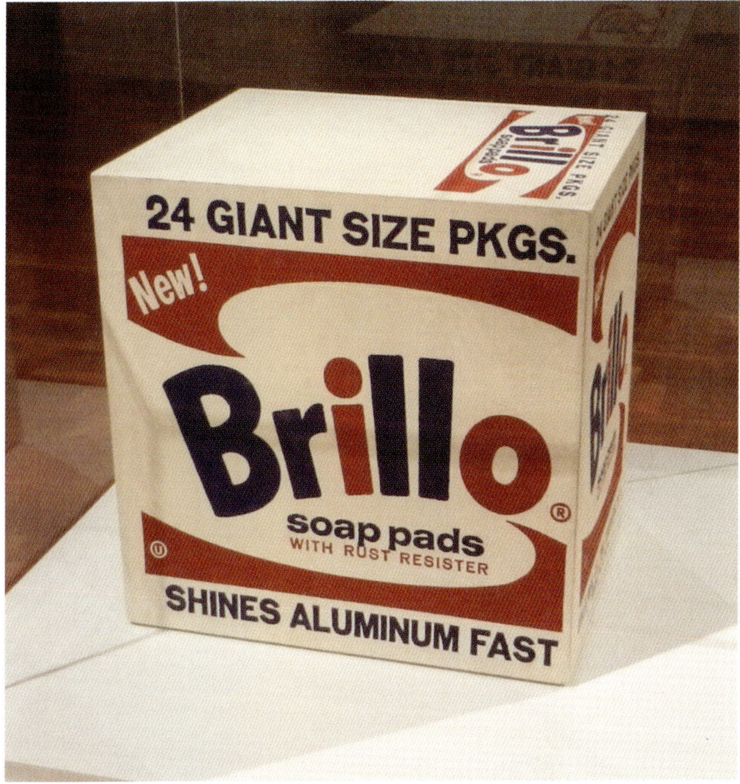

and not objects, as if they are in control of their lives and not as if they are simply at the mercy of the sundry social forces that surround them. What modern art did better than almost anything else, with its impetuousness, churlishness, abjection and the like, was give expression to that desire and to the pain, grief and longing born of that expression being thwarted or curtailed. If pre-modern artists were oracles, Boswells, barkers and jesters, modern artists were canaries in the mineshaft of modern life. The race to the bottom was, among other things, a competition in sensitivity, a competition for who could express best the rapidly metastasizing nervous condition of the industrializing world.

For artists like de Kooning, Park, Bacon, Dubuffet, Shiraga, Jorn and myriad other contemporaries and forebears, that expression was a decidedly boyish affair. Angst was actively, anxiously expressed; paint or mud or would-be semen, or urine or vomitus or blood was strewn about the canvas; powerlessness was rendered as rage, frenzy or temper tantrum; and the emotional range of art was ever approaching the impolitic and impolite directness and sensitivity of a two-year-old. In this way, it might be said, it was characteristically masculine. Art was like the skinny-boy-cum-welterweight in the old Charles Atlas ads, responding to power with power, to aggression with aggression, to phallic flare-ups of authority with its own spasms of prospective sovereignty.

Warhol and the postmodern tradition he helped to institute shared with the moderns that came of age before him the same sense of power and desire for autonomy, but his approach was opposite. Instead of acting out in response, he closed in; instead of responding with aggression, he responded with a form of self-containment; instead of filling out his identity with phallic presence, he refashioned it as a theatrical cocoon (illus. 55). While it is too strong to characterize this difference between modernism and postmodernism as a 'war', as Michael Fried famously did in 1967, it does seem fair enough to say with Fried that the 'explicit rejection of modernist painting and sculpture' (by the Minimalists that were the topic of his study, but it applies to Warhol and his affiliates as well) was 'not basically a matter of program and ideology but of experience, conviction, sensibility'.[1] That is, the turn that Warhol represents for us was not a matter of politics per se – from left-wing criticality to right-wing acquiescence, as some would have it, for example, or from high-bourgeois to working-class taste, as others would wager – but instead was one of 'sensibility', a matter of affective susceptibility and responsiveness. The new artists of the 1960s generally comported themselves differently than artists had previously, and Warhol did so particularly. There were pivotal antecedents, of course – Jasper Johns's flags, targets, stencils and so on perhaps more than any other – but it is only with Warhol that this new sensibility realized its full form.

In Johns's case, that form was derived on the one hand from the incongruity of the uninflected literalism (to use Michael Fried's term), facticity or machinic character of his repertoire of standardized compositions, and on the other from the highly inflected bodily expressiveness that came from his use of a thick, sometimes skin-like encaustic surface, his gestural application of paint and wax, his use of cast body parts and body contact prints, and perhaps even the one-to-one bodily scale of his early canvases. The contrast between body and machine, between effusive interior and self-possessed exterior, served as a figure for the closet-like constraint of desire and thus carried forward the old, modernist, Jorn-like boyishness as its inside, even as it set the stage for the postmodernism to come with its poised, protective, calcifying outside.

Warhol's single greatest accomplishment as an artist was to make it all about that exterior. As he put it in the opening lines of his book *POPism: The Warhol Sixties* (1980), 'Pop took the inside and put it outside, took the outside and put it inside' and, indeed, in that simple shift in sensibility, in that shift of affective susceptibility and responsiveness, in the sealing shut of the fluid, contested boundary between inside and outside by making them isomorphic, the postmodern was given its definitive form.[2] No longer a battle between inside and outside, self and social expectation, presentness and theatrical self-presentation, art under Warhol's tutelage would derive its freedom, its autonomy, by reimagining itself as a package, and the dynamic exchange across the border that differentiates self from society would be effectively sundered.

Warhol's emphasis on packaging – on cans, bottles, boxes and the like – at his moment of emergence as a fine artist makes

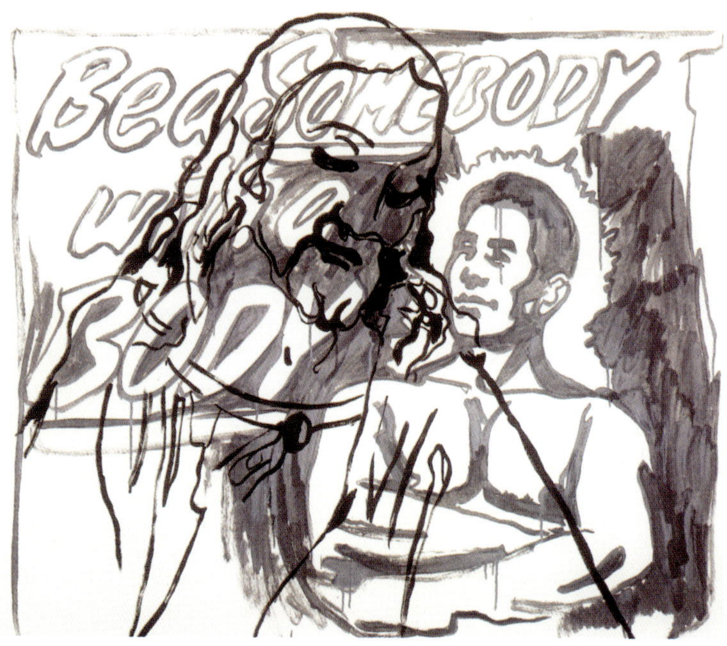

56 Andy Warhol,
*The Last Supper /
Be Somebody
with a Body,*
1985–6, synthetic
polymer paint
on canvas,
127 × 152 cm.

this clear enough, as did various other formal aspects of his
professional life: the silver-lined Factory, for example, or the
silver helium balloons; the photo booths and other recording
devices he used to capture his subjects; the standard 40-by-40-
inch canvas that he used for all his society portraits of the 1970s
and '80s (so that he could arrange them in grid formation for
museum exhibitions); the extensive cookie jar collection; the 612
standard-size cardboard boxes that he used to collect ephemera,
notes, correspondence, purchases, artworks and so on as a serial
artwork he called his *Time Capsules*. Everything and everyone
had its box, its closed container – Warhol himself as much as
anyone or anything else. In the end, it was really that container
and not its contents that made it art.

As Benjamin Buchloh pointed out in 1989, this had long been
the aim of visionary industrialists like Walter Paepcke, long-time
president of the Container Corporation of America, funder of

László Moholy-Nagy's New Bauhaus in Chicago and founder of the Aspen Institute, who saw the great commercial promise of Bauhaus design principles and modernist abstraction generally:

> Purged of the political and ideological idea that artistic intervention in the spheres of production and consumption would enable collective social progress, the cognitive and perceptual devices of modernity would have to be deployed simply for the development of a new commodity aesthetic (e.g., product design, packaging, and advertisement). The fabrication of that aesthetic would, in fact, become one of the most powerful and important industries in postwar America and Europe.[3]

The most effective package of all, the one that, in the end, carried the postmodern dream with the most enduring influence, was Warhol himself. Here is how that packaging is described by Warhol and his ghostwriters to great comic effect in a dialogue between A, Andy, and one of his series of interlocutors, who all go by the designation B:

> 'Okay, B, okay. So now the pimple's covered. But am I covered? I have to look into the mirror for some more clues. Nothing is missing. It's all there. The affectless gaze. The diffracted grace . . .'
>   'What?'
>   'The bored languor, the wasted pallor . . .'
>   'The what?'
>   'The chic freakiness, the basically passive astonishment, the enthralling secret knowledge . . .'
>   'WHAT??'
>   'The chintzy joy, the revelatory tropisms. The chalky, puckish mask, the slightly Slavic look . . .'
>   'Slightly . . .'

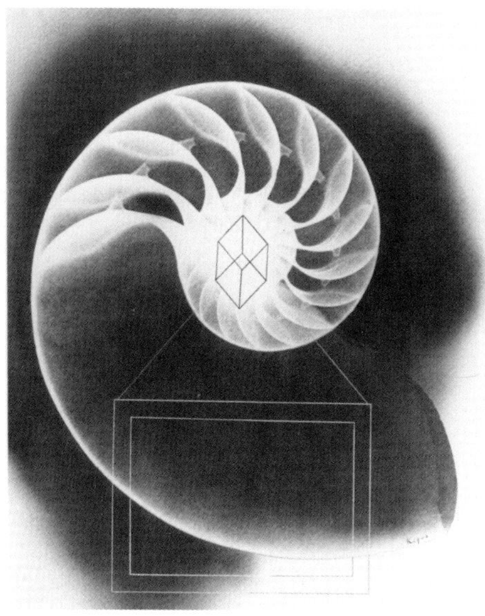

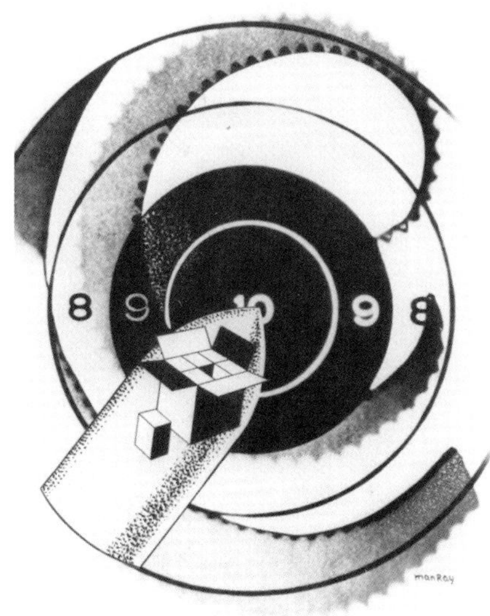

'The childlike, gum-chewing naiveté, the glamour rooted in despair, the self-admiring carelessness, the perfected otherness, the wispiness, the shadowy, voyeuristic, vaguely sinister aura, the pale, soft-spoken magical presence, the skin and bones . . .'

'Hold it, wait a minute. I have to take a pee.'

'The albino-chalk skin. Parchmentlike. Reptilian. Almost blue . . .'

'Stop it! I have to pee!!'

'The knobby knees. The roadmap of scars. The long bony arms, so white they look bleached. The arresting hands. The pinhead eyes. The banana ears . . .'

'The banana ears? Oh, A!!!'

'The greying lips. The shaggy silver-white hair, soft and metallic. The cords of the neck standing out around the big Adams apple. It's all there, B. Nothing is missing. I'm everything my scrapbook says I am.'[4]

57 György Kepes, *One Integrated Flow of Production, from the Early Series,* c. 1938, gelatin silver print, gouache and airbrush on board, 54.6 × 38.5 cm.

58 Man Ray, *Can Paperboard Stop a Shell?, from the Early Series,* 1942, gelatin silver print with collage on paper sheet, 43 × 35.6 cm.

With the drawing out of the caricature to its breaking point, this might as well have been a comic's stand-up routine or a skit from *Saturday Night Live*. Gone from such self-imagining were the days of modernist shibboleths like Jorn's: 'The form of a container is a form contrary to the form of its contents; its function is to prevent the contents from entering into process.'[5] Instead, self and society are synchronized by locating all the action at the boundary or screen that divides them rather than inside or outside, apart or together, such that it can be said: 'I'm everything my scrapbook says I am', leaving the interior to float free of the threat of other-determination or the burden of self-becoming.

The package or container wall represented by Warhol's pictures and sculptures of soup cans, Brillo boxes, Coca-Cola bottles and so forth was a scrim or boundary, a divider or enclosure, and the old, modernist dream of social, political and psychological transparency still carried by artists like Jorn and his ilk, or architects like Bruno Taut, Vladimir Tatlin, Mies van der Rohe, Le Corbusier and Philip Johnson, was placed in abeyance. This was obvious from the very beginning. David Bourdon made reference to a running joke in his interview with Warhol of 1962 ('I've heard your soup can is a symbol of the womb, expressing your deep-seated desire to return to the foetal state') but it was only half a joke, and the serious take on it was not so different from the comic relief.[6] One way to think of the idea of subject as container under discussion here is to say that it is a way of keeping oneself and one's world contained, orderly, protected by regimentation, by externalizing authority for who and what you are. As Koestenbaum puts it: 'Andy organized and boxed the world into digestible units, modular perceptual containers that can be stacked, repeated, and counted, and that might last forever.'[7] That containment represented the primary formal quality at issue and, like any such sustained, concerted emphases, cannot be divorced from root psychological issues. Put simply, this was Warhol's visual vocabulary of self and world understanding,

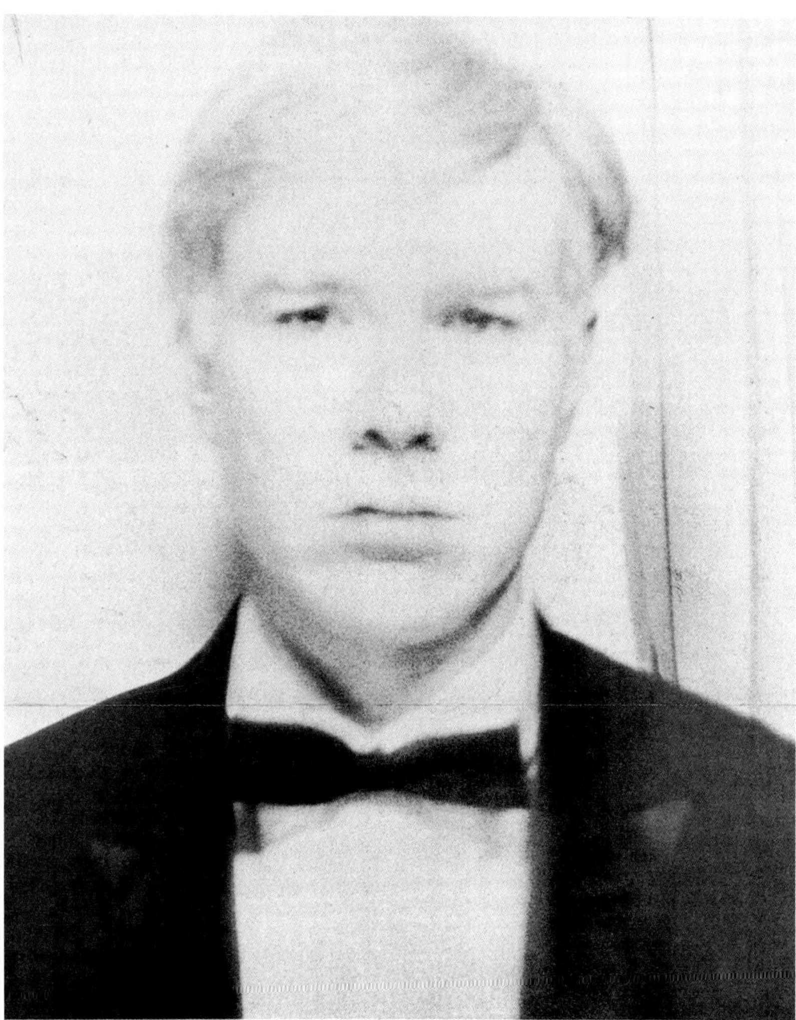

THE PERSONALITY OF THE ARTIST

An understanding of the works of Angus Sinclair, the late Scottish philosopher, might be helpful in understanding the paintings and boxes of Andy Warhol, although the artist might deny it. As for Warhol's images, we ought to be wary of reading any articulated philosophy into them. If anything, these objects on canvas and store boxes speak the "language in which inanimate things speak" (the language Hofmannsthal's Lord Chandos wanted to learn). "I want to be a machine," the painter has said, misleading many; his work does suppress those symptoms of modern art — personality and creativity — which have been sanctified to the point of blasphemy.

Art criticism has been as resistant to allowing the object to *make* feelings as most psychiatrists have been to allowing, for example, the head of government as a source for personal neurosis (except psychoanalytically through identification, a childhood fear of sexual authority, etc.). The paintings and boxes of Warhol *are* feelings, as much as paint in Abstract-Expressionist painting is paint; the artist's works have almost nothing to do with his white streaked hair or his pale skin.

Sinclair, in the "Sensations, Perceptions, Feelings, Emotions and Things" chapter of *Conditions of Knowing*, states that "experiencing things and objects as things and objects is the outcome of holding certain attitudes, and to hold and apply these requires a constant effort." That suggests an attitude to which few of us have come. Sinclair, in a footnote, suggests that we could probably develop a sensitivity to radar if it became necessary. To try to understand works of art which are not the result of personality may make us aware of an analogous need.

With a touch of prescience, Warhol's specific art has provided us with a means of seeing and feeling a place (things) which we have not seen and possibly have not sensed before.

59 Andy Warhol, *The Personality of the Artist,* invitation to Stable Gallery exhibition, 1964.

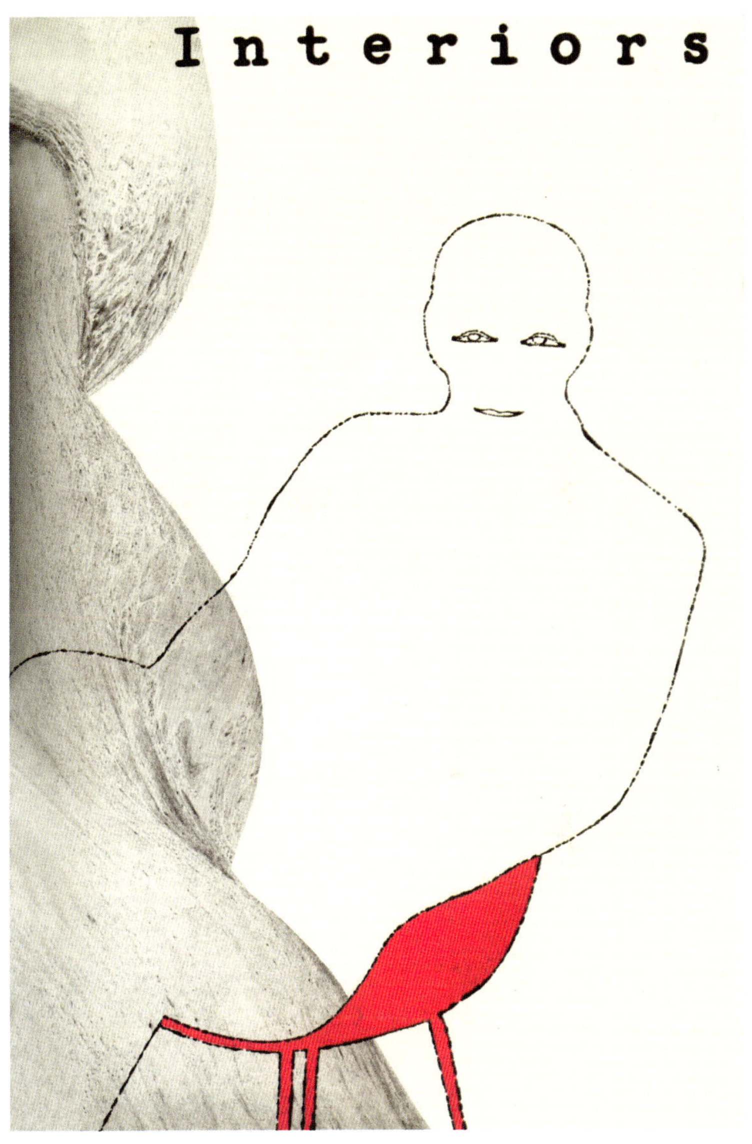

60 Andy Warhol, cover of *Interiors* (June 1952).

and it is that vocabulary which seemed to speak the truth to the audience that has responded so powerfully since to both him and his work. Gene Swenson's brilliant photograph of Warhol and short essay, 'The Personality of the Artist', made into an announcement for the show of the Brillo and other boxes in 1964, got this just right. The photograph's blur and blown-out highlights reducing its subject almost to an outline, together with its utter expressionlessness, was perfect, as was his effort to read the Brillo boxes in the shadow of the Kennedy assassination: 'Art criticism has been as resistant to allowing the object to *make* feelings as most psychiatrists have been to allowing, for example, the head of government as a source for personal neurosis' other than in the most mundane of ways, Swenson said, bringing his point home by insisting that the 'boxes of Warhol *are* feelings', that they speak of real human desire and need, of real neurosis or alienation.[8]

As commentators have endlessly noted, Warhol's personal life was resplendent with symptoms pointing the way to such issues and their larger meaning – not least of them being his own disciplined, ritualized, self-reflexive performance and documentation of those symptoms. Another such telltale sign was reported by his long-time live-in boyfriend/home manager/interior design consultant, Jed Johnson:

> He kept most rooms locked. He had a routine. He'd walk through the house every morning before he left, open the door of each room with a key, peer in and then relock it. Then at night when he came home he would unlock each door, turn the light on, peer in, lock up, and go to bed.[9]

Maybe there is a generic diagnostic description for such behaviour or for his *Time Capsules* and other related practices – 'obsessive-compulsive containerization', perhaps? – but, again, it matters little for our purposes. Suffice it to say that rooms, interiors, containers, boxes and so on were heavily cathected, and not so much because of the specific belongings that they held inside but instead for the containment itself. Like all his myriad symptoms – his shyness, say, or his self-conscious, working-class ethnicity, or his bad skin or wig-covered baldness, or his conflicted sexuality – this one was also routinely and effectively made into a joke and a point of ambivalence. 'When I look at things, I always see the space they occupy', the *Philosophy* tells us, for example, 'I always want the space to reappear, to make a comeback, because it's lost space when there's something in it.'[10] Or a little further on, 'shy people don't even want to take up the space that their body actually takes up' but 'I've always had a conflict because I'm shy and yet I like to take up a lot of personal space.'[11] Space, for Warhol, it seems safe to say, was a figure for ego, for identity, in the same way that it is for anyone – for oversized-SUV-driving McMansion owners, for example, or for proper, old-school, mansion-owning robber barons of Industrial Age Pittsburgh, or, more proper still, the castle- and estate-owning set of even further back, or really for any of us who recharge our sense of self from the warm embrace of home, community or nation, regardless of that space's proportions.

Characteristically, Koestenbaum has a good read on this: 'Warhol's mature practice takes its cue from the urban gay fetish of interiors'; collecting, decorating, nesting, working interior space is 'code for homosexual activity and identity'.[12] It was a way to communicate identity in the manner that a style of dress or tone of voice, bodily gesture or taste in art might, of course, but it was also a way to construct that identity, to flesh it out, to house it, to fortify it. Raw space, in other words, was as much a part of that code as was how that space was appointed, the raw spatialization of identity as important as the finesse of its decoration, stylization or attitudinization. Indeed, while Warhol was as ambivalent and as multifaceted about his taste for things as he was about everything else, on some level the particular qualities of the stuff inside did not matter. As one observer has it about the *Time Capsules*, for example, what was inside was a bit 'like the trashy contents of a teenager's bedroom', even if those trashy contents had been tidied up by being tucked away in a container.[13] Warhol himself would put it this way: 'That's what I have always wanted, not to own anything – to be able to get rid of all my junk – maybe just put everything on microfilm or holographic wafers' or in plain brown boxes, ' – and just move into one room.'[14] Or, more simply: 'I really believe in empty spaces.'[15]

Warhol's casting of himself as a container, with its accommodating way with people and things, was understood by many of his friends and associates as feminine. 'I think he's very feminine', said one, for example, 'he is the most receptive person I've ever met.'[16] 'Andy is the passive voyeur, the receiver', said another, 'He is feminine.'[17] He is 'a receiving station', another understood it, 'That's his way of working.'[18] Finally, 'What do you think he gives to people?', still another was asked, to which she responded, 'He takes them seriously and he considers them as remarkable.'[19] What he provided was recognition, a receptive space in which seemingly anyone and anything could exist – in the Factory, for example, or in his tape recordings or photographs or films – without being subject to the harsh, masculine judgment of laws, mores and the like. This is the other side of Warhol's hollowed-out interiority, his insistence on being the skin or shell, box or container: it created an empty space to be inhabited by others.

Some version or another of this feminine accommodation, it might be said, has always been the province of modern art. It is both central to its remove from the culture at large and the space of recognition for its boyish outbursts. Jeff Wall calls it 'this happy space of ours' and refers to the work that concerns him most as '*Kammerspielen*', or plays in and with the room, chamber or container.[20] But we might also say that the version of femininity at issue here is not the happy one that Wall refers to, the expressive, empathic, womb-like one that provides the space of recognition through emotional identification. Instead,

Warhol's femininity was really the sort given by his 'wife', as he liked to call his tape recorder. It was a form of feminine receptivity devoid of empathy or emotional identification and care. Warhol was 'a great listener', is how Ultra Violet put it, 'he just keeps listening all day and finally at the end of the day he does what has to be done. He's a computer.'[21] Phrased differently, the femininity of Warhol's wife was a femininity without a sense of place or sense of home. It was abstract, exchangeable interiority, the interiority of one cassette recording tape after another, one Brillo box after another, one Campbell's soup can after another, one standard brown cardboard 'time capsule' after another. Put another way again, it was the femininity of exchange value rather than that of use value, the femininity of the interchangeable prostitute rather than that of the contract-bound wife.

There is another period container form that we can refer to, one that has particular resonance with Warhol's role as a consummate figure for our epoch and lends perspective to the distinct form of femininity given by his tape-recorder wife. To jump from Warhol to empty container to a period form of femininity to shipping containers, as I will here, will seem a reach, but bear with me. The connection is a valuable one because it takes us by a series of steps from Warhol into the rudimentary visual vocabulary of globalization – a vocabulary we touched on in chapter One and with which we will conclude in chapter Nine – and then back again.

The shipping container, invented in the 1950s and made into the commercial standard that it is today in the early 1960s, was very much in the news as Warhol was developing his mature style. 'CONTAINERS CITED AS SHIPPING "MUST": Industry Officials Say Use Will Be Limited Only by Challenge of Labor', read one *New York Times* headline in 1959, for example; 'MINNEAPOLIS HOUSEWIVES are getting fresher meat because of containerized delivery service', proclaimed a large advertisement in the same paper later the same year.[22] President Kennedy championed containerization in speeches, international shipping companies took out full-page ad after full-page ad in major metropolitan newspapers, and academics and other industry supporters warned that 'the economy and safety of this nation and of the free world may depend, to a very important degree, on how well and how quickly we build a global transit pipeline, using the best tool that we have – containerization.'[23] As a result, from 1956 to 1966 the volume of international trade reportedly grew at better than twice the rate of global production, and the age of globalization found its stride.[24]

This shift in emphasis from production to distribution is inseparable from the larger post-war shift from a worker-centred to a consumer-centred economy, just as containerization's central design principle of abstract equivalence and its facilitation of the process of exchange are inseparable from the progressive hegemony of the commodity form. Indeed, the container form generally played a big role in the cultural consciousness of the period. From Tupperware, Saran Wrap, Styrofoam and other innovations of the packaging revolution made possible by the new plastics, to the suburb's 'Little Boxes' (as the new mass-manufactured housing was lampooned in Malvina Reynolds's much-covered song of 1962), to the box form standard that came to dominate Minimal art, the world seemed 'Better by the Box', as *Time* magazine summed up the container

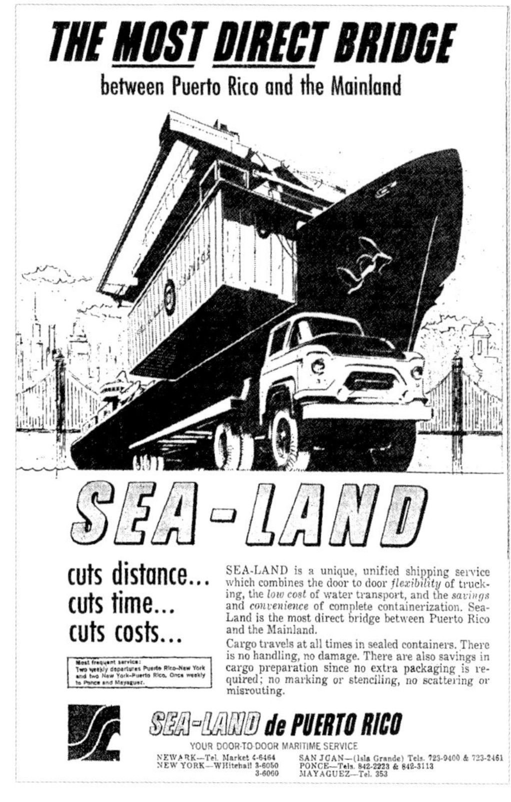

61 Sea-Land container advertisement, 1962.

revolution just a few weeks before Minimalism's triumphal 'Primary Structures' exhibition opened in 1966, with its kindred innovation (which *Time* would label the 'Engineer's Esthetic').[25] This new pervasiveness of the commodity's 'better by the box' abstract equivalence, in the end, is the single greatest meaning of Warhol's shift in the idea of art from interiority to the boundary between inside and outside, from soup to can, from product or good or creation or thing to the container for that thing.

Writing with no little tone of desperation during the heyday of Pop art, Theodor Adorno attempted to articulate what needed to be held on to in order to preserve the original promise of

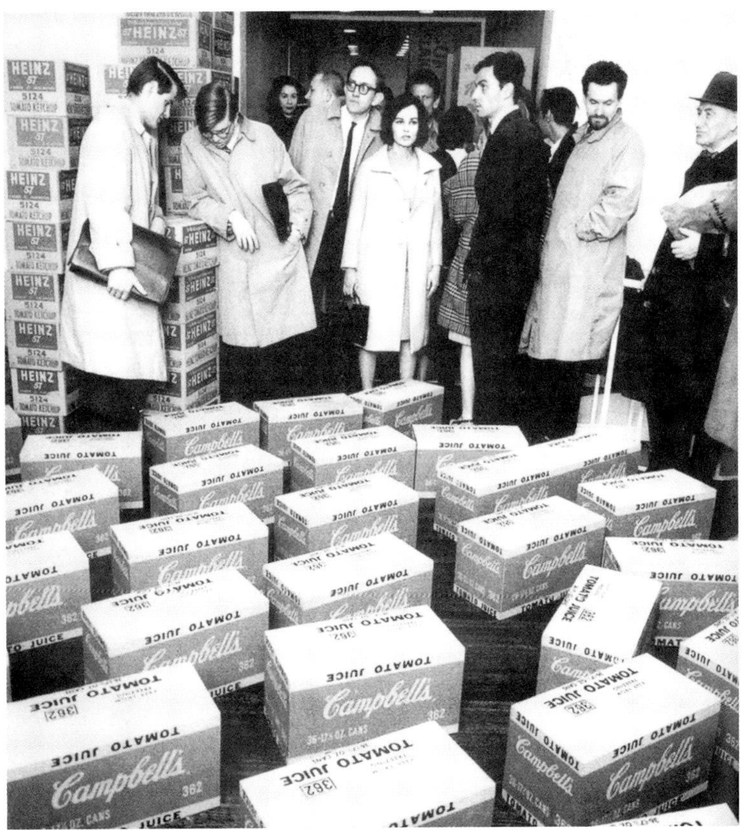

62 Ken Heyman, Stable Gallery opening, 1964.

modern art: 'Consciousness of the antagonism between interior and exterior', he stated, 'is requisite to the experience of art.'[26] What Warhol represents more than any other is the collapse of the great modernist dream that the tension between inside and outside was itself the realm of truth. Modern art in the manner of Willem de Kooning or Francis Bacon, Kazuo Shiraga or Asger Jorn, was a proclamation about the public value of the private self, and its motto was still the Enlightenment's motto: 'Have courage to use your own understanding!', as Kant famously put it, have courage to give public expression to the antagonism between one's own internal experience and the world outside. By making the container into our dominant artistic value – just as the bringing of pictorial space down to earth through the use of linear perspective did, beginning with Renaissance humanism (in the work of Leonardo, for example), or as did the bringing of pictorial space towards the surface of the canvas and thus towards the realm of the audience, beginning with Enlighten-ment idealism (such as in the work of David) – Warhol gave expression to the dominant experience of world available to us today. Like the earlier innovations of the Renaissance and Enlightenment, the abstract equivalence of Warhol's globali-zation aesthetic is a form of materialism that decentralizes authority. And like its predecessors, it is politically, socially çand psychologically ambivalent in its own distinctively historical way.

It is this ambivalence that Warhol recognized and knew how to work the edge of better than any other. The threat posed by that edge made it into the news in characteristic fashion in 1965, when the fortuitously named director of the National Gallery of Canada and Canada Customs arbiter for art, Charles Comfort, refused to certify that Warhol's Brillo boxes were art, thereby forcing Canadian customs officials to charge merchandise import tariffs to the gallerist who was bringing them in for an exhibition. As the enraged dealer, Jerrold Morris, said at the time, 'The rest of the world has recognized pop art as art – but our National Gallery seems to be afraid of the boxes.'[27]

Mr Comfort, it might be said, would have been right to be afraid of Warhol's boxes – of their empty interiority, their insistence on the thin interface between self and world, their reduction of meaning to the abstract equivalence of the container form – for what they meant for the old, hallowed ideals of modern art. The Brillo boxes also raised the question of homophobia: not only did they undercut both the boyish expressiveness of modern art and the femininity that accommodated it, they also stood clearly for the sensibility that Susan Sontag had made into a period vogue (with no little inspiration from Warhol) in her essay 'Notes on Camp' (1964). 'My desire to write is connected with my homosexuality', Sontag had written a few years earlier, 'I need the identity as a weapon, to match the weapon that society has against me.'[28]

Director Comfort, in his dual capacity to determine what is and is not art, would certainly have sensed the weapon-like status of Warhol's art, its assault on the conventional modernist register of the personality of the artist. Warhol's weapon, however, was not identity, homosexual or otherwise, and his method was not to challenge one identity with another. Instead, method and weapon alike were the systematic and sustained withdrawal from the founding Enlightenment tenets of bourgeois subject formation, a withdrawal outwards to the protective container wall that separated inside from out, id from superego, gut feeling from world. This was itself a form of repression and the end result a kind of armour that renders interior flaccid and unavailable and exterior hard and overwhelming, thereby reducing the elasticity negotiating inside and out that had been the medium for the bourgeois ideal. Again, it is our premise that this is who we are as postmoderns, who we have become, and it is the measure of Warhol as an artist that he was able to get it so right.

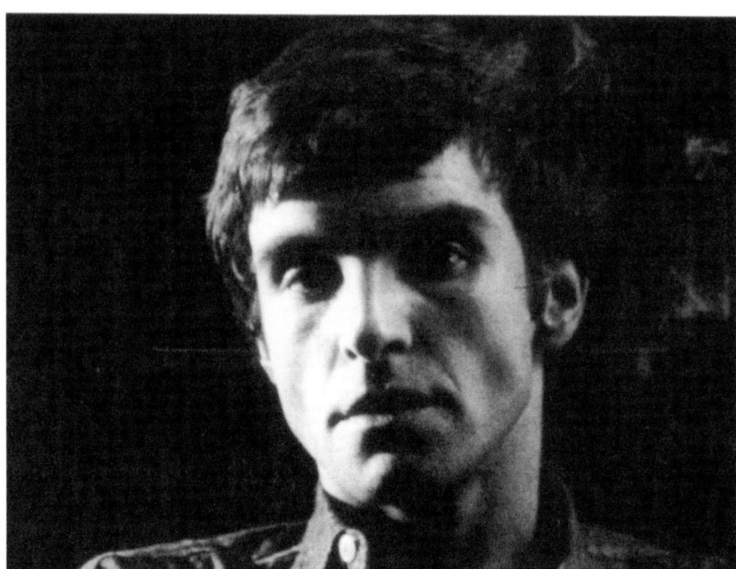

63 Andy Warhol,
film still from
Freddie Herko
screen test, 1964.

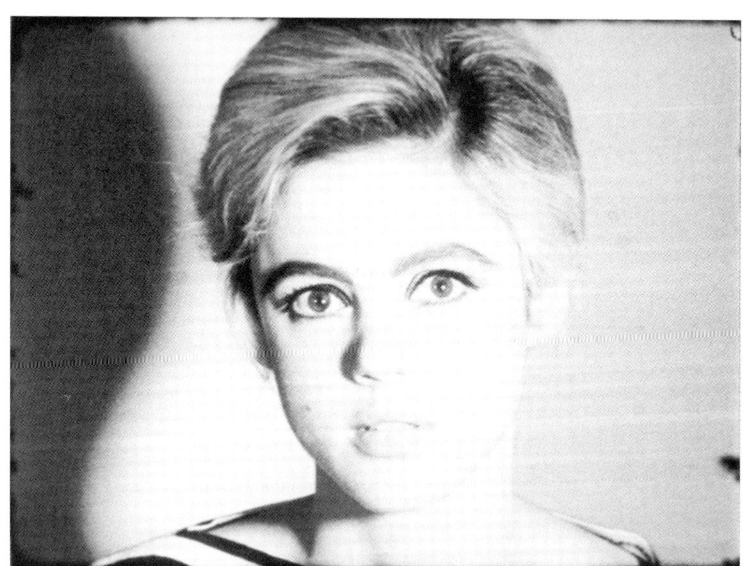

64 Andy Warhol,
film still from Edie
Sedgwick screen
test, 1965.

8

DRELLA

No matter which way you look at it, the 1960s were chilling, harrowing, scary times. From Patrice Lumumba's assassination in January 1961 and the international intrigue that swirled around it, to Marilyn Monroe's death by barbiturate poisoning in August 1962 and the terrifying threat of a nuclear war brought on by the Cuban missile scare in October, to the botulism outbreak in the 'housewife's standby' of canned tuna in March 1963, Martin Luther King Jr's civil rights campaign in Birmingham, Alabama, Bull Connor's response to it of April and May and John F. Kennedy's assassination in November, to the release of *Dr Strangelove* in January 1964, the Gulf of Tonkin incident in August and the release of *Fail-Safe* in October, to the assassination of Malcolm X in February 1965 and the Watts Riots that August, the early years of the decade were rife with death and disaster. It would only get worse, of course. There was a 'kind of death thing in the air then', reflected Mario Amaya, the only other besides Warhol himself to take a bullet from Valerie Solanas in June 1968, and Warhol 'maybe almost subconsciously captured the feeling, the kind of smell'.[1] Warhol had already said something similar when he was asked by Gene Swenson about the origin of his *Death and Disaster* series, published the same month as the Kennedy assassination: 'It was Christmas or Labor Day – a holiday – and every time you turned on the radio they said something like, "4 million are going to die". That started it.'[2]

Indeed, the smell of death was not just the residue of the big issues of the day – decolonization and recolonization, the cold war between First and Second worlds and the hot war in the Third, race relations and capital punishment, the mushrooming image culture and consumer economy, the bomb and organized crime – it was also evermore part of the culture that Warhol cultivated and surrounded himself with, at least until he was shot and nearly died in 1968. From the Juilliard School and American Ballet Theatre-trained performer in several Warhol films, Freddie Herko, dancing out of an apartment window to his death in October 1964, to Harvard-educated lighting designer, film editor, film-maker and possible Warhol lover Danny Williams apparently walking into the sea and never returning in September 1966, to beautiful and patrician 'Poor Little Rich Girl' (as her first Warhol feature was titled after the 1936 Shirley Temple film of the same name) Edie Sedgwick being committed to a series of psychiatric institutions for her drug-induced erratic behaviour beginning in December 1966 and finally dying of barbiturate poisoning in November 1971, death and disaster was a recurrent motif in Warhol's world. There were many others too, of course, including several more who would jump from windows; and so it seemed, the tragedy that surrounded Warhol in the 1960s and beyond was as much a sign of the times as were the assassinations, wars, police brutality, riots and all the rest of it.[3]

Warhol's death and disaster motifs of 1963 – car crashes, people leaping to their deaths from tall buildings, the electric chair, funerals and hospitals, the hydrogen bomb, race riots and, last but not least, deadly canned food – premiered at the Sonnabend Gallery in Paris in January 1964 with telling hype. 'The traditional feelings attached to death are banished', wrote catalogue essayist Alain Jouffroy, 'In front of these pictures we are preserved, cleansed, purified' – in a kind of baptism by fire. 'So what a lesson! And one not of morality but of lucidity!'

Indeed, Jouffroy promised, Warhol's pictures are nothing less than 'the sacred images of a godless world'.[4]

These works, together with the slightly earlier imagery of Marilyn Monroe produced immediately after her death and slightly later imagery of Jackie Kennedy made immediately following her husband's assassination, constituted a coherent and moving theme, even if Warhol characteristically fended off any such meaning in the Swenson interview of November '63: 'There was no profound reason for doing a death series, no "victims of their time", there was no reason for doing it at all, just a surface reason.'[5] Of course, it is often difficult to differentiate depth from surface, profundity from super-ficiality, emotionality from intellectuality – particularly in the context of trauma – and since Warhol was dredging some of the most weighty feelings of the period from their depths up to the surface, the matter was made all the more indistinguishable.

Early on, Warhol gained a reputation for being callous. The most renowned instance of this in the memoirs and interviews was his response to the news of Freddie Herko's suicide in 1964 when, according to one of many reports, he said: 'What a shame we didn't run out there with our camera to film it.'[6] This comment soon became part of Warhol lore and so may have influenced later reports about him saying that he wanted to have a camera on hand if and when Edie Sedgwick overdosed or committed suicide.[7] There is no doubt, however, that Warhol had the deeply troubled Sedgwick – whose two equally unstable brothers had died in 1964 and early 1965, one by hanging himself and the other by driving his motorcycle into a bus – re-enact the suicide of Hollywood actress Lupe Vélez at least three times for his film *Lupe* in late 1965, a role in all likelihood tailor-made for his leading star. There is no doubt either that that he had Lou Reed write a song about her as a femme fatale in 1966, shifting the meaning of her big-eyed, child-like beauty and well-bred charm from the domain of luxury and privilege into the register of death and disaster.

There are many other such reported instances of callousness around Edie and others, including an account provided by Warhol screenwriter Ronnie Tavel that summed up his sense of the period:

> My sense of the Factory . . . is caught in that filtered heat of the late summer, late afternoon sun falling through its streetside windows, and on Danny Williams at his desk, increasingly bizarre in appearance, his hair matted, his glasses broken, encounter by encounter progressively lost to amphetamine . . . And then one day Danny was gone. On September 5th I took a call at the Factory from his mother, asking anxiously if we had seen her son or knew of his whereabouts. 'Andy', I relayed, 'she wants to talk to you. She's very worried.'
>
> 'Oh', he groaned, 'what a pain. He's a pain, now she is. Tell her I'm not here.'
>
> 'She knows you're here: I just said I'll get you.'
>
> He didn't respond . . . After I hung up on Mrs Williams, by way of admonishing me, he concluded dismissively, 'I don't care where he is. He's just an amphetamine addict.'
>
> Three days later, Gerard told me that he'd learned they found his car by the water, he wasn't sure where, a river in Connecticut or the ocean off Cape Cod, with all his clothes piled neatly beside it. Danny had drowned himself.[8]

The name that Warhol came to be referred to by insiders, starting in 1964 and continuing until his shooting in 1968, was 'Drella', a combination of Cinderella and Dracula. The nickname was developed by the 'mole people', or speed freaks, who were part of the Factory circle, but was soon adopted by the larger community and eventually used by Warhol himself, including in his book *a, A Novel* (1968), which had largely been transcribed from 24 continuous hours of tape-recorded conversation centred on lead mole person and occasional superstar, Ondine. The title's lower case 'a' referred to Andy in the manner of e. e. cummings and to the amphetamine use associated with Ondine and his circle, the relatively casual use of speed by Factory habitués more broadly and with the drug-fuelled marathon recording session that became the book most immediately. Perhaps better than any of his many other sobriquets, 'Drella' sums up Warhol's tremendous resonance with the death and disaster of the period. Contrary to his own inclinations and to the jokiness of the nickname itself, we might think of it, in this regard, as bearing some profundity or depth. At minimum, we can see it carrying into the present some of the history associated with Cinderella's seventeenth-century coming of age and Dracula's nineteenth-century rejuvenation of the figure of the vampire.

The figure of Dracula was a recurrent theme in Warhol's work, starting before he became known as Drella with the film *Batman Dracula* of 1964 that featured Jack Smith in the role of Dracula.[9] Smith, probably the single most influential progenitor of the camp sensibility and the director of underground classics *Flaming Creatures* and *Normal Love*, would also play a leading role in Warhol's film *Camp* (1965), a response to Susan Sontag's essay on the topic of 1964, in which he, among other things, dramatically and symbolically opens a closet door. As Warhol's casting suggests, Bram Stoker's novel (1897) has long been taken to be an expression of closeted homosexuality, just as Stoker himself appears to have been a rather extreme closet case, rife with anxiety that circulated around his relationship with Oscar Wilde. 'In Dracula, written one month after Wilde went to jail', as one account has it, 'Stoker solved his guilty problem':

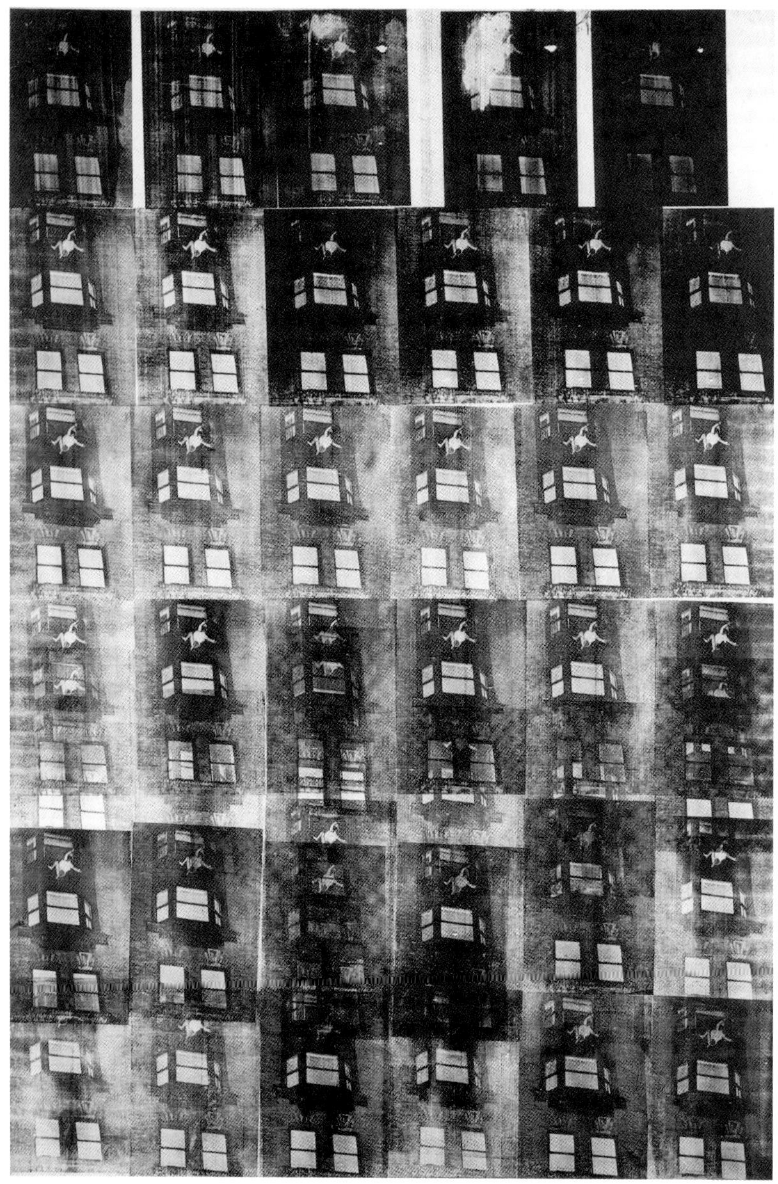

65 Andy Warhol, *Woman Suicide*, 1963, silkscreen ink on canvas, 313 × 211 cm.

> he produced a text that spoke about Wilde in a diffused,
> hidden, flowing, distorted way. Dracula reproduces Wilde
> in all his apparent monstrosity and evil, in order to work
> through this painful popular image of the homosexual
> and eventually transform it into a viable identity model.[10]

In this regard, Count Dracula's complex intertwining of sexuality
and violence was a natural subject for Warhol.

Perhaps the best account of *Dracula* – best because it was
the most encompassing and maybe even the most influential
– was the writer Maurice Richardson's description of it in
1959 as 'a kind of incestuous, necrophilous, oral-anal-sadistic
all-in wrestling match'.[11] The main theme in Richardson's
account (and most others since) was that the figure of
Dracula represented regression to a primitive and needy,
childlike state, a state of oral-anal aggression. Stoker is very
clear about Dracula's 'great child-brain' that can only 'creep . .
. into knowledge experimentally', that is, 'not by principle,
but empirically'.[12] Consistent with Freud's account of the
oral and anal drives that precede the ego and its province of
abstract reasoning, that aggression takes the form of narcissistic self-containment in a manner that eventually realizes
itself in the superego. 'Civilization', Freud wrote, 'obtains
mastery over the individual's dangerous desire for aggression
by weakening and disarming it and by setting up an agency
within him to watch over it, like a garrison in a conquered
city.'[13] Id and superego, self and society, inside and outside
are cast as mirror forms of aggression, with no mediating ego
in between.

Stoker's novel develops this theme at length, saying about
Dracula, 'as his intellect is small and his action is based on
selfishness, he confines himself to one purpose . . . he is intent
on being safe, careless of all'.[14] Vampiric aggression, in other
words, is also a form of shoring up the vampire's own boundaries

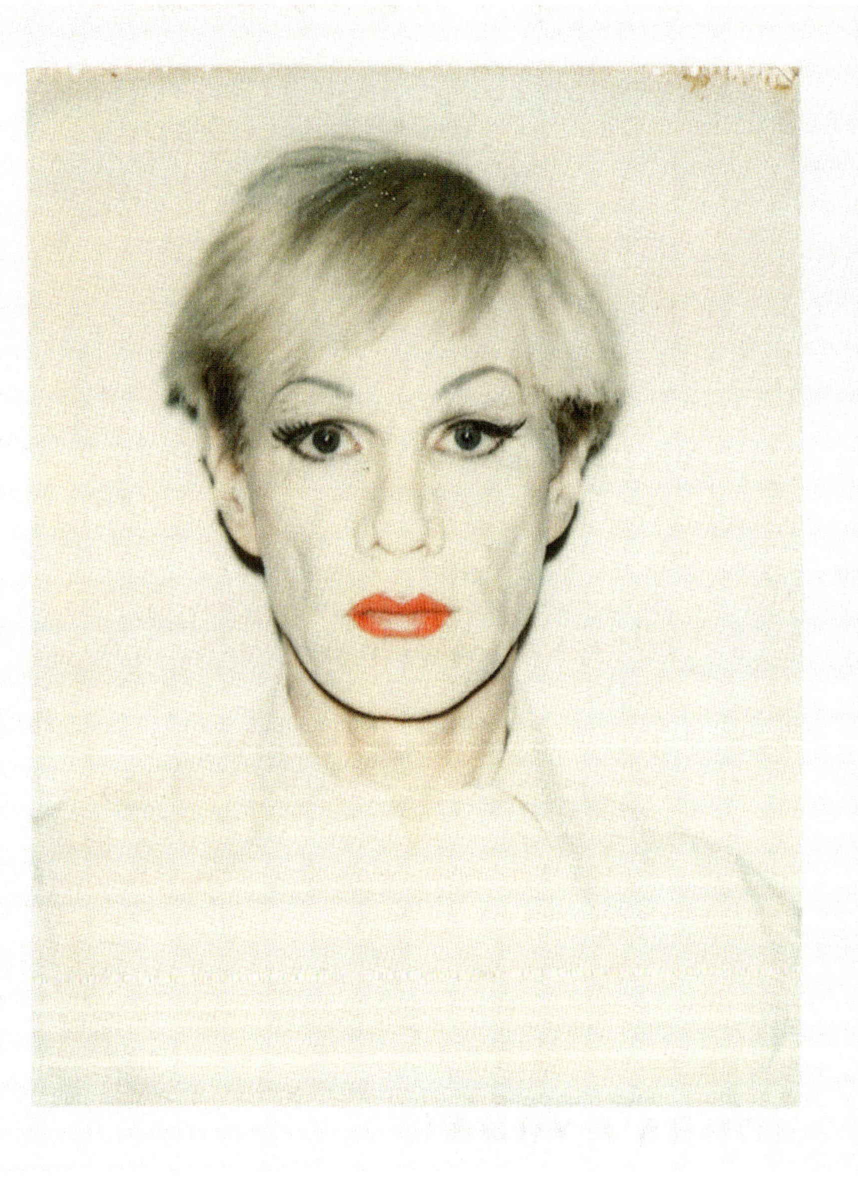

66 Andy Warhol, *Self-portrait in Drag*, 1981–2, unique polaroid photograph, 10.8 × 8.5 cm.

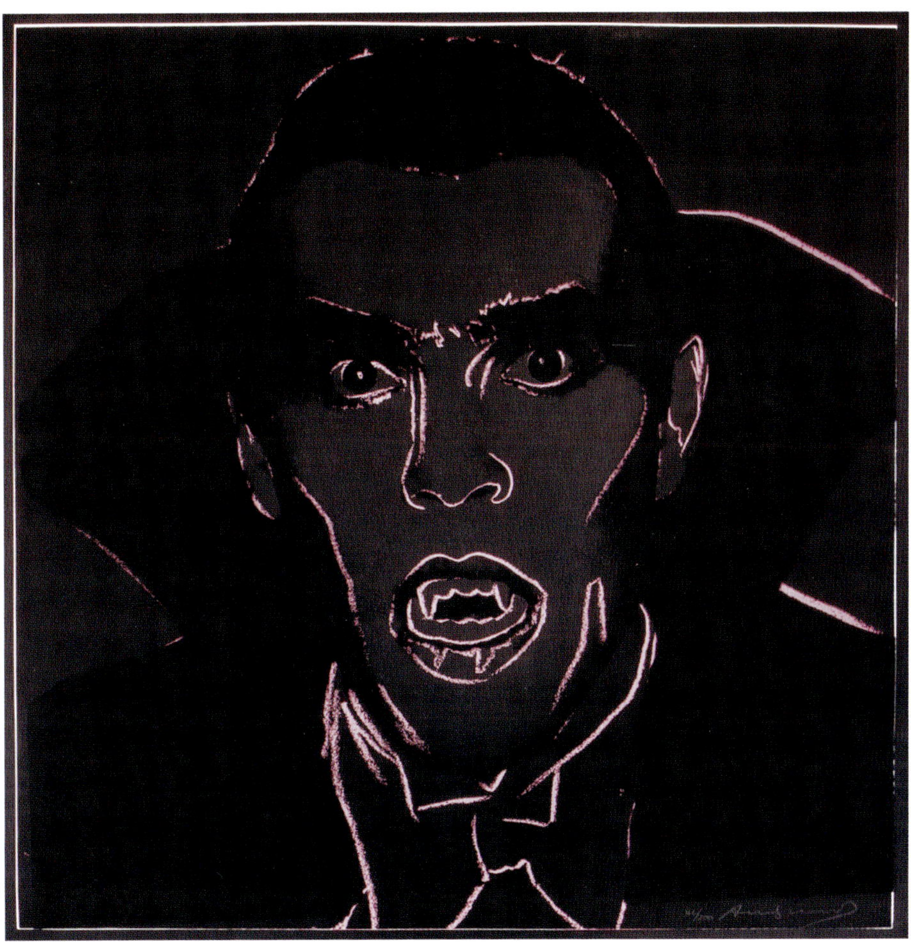

67 Andy Warhol, *Dracula, from Myths*, 1981, screenprint, 96.5 × 96.2 cm.

in a pre-egoic form of self-discovery and self-development by incorporating others in a manner consistent with the oral and anal stages of childhood development, rather than entering into the elastic, interpersonal give-and-take characteristic of a more mature psyche. Human relations, for the vampire, are all id and superego, all desire and fear, all interiority and exteriority, with a minimal role for the skin-ego or porous boundary that mediates between them.

Such egolessness is uncontrolled and thus scary, of course, but it is also ecstatic because it provides an experience of id that does not feel bound to reconcile itself to the superego or, alternately, of all superego that does not need to reconcile itself with id. In this way it is a form of letting oneself go and returning to a primitive psychical state. 'I long to go through the crowded streets of your mighty London, to be in the midst of the whirl and rush of humanity, to share its life, its change, its death, and all that makes it what it is', says Dracula. He brings home the meaning of this desire for anonymity amid the whirl and rush of humanity when he explains: 'a stranger in a strange land, he is no one; men know him not and to know not is to care not for. I am content if I am like the rest.'[15]

The bliss of egolessness, of losing oneself in the unknown, of experiencing others anonymously with access to one's own interiority sealed, was the pleasure of the vampire experienced as regression. This literary theme served as a figure for Stoker's own closeted homosexuality, and as a figure for the old-world aristocracy of the bourgeois *flâneur*. *Flânerie* was a kind of tourism or consumption or cruising, and in so being represented a specific kind of subject–object relation, one that addressed the world as if it were an image that lies on the other side of a screen. The department store, as Walter Benjamin noted, would be the *flâneur*'s 'last haunt' as his unique form of bliss began to be generalized in the figure of the consumer's anonymous drift through the fantastic world of commodities.[16]

What is important in all this, for our purposes, is the figure of the closet or coffin, or the commodity as container. Each of these in the same way stands for the hard divide between id and superego, between desire and its object, between self and world, and as such for the same form of alienation. The psychopathology of the closet – the experience of sexuality not permitted to acknowledge itself – like the psychopathology of the commodity form – the experience of being 'a thing which transcends sensuousness' – like the living death of the vampire, finds its only outlet under cover of anonymity, of being an isolated thing rather than a knowable being. All of Warhol's containers give expression to this experience of isolation – the Brillo and other boxes, of course, the *Time Capsules* (illus. 68), the refashioning of the artist's studio into a 'factory', the avowedly empty container of the artist's persona, and so on – but perhaps the most vivid expression of what was at stake can be seen in his plan to sell a series of boxes, each with an individual screen test looping endlessly inside, 'for $1,000 or $1,500 each', as 'LPBS', or *Living Portrait Boxes.*[17]

The psychosocial effect of the screen tests, as one sensitive description has it (simultaneously betraying the effect it describes with a shift in grammatical subject), was 'what it is like to sit for your portrait, with each poser trapped in the existential dilemma of performing as – while simultaneously being reduced to – his or her own image'.[18] The screen-test subject oscillates back and forth between subject and object positions, between actor and audience, between being themselves and performing themselves, between first person and third, and in so doing enacts their own isolation in the image. Doing so restricted to the solitary confines of a 'Living Portrait Box' and repeating the oscillation over and over again endlessly would have only made it worse.

Insofar as the experience of one's own subjectivity is defined by the enclosure of coffin, closet or commodity, in other words, the dynamic range of one's humanity is reduced. Each divorced from a different key element of sociality, the vampire, the closeted homosexual and the worker or consumer as commodity is forced to realize his or her place in the world not through the elastic give-and-take of human beings progressively revealing them-selves to each other but through the violent act of incorporation characteristic of the oral-anal phase of psychical development. As Ellis Hanson has put it about the closet, for example, to

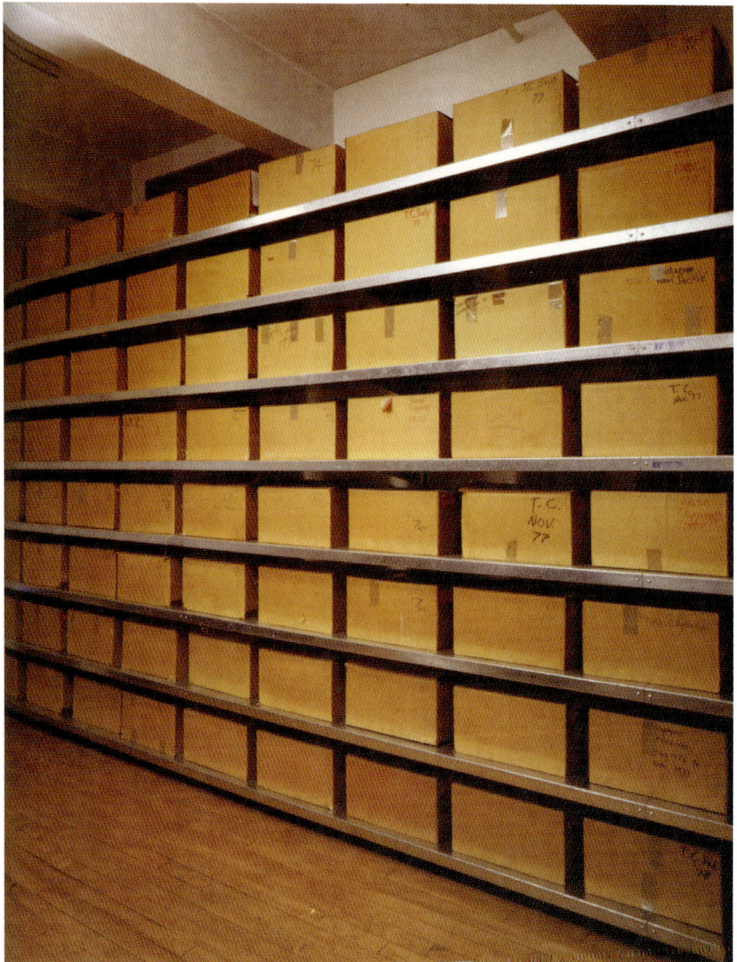

68 Andy Warhol, *Time Capsules*, displayed at the Andy Warhol Museum, Pittsburgh.

'comprehend the vampire is to recognize that abjected space that gay men are obliged to inhabit; that space unspeakable or unnameable, itself defined as orifice, as a "dark continent" men dare not penetrate'.[19] So too we might say this about the boxed interiority, the unspeakable and unnameable dark continent of experience given to the consumer that is brilliantly, agonizingly, ecstatically figured by Warhol.

The theorist Franco Moretti got this experience right when he described Dracula as 'an ascetic of terror', as a figure for 'the victory "of the desire for *possession* over that of *enjoyment*"'.[20] All desire and no love, all id and no ego, the vampire exudes repression – not repression of libido per se but of the pleasure of human relations that fill out the exercise of that libido, repression of sublimated sexuality, repression of the public life of private sexual relations. There is no socially acceptable way for the vampire to act on his desire, so it can only realize itself as a symptom in both the craving for the immediate, anonymous, lustful experience of possession and in the alienation born of desire satisfied too quickly or easily without the intermediary process of human sociality. 'Capital is dead labour, which, vampire-like, lives only by sucking living labour', Marx wrote in a famous analogy.[21] The pleasure of labour, of collective self-realization, the sociality of desire, is substituted by possession or being possessed by others.

Sublimation works in two ways, either horizontally or vertically. It either spreads libido evenly across the field of objects or it inflates and elevates an ideal. Our desire is our own but it is also directed by social institutions of all sorts. On the whole, the market acts as a force of sublimation to distribute our desire horizontally, while institutions like Church and state often act to direct it vertically. The problems with the latter approach are legion, of course, and we need only remember any of the over-inflated religious or political ideals of the past and present to not think otherwise. The market approach is not without its downside as well, however: cruising with only one thing in mind, with its desire festering inside and its shiny social veneer projected outside, the capitalist marketplace turns everything into sex, into market share and market penetration, into notches in its belt. As a result, all exchanges are private and the expression of desire as a public act, as an act of citizenship or faith or conviction, is repressed.

The literary and cultural critic Michael Warner offered a rich sense of this correspondence in a 1993 discussion of 'the close connection between consumer culture and the most visible spaces of gay culture: bars, discos, advertising, fashion, brand-name identification, mass-cultural camp, "promiscuity"', albeit without casting it as the alienation wrought by both closet and commodity form that is our concern:

> Gay culture in this most visible mode is anything but external to advanced capitalism and to precisely those features of advanced capitalism that many on the left are most eager to disavow. Post-Stonewall urban gay men reek of the commodity. We give off the smell of capitalism in rut, and therefore demand of theory a more dialectical view of capitalism than many people have imagination for.[22]

We can get to our central questions (and, perhaps, to something of Warner's called-for more dialectical approach) if we shift his periodization of the 'smell of capitalism in rut' slightly, by characterizing it as post-Warhol rather than post-Stonewall (with the idea that Warhol helped to create the cultural foundation for Stonewall as a political watershed) and add that Warhol and urban gay men since have played the role of vanguard class for the rest of us. With this is mind, the first question we might attend to is whether the form of citizenship to which Warhol gave such effective expression and that we have come to adopt as our own continues to bear the psychosocial repercussions of having been closeted. The second takes up the degree to which the closet can be understood as a form of alienation that is intertwined with that of the commodified desire of the consumer.

These are larger contextual questions that cannot be fully resolved here, of course, but it seems fair to say that they represent concerns that were already central to Warhol in his role as Drella. The critical measure is whether both commodified desire and closeted desire are forced to be Moretti's 'desire for *possession* over that of *enjoyment*'. Put differently, it is a question of the isolation and privatization of desire. This has nothing to do with desire itself or object choice per se – it is not determined by the id, which is what it is, but instead is a matter of how the id's desire is negotiated with the superego by the ego. In other words, the issue is not about what happens behind closed doors but about the ways in which desire reaches beyond such boundaries to find its fullest realization and satisfaction in public expression and acceptance. Or, differently again: the distinction between possession and enjoyment is a question not about the social sanctioning of individual pleasure but about the horizon of possibility for that pleasure to be not only socially sanctioned but also realized in and expanded on through social customs, mores, institutions and events.

The commodity relation is one that is contained by the anonymity of consumer and commodity alike, by the consumer's inability to get to know, or be known to, her object as a subject. In this way the consumer maintains an illusory sense of control through her objectifying gaze, even as that power relation is flipped on its head by the market's invisible hand. This is what Gene Swenson meant when he said that the 'boxes of Warhol *are* feelings': they embody the affective dimension of the commodified desire's isolation from social recognition and self-determination as an expression of asocial subjectivity. So too, Warhol's boxes were the feelings of the closet, of desire isolated and unrecognized except through private exchanges. Warhol's boxes gave expression to both commodity and closet as alienation, as id forced to do its work against superego without the mediating benefit of a socialized ego. As such, superego is experienced as all outside and id all inside, without the two ever coming to common purpose via the agency of the ego.

'A commodity appears, at first sight, a very trivial thing, and easily understood', Marx famously wrote; however, 'it is, in reality, a very queer thing, abounding in metaphysical subtleties and theological niceties.'[23] Put most simply, the theological nicety of the commodity at issue is about maintaining a hard boundary between inside and outside, self and world, subject and object, individual and collective life, man and God. The commodity Balkanizes human experience by substituting the private relations of the market for the public life of citizenship. It obscures from view the social contract that the project of enlightenment worked so hard to keep visible and available for renegotiation. The closet performs the same role, by privatizing desire and thereby disenfranchising it from political will and collective self-determination. This theological split, in Moretti's words, is 'the *ambivalent* root, interweaving hate and love, that underlies vampirism'.[24] Warhol appreciated and understood the mix of individualized desire and disavowal of collective life that are the primary social roles of commodity and closet alike, and he gave expression to their common cause better than any other.

In order to fully understand how this distinctive subject–object relation really works for our purposes, we also need to consider the other half of Warhol's Drella, the Cinderella half, the vulnerable and accommodating half rather than the anonymous and exploitative half. He was not all vampire, of course, but also bore a sweetness and openness that his associates found endlessly and enduringly sympathetic. His diarist and ghostwriter Pat Hackett, for example, reports that he always 'made everyone feel important, soliciting their opinions and probing with questions about their own lives' and that the worst thing he 'could think to say about someone was that he was "the kind of person who thinks he's better than you" or, simply, "He thinks he's an 'intellectual'"'.[25] On some level, this was just the flipside of the vampire's relation to death and disaster, and it was already there in the thin-skinned, traumatized innocent,

Andy Paperbag. But Andy as vampire and Andy as victim do not complete the picture – there is also the Andy that turns out to be just the right fit for the prized glass slipper.

Cinderella is a story about recognition that is unexpected but nonetheless deserved because of the recipient's genuine niceness. Some version or another of this story is applied to Warhol again and again in the literature: he achieved his unique version of the American Dream not just because he worked hard or because he played up his vulnerability and capitalized on the pity of others, or because he was a bloodsucking vampire, but also because he was generous, well-meaning, accommodating or, in a word, nice. Many accounts would serve here, but Paul Morrissey's is one of the most expressive, in significant measure because he also feels more strongly than most (because his contribution to Warhol's enterprise was greater than most) that the recognition he himself deserves has erroneously gone to Warhol. 'He was shy, incredibly insecure, very timid, but if you paid attention, you could see that he was genuinely trying to make an effort, trying to come up with something to say, something that was positive, something nice just to engage in conversation', Morrissey said in a recent interview, adding that, not only did Warhol not drink, do drugs or go into debt (none of these exactly true but probably close enough) but, astoundingly given the history between the two men, 'I don't think he ever took advantage of anybody.'[26]

Just as we can see the legacy of the nineteenth century in Warhol's Dracula, so we might see that of the seventeenth century in his Cinderella. One of 'the most striking trends in seventeenth century thinking about art', writes the literary scholar Philip Lewis in his incisive study of Charles Perrault's *Mother Goose* fairy tales, is

> its tendency to anchor itself in the authority of the visible,
> to treat visual experience in its diverse aspects – the pleasures

of looking or being looked at, the form and formation of
images, the bonding and communication at work in eye
contact – as pivotal human activity and source of value.[27]

His point is that this pleasure of looking and being looked at
is born in reaction against the decentralized, proto-democratic
humanism of Descartes and others, and as an apologia for the
triumphant absolutism of Louis XIV. By 'turning away from the
authentic revelation achieved in the *cogito*' – the revelation that
one's being is derived not from the grace or the tyrannical will
of God but instead from one's own innate capacity for reason
and self-reflection – 'the relation of the *cogito* to its *cogitatum*',
of thinking to its thought, is substituted for the *cogito* or the act
of thinking itself. It is a 'fall of the subject's radical interiority
into representation', Lewis says perfectly for our purposes,
a fall into image rather than being, into persona rather than
person.[28] In so doing, the great humanist category of subjectivity is absorbed by objectivity, by the tyranny of what is, by
the mechanical, proto-photographic facticity of the visual
world out there rather than vision as an act of self-realization.

'I always feel that my words are coming from behind me,
not from me', is how Warhol himself put this idea, just as all
of his work makes the same sort of feint to passivity, to other-
creation rather than self-creation, to another voice rather than
to his own.[29] When Louis pronounced himself to be the Sun or
when he said '*l'état, c'est moi*', he was saying to his subjects –
against Descartes – that being is given from the outside, not
created from the inside, that the sources of political being
and natural being are exterior to individual subjects. The story
of Cinderella replays this anti-humanist, anti-Cartesianism
by exteriorizing the authority of her recognition. Vision as
recognition, as seeing and identifying the truth of Cinderella's
niceness, thus, is not the exercise of self-realization but instead
a form of passive subjection to the authority of fairy godmothers

and princes, just as Cinderella's exploitation had been a matter of passive subjection to her stepsisters and stepmother. The moral of the story is that passivity and quiescence in the face of authority – in a word, being 'nice' – will be rewarded at the discretion of that authority.

For us to assume that the Dracula and Cinderella roles in Warhol and his work somehow reduces its meaning or significance – for example by casting it as simply a rehash of old myths, or assuming that they merely function as roles to occupy for camp countercultural or subcultural identifications – would miss the significance at issue here entirely. Mario Amaya, the second Solanas shooting victim, put this well, and I think not at all too grandly when he said,

> This may sound a bit pretentious, but it is really what Leonardo was all about, on a totally different level, on a more intellectually organized level. It is sort of the artist as everyman; the artist as all men, and the artist working and thinking on every level of society at once and in many different areas at once.[30]

That is, Warhol was a manner of polymath, of Renaissance man or *homo universalis*, because his way with the world spanned a wide range of media and interests and was one that applied to everything and everyone, 'on every level of society'. Like Leonardo's scientism and humanism, he had his finger on the pulse of the times, on the way the world was changing, and was able to give expression to it and thereby help pull it into being. As with Leonardo as well, that universal meaning for our epoch was to be found not so much in what was depicted but in how it was depicted, not so much in subject-matter as in form. As Amaya said: 'he isn't trying to say something as such, but he's trying to show something', show us 'a little bit about what's happening with us and to us, for us, in us, and all that'.[31]

What was happening with, to, for and in us can, for the purposes of this discussion, be simply called 'postmodernity'. To see the meaning of Warhol's work in any way other than the death and disaster of modernity – the death and disaster of everything that the humanism, scientism, subjectivism and politicism of Leonardo or David or Speer meant – would be to psychologize, culturalize and trivialize Warhol by reducing him to his biography. Ultimately, therefore, this brings us back to the social life of Warhol's psychology, or sensibility, or sexuality, its relation to the world we find ourselves in today. Art, for Warhol, was, as we have said with Koestenbaum, 'a means of having sex'. In this regard he 'surprises us by epitomizing civilization, since he channelled every impulse, sexual and otherwise, into work'. He is thus like Leonardo and the others in this way too, but he also represents a marked shift in the meaning and function of sublimation. Koestenbaum has it that Warhol did not really sublimate his sexuality but instead 'extended its jurisdiction', spreading it across the world he encountered. 'Warhol's art' – meaning, really, everything he did – 'was the sexualized body his actual body refused to be.'[32]

As smart as this account is, I'm not sure that its orgiastic or polymorphously perverse connotations quite get at the frustration or lack of satisfaction or completion – the *repression*, really – that drove Warhol's work. The *Philosophy* puts it well, I think, when it says, 'Frigid people can really make out.'[33] Or we might get a good sense of it from one early audience response to *Blow Job*, at a screening for a capacity crowd at Columbia University in the autumn of 1966, with Warhol present. According to the film critic Rex Reed, at some point into the 33-minute film the audience grew restless with its tease (showing just the face of the film's star and recipient of the action specified by its title), and some in the crowd began to sing the great period protest anthem popularized by Pete Seeger and Joan Baez, reworded as 'We Shall Never Come'. Reed continued:

> They finally began to yell things at the screen, most of them
> unprintable. Total chaos finally broke out when one voice
> (a girl's) screamed: 'We came to see a blow job, and we
> stayed to get screwed!' Tomatoes and eggs were thrown at
> the screen; Warhol was whisked away to safety through the
> raging, jeering, angry mob and rushed to a waiting car.[34]

Or, finally, we might refer to any of the many accounts of his
relationship with his tape-recorder 'wife' and other such
surrogates. These techno-erotic liaisons, as he put it, 'really
finished whatever emotional life I might have had', adding,
'I was glad to see it go.'[35]

As we noted above, sublimation works two ways. In either
case – vertical or horizontal, progressive or entropic, affective
and concentrated or disaffected and disseminated – it is a routing
of libido. The form that routing takes, like anything else, has
a history, and the two historical categories at issue, for our
purposes here, are the modern and the postmodern. We might
take the Warhol photograph of the Washington Monument with
his superimposed statement, 'America really is The Beautiful'
that we opened this book with as our figure for the modern.
On the one hand, it has all the affect of the old, progressive
ideals concentrated into its formalized principle of beauty –
the 'Cinderella of the transcendentals', in the words of one
aesthetician.[36] On the other hand, its resolute verticality and
austere, modern, neoclassicizing simplicity of form can be seen
(should we look for long enough!) in the words used by Warhol
to describe the duration for which he filmed the Empire State
Building, for his work *Empire* (1964): an 'eight-hour hard-on'.[37]
In this way, it serves us by standing for both the old, modernist
form of sublimation – of libido become culture, we might call it
– and for the postmodern reading of those old ideals as culture
remaking itself as libido, as monuments becoming sex. For
our figure of the postmodern itself, by contrast, we might take

a work by Warhol heir Vito Acconci, whose piece *Seedbed* (1972, in which he lay in a gallery hidden under a ramp and masturbated to the sound of the art viewers' footsteps above, speaking about his excitement through a loudspeaker), perhaps more than any other, literalized the horizontal form of sublimation concerned here, the form that extends sexuality like a blanket across the horizon of the world encountered by the artist. That Acconci enclosed himself in a box-like, tomb-like container only made that postmodernization all the more real, all the more felt as a lived symptom (illus. 69).

Later, Acconci would reflect back on that moment. 'What we did', he said, 'was the cause of the 1980s',

we made galleries stronger. We were naïve about business. Our work didn't sell, but it did provide window dressing, which tied right into the business interests of the galleries.

69 Vito Acconci, *Seedbed*, 1972, film still of performance at Sonnabend Gallery, New York.

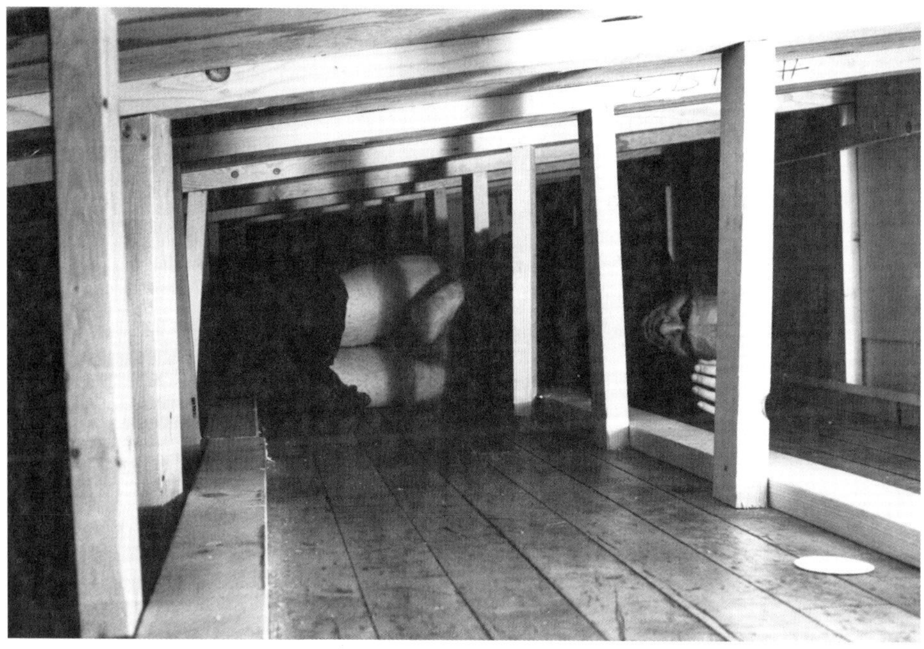

> The attention brought people in so that backroom sales of other artists' works could be made. It was no accident that the first year 420 West Broadway opened, Sonnabend had my *Seedbed* show, a Dennis Oppenheim show, Gilbert and George's *Singing Sculpture* – none of which brought in any money but all drew attention. The attention put SoHo on the map. Our work enabled galleries to exert power.[38]

This, of course, was exactly what Warhol did as well, although, in his case, he would be both the gallery exerting its power and the window dressing that served as the mechanism for that exercise.[39] While it was the spectacle of *Seedbed*, *Blow Job* and the like that generated audience interest, it was the overall aesthetic sensibility – the foiling of the old ideals, the undoing of the concept of progress, the debunking of the dream of beauty, the dissipating of the transcendental of love, and all the rest of it – that would carry the new, burgeoning art economy.

In the end, it is hard not to read this radical democratization of aesthetic sensibility, with its spreading of libido widely and thinly across the object world, as a figure for the collapse of thesubjectivityinteriority of the bourgeoisie, a collapse of the old elastic container that dreamed democracy and subjectivity, publicness and desire, citizenship and sexuality as if they were the same quivering, resilient, expanding skin. There are two figures of this collapse, two outcomes, that have historically fallen on either side of the bourgeois imagination: the proletarian one and the aristocratic one, the one that is hardened by the meanness of industrial labour, the meanness of becoming a thing, and the one that is hardened by embodying the law, by carrying the burden of its birth into entitlement. At rare moments one can see these coalescing into the same thing, into the same historical closure or disintegration of the old dream of the bourgeoisie. This reduction of humanity is the meaning of Warhol's Drella, the meaning of his affinity for death and disaster, the meaning of his collapse of the roles of artist as window dressing and the backroom machinations of the businessman, but we might close by seeing it already suggested in his progenitor, Jasper Johns.

Responding to the sympathetic and unassuming elder statesman Johns in this way risks seeming ungenerous, of course, but I do not mean it that way. Instead, heed this diary entry by Johns admirer Susan Sontag with an ear for the alienation or trauma, the solitary confinement of the closet and the commodity, that has been our theme: 'Jap's authority, his elegance', mused Sontag in 1966 with no little awe, 'He is never flustered, apologetic, guilty, ashamed.' Seamlessly self-contained, she observed, he comported himself with 'Perfect certitude'; even when 'he picks his nose or eats in the Automat, he's being elegant.'[40] Like Warhol, the lowly-born Johns had a tough and unstable childhood, so the strong sense of composure signalled in both the standardization of form in his art and his aristocratic personal bearing can likewise be understood as symptomatic coping or compensation, as a form of overcoming the difficult life he was born into.

Such a triumphant personal narrative is certainly true, certainly noble, but seeing these symptoms only in such a psycho-biographical manner misses the ways in which symptoms pile up, the way in which afflictions of class, closet and commodity meet, cross-determine and co-elaborate each other. Like all the rest of the death and disaster of the period, this reaching for the cover of certitude, like the protection offered Warhol by his recording devices, is inseparable from the scariness of its time. Johns continues to this day to play out the endgame of the closet, of subjectivity operating under the cover of image, of 'a thing's not being what it was, with its becoming something other than what it is', as he had it early on, or in the manner of 'sensuous things which are at the same time suprasensible', as Marx did.[41] With Warhol as measure, however, we can see, more and more, the risk of the closet collapsing in on itself. The hard, universal subjectivity of the seventeenth-century aristocrat's God-given right and the hard, universal objectivity of the nineteenth-century proletarian's systemically derived thingness unwittingly join sides. This is our postmodernization. In the process, the old interiority of the eighteenth-century bourgeoisie – that of enlightenment, of ego as mediator, of publicly exercising 'one's understanding without guidance from another', the vestigial modernist enterprise – is squeezed from the middle.

9

CITIZEN WARHOL

On the whole, Warhol's politics were pretty transparent. For example, he made an anti-Nixon, pro-McGovern poster in 1972 but came to have second thoughts about it when the IRS started auditing him the same year (and continued to do so annually for the remainder of his life). Pat Hackett summed it up this way: 'Philosophically, Andy was a liberal Democrat, although he never voted because, he said, he didn't want to get called up for jury duty. He did, however, offer his employees bribes of Election Days off if they gave their word they'd vote Democratic.'[1] In a word, we might say that he was a liberal in the sense caricatured by Phil Ochs as he introduced his great song 'Love Me, I'm a Liberal' (1965) to a concert audience:

> Every American community has varying shades of political opinion. One of the shadiest of these is the Liberal. An outspoken group on many subjects: ten degrees to left of centre in good times, ten degrees to the right of centre if it affects them personally.[2]

This is only to highlight what we have been saying all along: that Warhol had the post-war liberal consensus and its consumer economics just right.

In the mirror image that Warhol provides for us, the American and Americanized consumer does not simply replace the earlier ideas of what it means to be a social subject – of being a believer, a citizen or a labourer – but instead carries them forward as residual parts of its formation by remaking them in accord with its new hegemony and the corresponding new world order. Religion, politics and industrial production continue to exist for us as much (or nearly so) as before, but they have been subordinated to consumption socially and culturally by personalization (as in the attribute 'spiritual but not religious'), by wholesale devaluation (as in the slogan 'government is not the solution to our problem; government is the problem') and by financialization and offshoring of production in the economy. As a result we, like Warhol, have become consumers more than constituents of religious belief, political participation and the global industrial economy.

'Andy had no idea of bourgeois life', is how one commentator explained Warhol's distinctive persona when called on to do so for a PBS documentary in 2006.[3] He had no middle register because at one minute 'he's in the ghetto' and the next 'he's hanging out with Liza'; one minute he's the Pittsburgh proletariat, the next the uptown aristocracy; one minute he's a cinder sweeper longing to become the princess of the ball, the next an old-world count longing to lose himself among the 'teeming millions' of the modern metropolis.[4] While the idea of bourgeois life here is different from the one that concerns us, the idea that Warhol had no meaningful middle register between the two social and economic extremes of his life is dead-on for our purposes. One way to explain this is to say that, like the protagonists in many other rags-to-riches stories, Warhol did not have the time or energy to develop much of a personal life had he wanted to, simply because he was working too hard. As countless observers have noted and as Warhol himself would routinely say, everything, every aspect of his life, was work or work-related, everything was professional rather than personal, with the possible exception, early

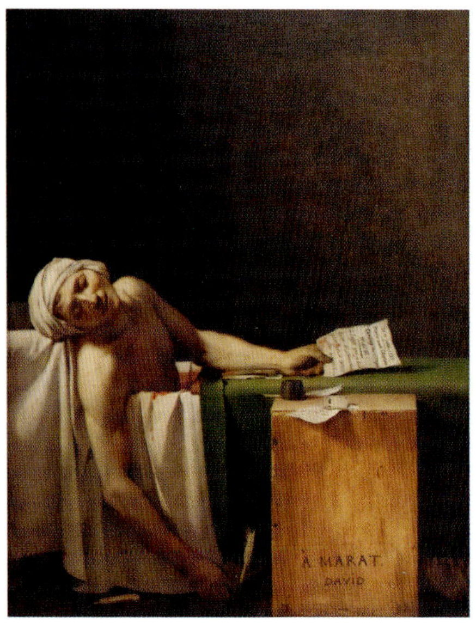

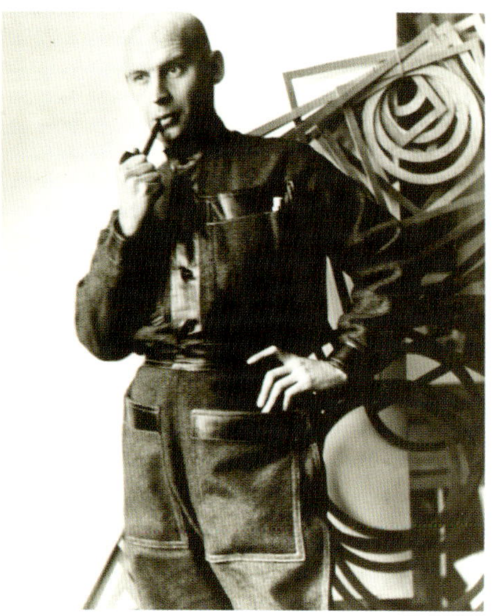

on at least, of the religiosity that did not make it into his endless, obsessive documenting of his daily activities. A better way to describe Warhol's missing middle, thus, might be to say 'Andy had no idea of life.'

This, of course, depends on what we mean by 'life'. Like his heroes – the Howard Hughes character in *The Carpetbaggers*, who we have already discussed, and the William Randolph Hearst character of *Citizen Kane*, who we will touch on briefly below – Warhol's obsessive work habit almost certainly orbited around a central trauma or loss. It doesn't matter so much for us here which trauma this was – it could have been his family's poverty, or the scary world he found himself born into in industrial Pittsburgh, for example, or his sickliness as a child, or the deeply conflicted body image that resulted from his bad skin and other ailments, or his father's regular absences and early death, or the violent sexual scene he witnessed at a very tender age, or simply growing up homosexual in a heterosexist world – or it might have been something else, or any combination of

70 Jacques-Louis David, *The Death of Marat*, 1793, oil on canvas.

71 Mikhail Kaufman, *Rodchenko standing in front of dismantled hanging spatial construction*, 1922, gelatin silver print.

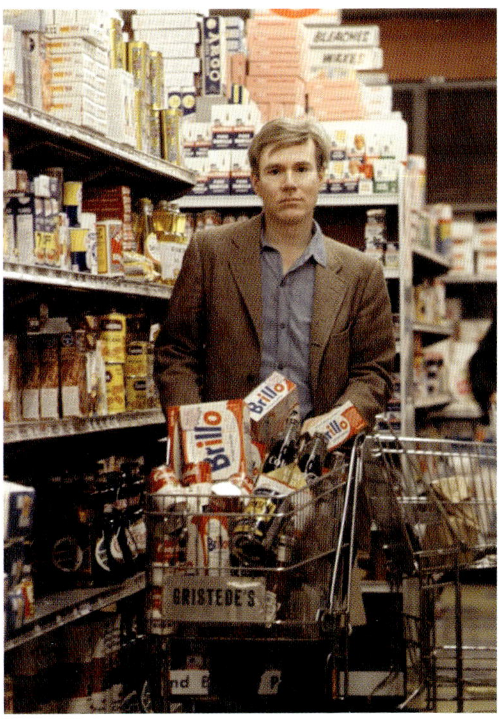

72 Bob Adelman, *Andy Warhol shopping at Gristede's super-market on Second Avenue,* executed 1964, printed 2008, archival inkjet print, 48.4 × 35.6 cm.

the above. Whatever it was, something of this sort was surely his 'Rosebud'.

While many of these experiences can be attributed to the harsh circumstances of Warhol's proletarian childhood, trauma itself is largely universal and not generally structured by class. How that trauma is nego-tiated, however, is typically a function of class and Warhol's position, oscillating back and forth between cinder sweeper and princess, between aristocrat and anonymous mass, may be said to be exactly the 'idea of bourgeois life' that we began with. In this sense, therefore, we might say that Warhol's great legacy, his great gift to us, was that he had the idea of bourgeois life exactly right and what he had right about it was its own suicide, its own movement towards having no life.

This, of course, depends on what we mean by 'bourgeois'. One definition we can work with is to say that a bourgeois, as we generally use the term, is someone defined by the dynamism of his or her position in the middle, someone caught betwixt and between labour and the autonomy of life-sustaining, society-influencing wealth, between having no choice but to work and not needing to work at all, between cinder-sweeping misery and castle-keeping entitlement. This dynamic role is often exciting, certainly, but it also serves as a kind of vortex animated by these oppositions – by becoming a factory owner or a brand name on the one hand and relinquishing existing

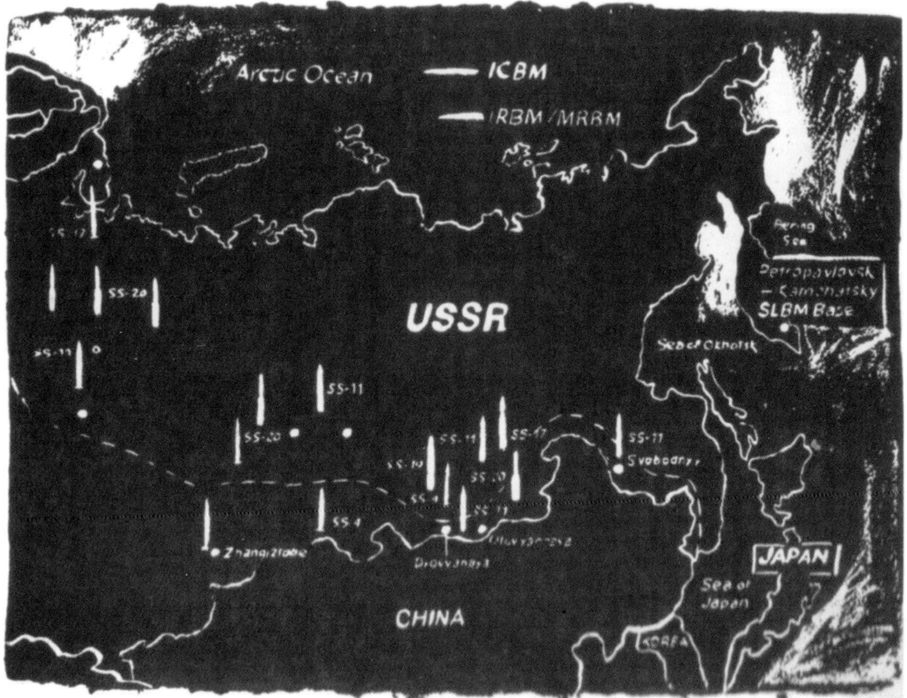

73 Andy Warhol, *Map of Eastern U.S.S.R. Missile Bases*, 1985–6, acrylic paint and silkscreen on canvas.

measures of a fulfilling life on the other. Leisure, relaxation and self-reflection, say, or taking deep, self-affirming aesthetic pleasure in art or nature or people or things, or the human bonding that comes from building understanding and a collective sense of autonomy through the exercise of that understanding and collectivity – these constitute one side of the American Dream that cannot be separated from its flipside, the American Nightmare.

At its base, 'bourgeois' is a brute sociological category – one that is properly understood as 'the owners of the means of production' and all the rest of it – but the meaning that we need in order to really make sense of Warhol's life is more historical than sociological, more about becoming bourgeois than about already being there. In this sense it incorporates its sometimes wayward subcategory, the petty bourgeoisie, rather than falsely cleaving the two apart into separable sociological entities. In the end, the term we have used a couple of times now, 'workaholic', will do as the measure of being bourgeois because it conveys the central psychosocial principle of substituting social mobility for other more innately human objects of desire – 'the desire for *possession* over that of *enjoyment*' as discussed above, for example. Warhol's lesson and the meaning of the Factory was: 'if you want to do whatever you do, then you should work very, very hard', according to Lou Reed, 'If you don't work very hard all the time, well then nothing will happen.'[5] This is just to say that Warhol as persona, like the cinematic portrayals of Howard Hughes and William Randolph Hearst, was structured by trauma. That structure was fundamentally bourgeois because its symptomatic patching over of the trauma was defined by endless and obsessive work, by reaching for ever more

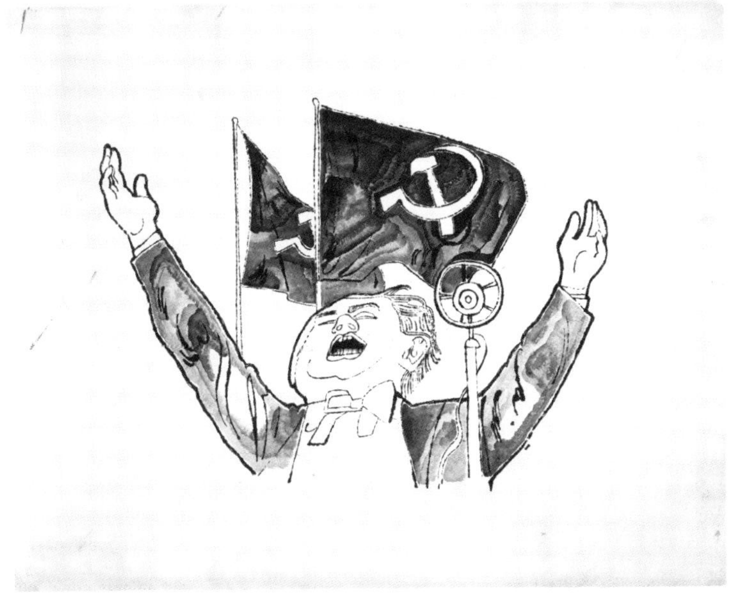

74 Andy Warhol, *Communist Speaker, c.* 1950, ink on paper, 58.4 × 73.7 cm.

business opportunities, by the manifold development of private enterprise, by endless hustling.

This was the drama governing the early years of Hearst's corporation and the array of Hughes's companies, just as it drove and regulated the multifaceted undertaking that came to be known as Andy Warhol Enterprises.[6] Jorge Luis Borges described the structure of this drama well in 1941 in his review of *Citizen Kane*: 'Overwhelmingly, endlessly, Orson Welles shows fragments of the life of the man', a man who is 'a simulacrum, a chaos of appearances', 'a labyrinth without a centre'.[7] While Borges was characteristically more concerned to make sense of this centrelessness in universal terms, as a condition of being human, ours is to see it more narrowly or historically, as a function of becoming bourgeois. To reiterate, this is not to say that only bourgeois subjectivity is structured by trauma; instead it is to say that, symptomatically, bourgeois reaction to trauma follows a distinctive path.

There are a number of references to Warhol's fascination with the figure of Hearst/Kane in the literature, including this one by superstar Ultra Violet:

> Andy's secret wish is to become Citizen Kane, a tycoon of fame . . . he identifies with every minute of the famous Orson Welles film that portrays William Randolph Hearst as an idealist corrupted by power. It gives Andy white goose pimples to have Brigid Berlin, daughter of Hearst's surrogate, cavorting around the loft, with or without clothes on. It lends tangibility to his dream of power, fortune, glory.[8]

It would be easy to say that this desire is a form of egomania that applies equally to the Hearst figure in *Citizen Kane*, to the Hughes figure in *The Carpetbaggers* and to Warhol in the media spectacle he generated around his own life, but such an analysis does not adequately make sense of the other pole of that mania, the empty moment rather than the full moment, that is so central to the two films and so much a part of Warhol's own self-portrayal. What is so compelling about Warhol's life and work is that he makes emptiness into something more than the standard tragic fare we are given in the two films by endowing it with the self-reflexivity and thus the self-determination of modern art.

We can see this self-reflexivity at work in the first mature version of his idea of 'business art' – the small classified advertisement in the *Village Voice* in 1966 that read:

> I'll endorse with my name any of the following: clothing AC-DC, cigarettes, small tapes, sound equipment, ROCK N' ROLL RECORDS, anything, film, and film equipment, Food, Helium, Whips. MONEY!! love and kisses ANDY WARHOL. EL 5-9941.[9]

The key point of this ad, for our purposes, is not so much that it was an advertisement or that it offered to endorse products – these qualities already existed, at least more or less, in the earlier Pop work – but instead lies in its emphasis on Warhol's endorsement. The brand at issue was no longer Campbell's or Brillo but instead Warhol, and the product was no longer art but rather anything and everything that could be profited from under the Warhol brand.

This was the gist behind the art book, *Andy Warhol's Index (Book)* (1967), which leads with images from the Brillo box exhibition on the cover and front endpapers but then turns to, among other things, a number of fun pop-ups and inserts, all eight or so initialled by Warhol (or a surrogate) on most or all of the several hundred copies produced (illus. 76). The shift from Brillo and other brand names to his own branding is marked in a number of ways beyond signing the book's cover and initialling all the inserts: it also makes liberal use of a Warhol signature stamp, including as the identifying emblem for a sheet (presumably unloaded) of LSD tabs and as a moustache tattoo on the back cover. From Brillo on the front to Warhol on the back, the book thus symbolizes and enacts the transition from an artist who represents the products of others to an enterprise that markets its own. That the brand was being associated with the bodily and psychical immediacy of tattoos and hallucinogens – not completely unlike the bodily and psychical immediacy of the Campbell's soup that Warhol's mother served him as a child – only reinforced the tremendous inroads into the kernel of consumer taste that the Warhol brand was striving for and effecting. This deep-seating of its meaning was already indicated by casting the volume as an 'Index', a conceit taken from the *Index Librorum Prohibitorum*, the Catholic Church's list of prohibited books, which had been in place from 1559 until it was abolished the previous year, 1966, by Pope Paul VI (illus. 75).

Representing himself as a brand was one thing, of course; truly functioning as if he were Brillo or Campbell's was something

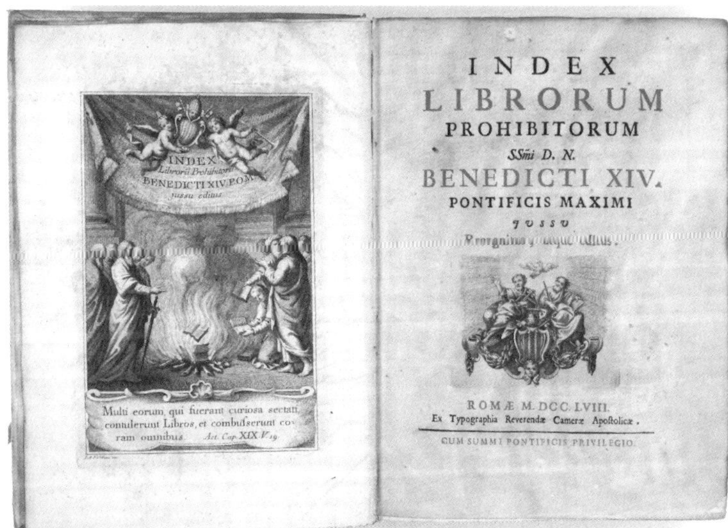

75 *Index Librorum Prohibitorum* (Typographia reverendæ Cameræ apostolicæ, 1758).

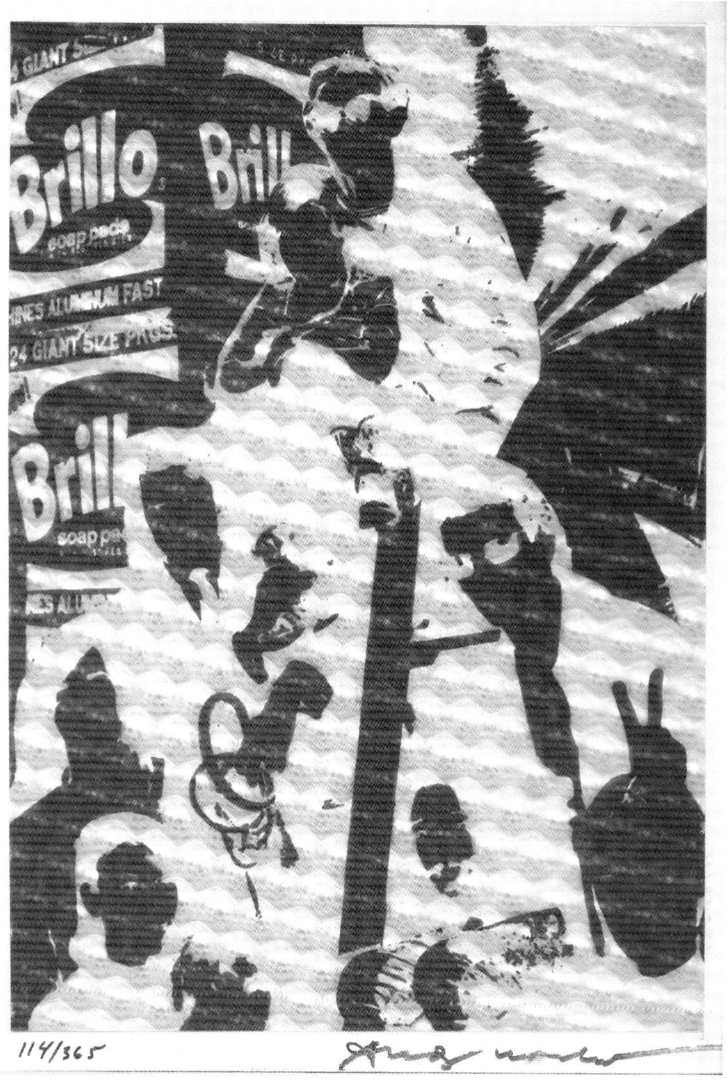

76 Cover of *Andy Warhol's Index* (1967).

different. Paul Morrissey, who reports being paid a 25 per cent commission for any income he could generate for Warhol's enterprise, helped advance Warhol's place in the world from artist to that of producer. This new role would be something like what the music promoter Bill Graham was doing in San Francisco but with Warhol functioning more as a 'presenter', less involved in financing and managing the production (although there was some of that) and more with lending his name to the production and inflecting it with his artistic sensibility and brand-name legibility. This was true for the Velvet Underground, beginning in 1966, and it was true for the films that Morrissey would make, increasingly without any managerial or direct artistic contribution from Warhol, starting in 1968. It was also true of nearly all of Warhol's later enterprises: *Interview* magazine, the music video and cable television operations and, to a signi-ficant extent, the sequence of books and the society portrait business. More than anything else, Warhol was a savvy and entrepreneurial businessman.

To varying degrees, these were Warhol-branded corporate productions. Bob Colacello, who together with Pat Hackett, Brigid Berlin and Warhol authored the *Philosophy* in 1975, provides this account of his experience:

> I hadn't fully comprehended what I'd gotten myself into by ghostwriting the book, until Andy was photographed for the cover of *New York* magazine, which had bought the serial rights. They posed him in a closet, sitting at a typewriter, under a headline that read: *Andy Warhol's Greatest Secrets: He Likes To Write.* It finally hit me then – I was part of a big lie and while it had lined my pockets, it robbed my ego of any hope of recognition.[10]

Colacello's lament is understandable, of course, but from our perspective the Warhol name coming to stand for a corporate entity or brand rather than an individual expressive artist only fleshes out the meaning and historical significance of his art. It was this turn in Warhol's career, more than anything else, that made him the Leonardo of our day, the figure that has best expressed the lived experience of our consumer age.

Considering Warhol's life and work as art in such a manner, rather than merely as business, requires evaluating the artistic or aesthetic value of his 'business art' accomplishment. In a recent interview, Pat Hackett explained that Warhol's driving force was never just about maximizing profit but instead was about spreading himself as widely as he could. 'He wanted to make a place for himself in all the fields that he admired', she said, 'the more enterprises you could have, the better', even if many of them were money-losers. Putting this insight into the formal vocabulary we have already highlighted, Hackett added, 'He really believed in horizontal expansion', 'He never got that vertical, but he had a lot of horizontal.'[11] Indeed, Warhol's business practices were like – and in the end were really inseparable from – his sex life and his art practice. Everything was a business opportunity, just as everything was sexual, just as everything was art. Warhol superstar Viva put it thus, in response to the question 'What do you think you've learned mostly from Andy?': 'if you consider yourself as an artist, everything you do is equally valuable.'[12] Morrissey, who would, beginning in the 1970s, increasingly return to the conservative Catholic values that he was raised with, put the same idea in more judgmental terms: 'once you stop accepting everything on a moral basis you begin to accept everything literally.'[13]

That horizontality was never understood as democratization in the public sense of Enlightenment but instead always functioned in the lowest-common-denominator manner of the marketplace. 'He wasn't a culture hero, really, he was a culture zero!', as Billy Name had it, and the theme that Warhol and those around him would return to again and again was that of

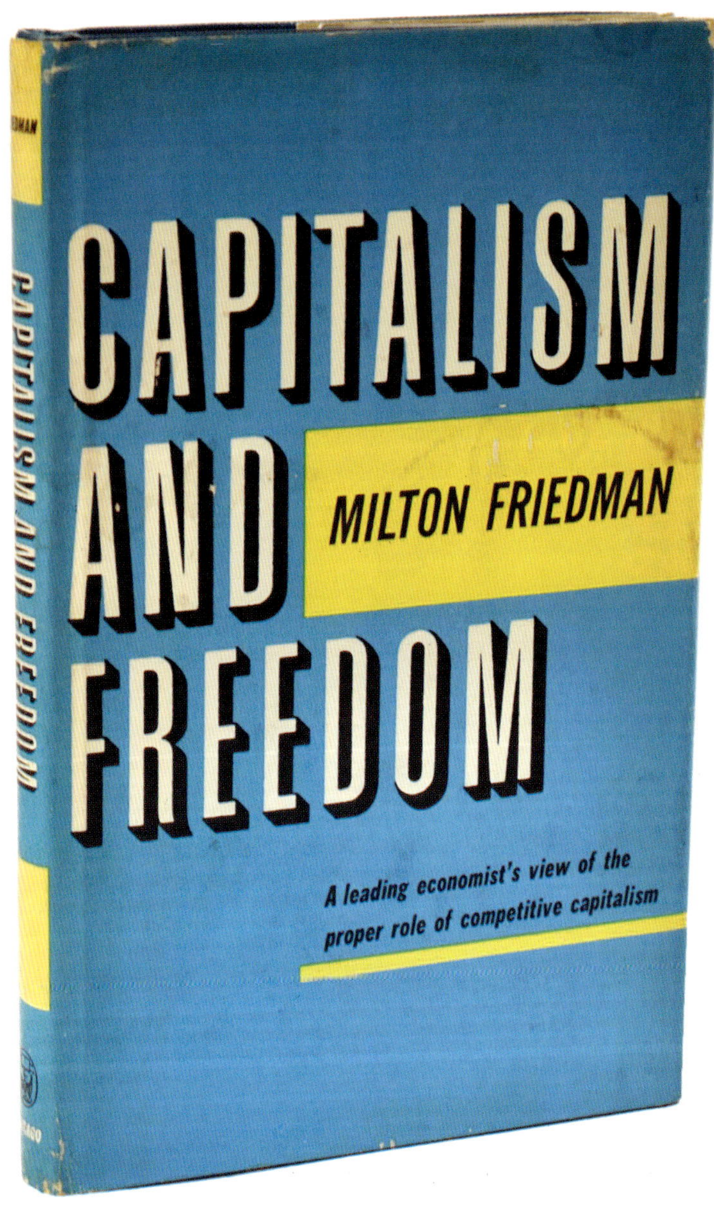

77 Cover of Milton Friedman's *Capitalism and Freedom* (1962).

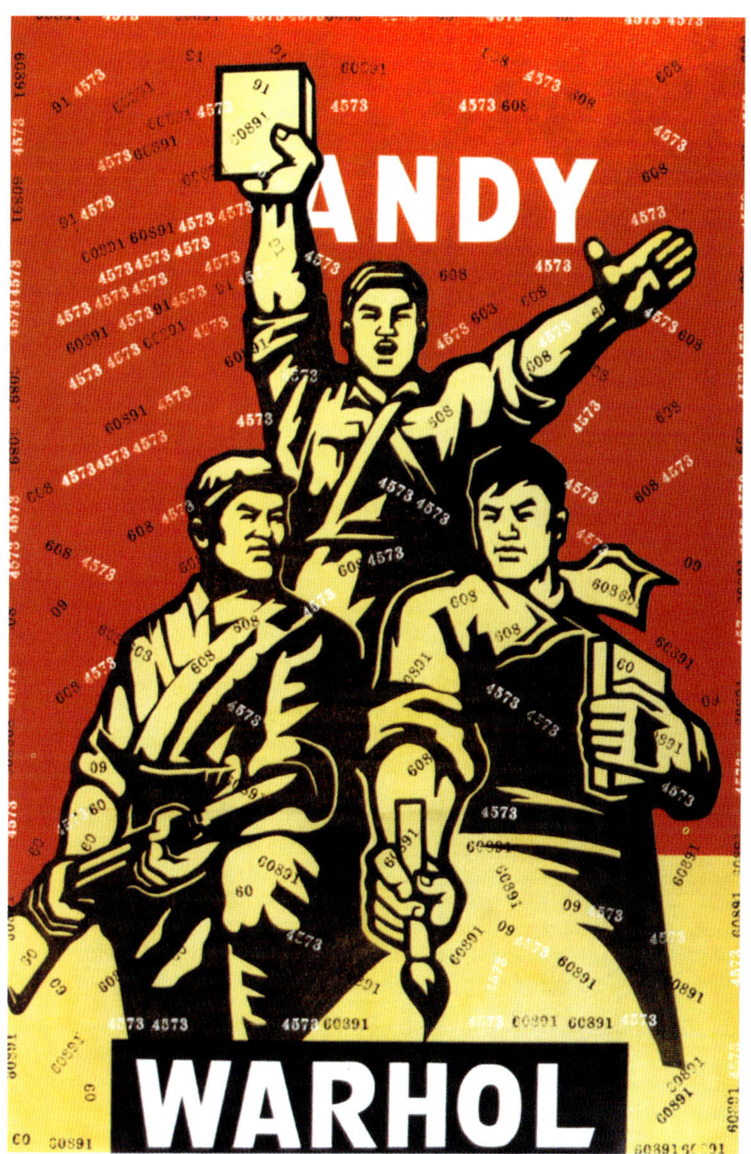

78 Wang Guangyi, *Great Criticism – Warhol*, 2002.

all things American.[14] 'I don't believe in Europe', Warhol said early on, for example.[15] This lack of faith in the old ideals and belief in the new world of global Americanism was infectious. 'Andy was contaminating society by entering it, just as he was contaminating art by his adventures in society', is how Koestenbaum puts it, and there is endless evidence to support this conclusion.[16] The French, high-born Ultra Violet initially felt sorry (in a patronizing manner) for Warhol's clumsy, immigrant American ways, but by the time she wrote her memoir in 1988 she felt herself to be fully contaminated by that Americanism and unable to relate any longer to her own kind: 'I'm a stranger to my family. When I first came to New York, never for an instant did I feel like a stranger. But here, now, at home among my own people, I am a stranger.'[17] Americanized, Warholized and stripped of her upper-class French birthright, she could no longer feel or experience the verticality of European culture and tradition, its sense of value and integrity, its sense of elite standing and purpose, its enduring chauvinism and sense of innate superiority.

Warhol's withdrawal from judgment offered a distinctively American, distinctively postmodern feeling of safety or home or belonging, and in the end that feeling was the meaning of his work. Sontag was once again dead-on with her analysis:

> The best works among those that are called pop art intend, precisely, that we abandon the old task of always either approving or disapproving of what is depicted in art – or, by extension, experienced in life. (This is why those who dismiss pop art as a symptom of a new conformism, a cult of acceptance of the artifacts of mass civilization, are being obtuse.)[18]

Indeed, the Warholian art object was not about artefacts or cults at all. It had little interest in its own object status and was concerned instead with the atmosphere of liberty or freedom from judgment that it produced by disavowing that status. In this way Warhol's art functioned as a kind of social sculpture by establishing mores or means of social interaction based on non-judgment, on suspending the old habits of approving and disapproving, of thinking for oneself, that had so characterized modern art as a project of enlightenment.

The way it achieved this social effect, this community of nation building, was simply to empty out its centre, its interior being. Rather than rising up as a monument to Frenchness, or to some form of top-hat-wearing, walking-stick-carrying, wannabe-aristocratic bourgeoisness, or to the great old dream of enlightenment itself, Warhol's art was richly, effectively, meaningfully, presciently a monument to nothing. It was a monument to the hole, trauma or void that had always been the constitutive core of the bourgeois subject seeking to disavow its universalist principle of enlightenment in order to preserve its particularist sense of entitlement. This had always been the object of modernism's bad faith – either as symptom or negative ideal – it just had not been fully expressible before the post-war epoch of the consumer. By finally giving itself over to its empty centre, modernism realized itself in postmodernism and Warhol came to stand as the single most important artist of our time, as our Leonardo, as the artist who provides us with the greatest summary expression of the world we find ourselves in today.

Henry Geldzahler put this well when he said, 'It was Andy as much as anybody else who extended the Marshall Plan beyond consumer goods' to a general 'Americanism that could be exported and make sense to people all over the world'.[19] This is really the point: what Warhol depicted in his art and persona was a way of being in the world, a way of being bourgeois with no guilt, no illusions, no holds barred, no ideals. It was the ultimate freedom – the freedom that the bourgeoisie had always championed, the abstract freedom that the Statue of

Liberty or the Washington Monument commemorated, the containerized freedom that the Marshall Plan exported – and so made for the quintessential expression of the lived experience of what we have come to call globalization. This came at a price, of course – the closing of the bourgeoisie's founding dream of its own interiority, open to the outside world in dynamic and reciprocal exchange, the dream of enlightenment or the public sphere – but, good shoppers that we are, that price was one we have always been willing to pay.

In the end, this is what we can see in the mirror that Andy Warhol still offers us when we sensitize ourselves to its reflection: our own aspiration to the great American Dream, of course, our sense that America and the free-market liberty it stands for better than any other nation 'really is The Beautiful', but we also see our own lived sense of the anxiety, turmoil and unease of the American Nightmare, of bourgeois social being that has stepped away from its own founding project of judgment. In its place there is the (un)easy, horizontal self-expressiveness and (un)easy, horizontal equality of the commodity, the equality that comes from everybody drinking Coke or from everybody wearing blue jeans or everybody liking Pop art.

The freedom arising from this equality should never be underestimated. The market works its magic on prejudices, biases and hatreds, on old boys' clubs and familial dynasties, on nationalisms, racisms, sexisms and homophobias, just as the neoliberal ideologues have always claimed. After all, it was not for no reason that Milton Friedman's world-changing book was titled *Capitalism and Freedom* (illus. 77). But the market also works its sorcery on our capacity for reason, pleasure and self-governance by taking all experience of value down to the baseline of the lowest common denominator of individual need or desire. In so doing it undercuts our primary means for realizing those base needs and desires – the public exercise of reason, the regular and fluid exchange of inner thoughts and feelings across the boundary of the self with the world of ideas and attitudes outside.

That he got the intertwining of the American Dream and the American Nightmare so right is why Warhol, more than any other, remains our genius, our *artiste extraordinaire*, the exemplary mirror image for our unprecedented time. There are signs that the world as we know it is changing once again, and it is possible that the epoch of the citizen-as-consumer is coming to a close. Whether a resurgence of the European social-democratic tradition or the triumph of 'capitalism with Chinese characteristics' or something else, such a change still only means that making sense of Warhol as the enigma of our period, our period genius, is that much more important if we hope to glimpse a way forward into the densely layered, psychosocial being of our new beyond.

REFERENCES

Preface: The Citizenship of Artists

1 Isabelle Bruno and Christopher Newfield, 'Can the Cognitariat Speak?', *e-flux* (14 March 2010), available at www.e-flux.com.

2 Jon-Ove Steihaug, 'Catastrophic Modernity' (interview with T. J. Clark), *Kunstkritikk* (7 December 2010), available at www.kunstkritikk.com.

3 Gilles Deleuze, 'Du Christ à la bourgeoisie', *Espace* (1946), p. 105; translation Raymond van de Wiel, available at www.raymondvandewiel.org.

4 Here is the relevant passage from Rand's book:

> 'Mr. Reardon', said Francisco, his voice solemnly calm, 'if you saw Atlas, the giant who holds the world on his shoulders, if you saw that he stood, blood running down his chest, his knees buckling, his arms trembling but still trying to hold the world aloft with the last of his strength, and the greater his effort the heavier the world bore down on his shoulders – what would you tell him to do?' 'I . . . don't know. What . . . could he do? What would you tell him?'
>
> 'To shrug.'

Ayn Rand, *Atlas Shrugged* (New York, 1996), p. 450.

5 Gene R. Swenson, 'What is Pop Art?', *Artnews*, 62 (November 1963), p. 26.

6 Ibid.

7 *Dr Strangelove or: How I Learned to Stop Worrying and Love the Bomb*, dir. Stanley Kubrick (Columbia Pictures, 1964).

8 Arthur Danto, 'The Artworld', *The Journal of Philosophy*, LXI/19 (15 October 1964), p. 581.

9 Karl Marx, *Capital*, vol. 1: *A Critique of Political Economy*, trans. Ben Fowkes (New York, 1992), p. 163.

10 Hal Foster, *The Return of the Real: The Avant-garde at the End of the Century* (Cambridge, MA, 1996), p. 130; see also Douglas Crimp, 'Getting the Warhol We Deserve: Cultural Studies and Queer Culture', *In Visible Culture*, 1 (Winter 1999), available at http://ivc.lib.rochester.edu.

Introduction: America Really is The Beautiful

1 Henry Geldzahler, 'The Recording Angel', in *Andy Warhol: A Memoir*, exh. cat., Dia Art Foundation, Bridgehampton, New York (Bridgehampton, NY, 1987), n.p.
2 Immanuel Kant, 'What is Enlightenment?', in Paul Hyland, Olga Gomez and Francesca Greensides, *The Enlightenment: A Sourcebook and Reader* (New York, 2003), p. 54.
3 See the interview with Warhol, 'What do you think of Jasper Johns?', at YouTube.com, accessed 11 March 2013.
4 Gretchen Berg, 'Andy Warhol: My True Story', *The East Village Other* (1 November 1966), reprinted in *I'll Be Your Mirror: The Selected Andy Warhol Interviews, 1962–1987*, ed. Kenneth Goldsmith (New York, 2004), p. 85.
5 For one discussion of the two forms of the everyday, see Henri Lefebvre, 'The Everyday and Everydayness', *Yale French Studies*, 73: *Everyday Life* (1987), pp. 7–11.
6 Victor Bockris, *The Life and Death of Andy Warhol* (New York, 1989), p. 204.
7 Ibid., p. 29. That Warhol could be so readily impersonated – and he was routinely by staffers, associates, ghostwriters and others – testifies to the clarity and purpose of his vision or dream of freedom, his vision of America the Beautiful.
8 Gerard Malanga, 'Andy Warhol on Automation: An Interview with Gerard Malanga' (1964), first published in *Chelsea*, 18 (1968), reprinted in Goldsmith, ed., *I'll Be Your Mirror*, p. 61.
9 Jean-François Lyotard, *The Postmodern Condition: A Report on Knowledge*, trans. G. Bennington and B. Massumi (Minneapolis, MN, 1984), p. xxiv.
10 Terry Eagleton, *The Ideology of the Aesthetic* (London, 1990), p. 72.
11 David Hume, *A Treatise of Human Nature: Being an Attempt to Introduce the Experimental Method of Reasoning into Moral Subjects* (London, 1739–40), p. 415; Kant, 'What is Enlightenment?'.
12 'Topics of the Times', *The New York Times* (6 May 1938), p. 20. See also, for example, Betty Kirk, 'Rivera, the Fiery Cellini of Mexico', *The New York Times* (25 April 1937), p. 134.
13 See for example Didier Anzieu, *The Skin Ego* (New Haven, CT, 1989).
14 Andy Warhol, *The Philosophy of Andy Warhol (From A to B and Back Again)* (New York, 1975), p. 7.
15 Truman Capote quoted in *Edie: An American Biography*, ed. Jean Stein and George Plimpton (New York, 1982), p. 183.
16 Correspondence from Friedrich Engels to J. Bloch in Königsberg (London, 21 September 1890), in *Marx, Engels, Lenin: On Historical Materialism* (Moscow, 1972), pp. 294–6, available at www.marxists.org.
17 Barack Obama quoted in Peter Baker, 'Whose President is he Anyway?', *The New York Times* (15 November 2008), available at www.nytimes.com.
18 Quoted by Stein, in Stein and Plimpton, eds, *Edie*, p. 239.

19 Frank Stella as reported by Barbara Rose and quoted by Stein, in Stein and Plimpton, eds, *Edie*, p. 292. Rose on Stella: 'He saw the whole thing as an American parable.'

20 See Luc Boltanski and Eve Chiapello, *The New Spirit of Capitalism* (London, 2007).

21 Michael Denning, *Culture in the Age of Three Worlds* (London and New York, 2004), p. 1.

22 Immanuel Kant, *Critique of Pure Reason*, trans. Paul Guyer and Allen W. Wood (Cambridge, 1999), A12, p. 149.

23 *Fortune* (May 1956), quoted in Lizabeth Cohen, *A Consumers' Republic: The Politics of Mass Consumption in Postwar America* (New York, 2003), p. 121. Among the many more recent examples of the primacy of the political economy of consumerism, see George W. Bush's urging of American citizens in 2006: 'As we work with Congress in the coming year to chart a new course in Iraq and strengthen our military to meet the challenges of the 21st century, we must also work together to achieve important goals for the American people here at home. This work begins with keeping our economy growing . . . I encourage you all to go shopping more.' Transcribed in 'President Bush's News Conference', *The New York Times* (20 December 2006), available www.nytimes.com.

24 Roland Barthes, 'That Old Thing, Art . . .', in Barthes, *The Responsibility of Forms*, trans. Richard Howard (New York, 1985), p. 204.

25 Clay Shirky, *Here Comes Everybody: The Power of Organizing Without Organizations* (New York, 2008).

26 T. J. Clark, 'Modernism, Postmodernism, and Steam', *October*, 100 (Spring 2002), p. 172.

27 'The world, it said, is more and more a realm of technical rationality, made available and comprehensible to individual subjects by being made mechanized and standardized. The world is on its way to absolute material lucidity. In the end it will become (and if you look hard, it is already becoming) a world of relations rather than entities, exchanges rather than objects, symbol management rather than bodies engaged in physical labour or gross struggle with the realm of necessity.' Ibid., p. 165.

1 Jesus Christ

1 'Andy's Mother', The Andy Warhol Family Album, at www.warhola.com, accessed 17 May 2009.

2 On the latter for Rusyn immigrants in particular, see Walter C. Warzeski, 'The Rusin Community in Pennsylvania', in *The Ethnic Experience in Pennsylvania*, ed. John E. Bodnar (Lewisburg, PA, 1973), pp. 175–215; and, particularly, Keith P. Dyrud, *The Quest for the Rusyn Soul: The Politics of Religion and Culture in Eastern Europe and in America, 1890–World War I* (Philadelphia, PA, 1992).

3 Philip Pearlstein quoted in *Edie: An American Biography*, ed. Jean Stein and George Plimpton (New York, 1982), p. 187.

4 Patrick O'Higgins quoted by Stein, ibid., p. 188; Ronald Tavel quoted by Stein, ibid., p. 237.

5 John Richardson, 'Eulogy for Andy Warhol', given on occasion of his memorial service at St Patrick's Cathedral, New York, 1 April 1987. Published in Jane Daggett Dillenberger, *The Religious Art of Andy Warhol* (New York, 1998), p. 13.

6 Ronnie Cutrone quoted in John O'Connor and Benjamin Liu, *Unseen Warhol* (New York, 1996), pp. 69–70, and in Peter Kattenberg, *Andy Warhol, Priest: 'The "Last Supper" Comes in Small, Medium, and Large'* (Leiden, 2001), p. 12.

7 Christopher Makos, *Warhol: A Personal Photographic Memoir* (New York, 1988), p. 53.

8 Richardson, 'Eulogy for Andy Warhol', p. 13.

9 Bob Colacello, *Holy Terror: Andy Warhol Close Up* (New York, 1990), p. 19.

10 The 'flaw in [the iconoclasts'] reasoning, which those who defended icons did not fail to point out, consisted precisely in their basic understanding of the dogma of the God-Man. Chalcedon makes a very clear distinction between nature on the one hand, and person or hypostasis on the other. It is precisely this clarity which is lacking in iconoclastic thought. The iconoclasts see only two possibilities in the image of the incarnate God the Word: Either, in representing Christ, we represent His divine nature, or in representing the man Jesus, we represent His human nature distinct from His divinity. Both possibilities are heretical. There is no third option.' 'But the Orthodox, fully aware of the distinction between nature and person, maintain precisely the third possibility, which abolishes the iconoclastic dilemma. The icon does not represent the nature, but the person: . . . "Christ is describable according to his hypostasis, remaining indescribable in His Divinity", explains [the great iconodule] St Theodore the Studite.' Leonid Ouspensky, *Theology of the Icon* (Crestwood, NY, 1992), vol. I, p. 125.

11 'The iconic form is justified by the need for remembrance of the humiliation of the Logos in becoming flesh.' Charles Barber, *Figure and Likeness: On the Limits of Representation in Byzantine Iconoclasm* (Princeton, NJ, 2002), p. 42.

12 Hans Belting, *Likeness and Presence: A History of the Image before the Era of Art* (Chicago, 1997), pp. 15–16. 'Humankind has never freed itself from the power of images, but this power has been exerted by different images in different ways at different times. There is no such thing as a historical caesura at which humanity changes out of all recognition. But the history of religion or the history of the human subject, both of which are inseparable from the history of the image, cannot be narrated without a schema of history. Certainly, it is impossible to deny that the Reformation and the formation of art collections changed the situation. The aesthetic sphere provided, so to speak, a kind of reconciliation between the lost way of experiencing images and the one that remained. The interplay of perception and interpretation that is pursued in the visual arts, as in literature, demands the expert or connoisseur, someone who knows the rules of the game.'

13 Bissera V. Pentcheva, 'The Performative Icon', *The Art Bulletin*, LXXXVIII/4 (December 2006), p. 632. See also Barber, *Figure and Likeness*, for example his account of Byzantine visuality constituted by 'a very rich sense of representation, suggested by the lack of any clear distinction between painting and relics as forms of representation. Both are matter transformed into a holy state – the relic having become holy by contact and the icon having a specific form, a likeness, impressed into its material nature . . . The icon not only demonstrates the existence of a historical subject, it also makes that subject present to whoever looks at that icon . . . It marked a trace of a continuing presence of the holy in the world' (pp. 36–7).

14 Pavel Florensky, *Iconostasis* [1922], trans. Donald Sheehan (Crestwood, NY, 1996), pp. 62–3.

15 Pentcheva, 'The Performative Icon', p. 631.

16 'This basic principle of Byzantine art of the Middle Ages results, I believe, from a distance imposed between object and viewer. The consequences of so fundamental a shift from the period of Late Antiquity were many. The Byzantines' distance allowed the portrait icon to be objectified and used in a variety of ways, many of which . . . clearly provided the setting or opportunity for public acts witnessed by communities of believers. Whereas the early panel offered individual access to God that was apparently perceived by iconoclast emperors as a threat to society, the medieval icon fostered social cohesion.' Jeffrey C. Anderson, 'Byzantine Panel Portraits', in *The Sacred Image East and West*, ed. Robert G. Ousterhout and Leslie Brubaker (Champaign, IL, 1995), p. 39.

17 Karl Marx, *Capital*, vol. I: *A Critique of Political Economy*, trans. Ben Fowkes (New York, 1992), p. 165.

18 Gabriel Daly, O.S.A., *Transcendence and Immanence: A Study in Catholic Modernism and Integralism* (Oxford, 1980), pp. 8, 45.

19 Florensky, *Iconostasis*, pp. 107–8.

20 Ibid., p. 109.

21 Ibid., pp. 124, 112.

22 From Florensky's entry on 'Point', in P. Florensky and A. Larionov, 'Symbolarium', quoted in Nicoletta Misler, 'Pavel Florensky as Art Historian', in *Beyond Vision: Essays on the Perception of Art*, ed. Nicoletta Misler (London, 2002), pp. 92–3.

23 Pavel Florensky, *The Pillar and the Ground of the Truth* [1914] (Princeton, NJ, 1997), p. 374.

24 Jacques Maritain quoted in Stephen Schloesser, *Jazz Age Catholicism: Mystic Modernism in Postwar Paris, 1919–1933* (Toronto, 2005), p. 88 (emphasis in original).

25 Jacques Maritain, *Art and Scholasticism* (Minneapolis, MN, 2007), p. 25.

26 Ibid., appendix.

27 'Via the computer, we could logically proceed from translating languages to bypassing them entirely in favour of an integral cosmic unconsciousness somewhat similar to the collective unconscious envisioned by Bergson. The computer thus holds out the promise of a technologically engendered state of universal understanding and unity, a state of absorption in the logos that

could knit mankind into one family and create a perpetuity of collective harmony and peace. This is the real use of the computer, not to expedite marketing or solve technical problems but to speed the process of discovery and orchestrate terrestrial – and eventually galactic – environments and energies.' 'The Playboy Interview: Marshall McLuhan', *Playboy* (March 1969), reprinted in *Essential McLuhan*, ed. Eric McLuhan and Frank Zingrone (New York, 1997), p. 253.

28 Quoted in Eric McLuhan, 'Introduction', in Marshall McLuhan, *The Medium and the Light: Reflections on Religion* (Toronto and New York, 1999), p. xxvii; quoted ibid., p. xvii.

29 Marshall McLuhan, 'Communication Media: Makers of the Modern World' [1959], in ibid., pp. 37–8.

30 Ibid., p. 35.

31 Terry Eagleton, *The Gatekeeper: A Memoir* (London, 2001), p. 31, quoted in Ruth Adams, 'Idol Curiosity: Andy Warhol and the Art of Secular Iconography', *Theology Sexuality*, X (2004), p. 95.

32 Eagleton, *The Gatekeeper*, p. 32, quoted ibid.

33 Eagleton, *The Gatekeeper*, pp. 35–6, quoted ibid.

34 Lou Reed and John Cale, 'Work', *Songs for Drella* (Sire Records, 1990), album; Ellis Hanson, *Decadence and Catholicism* (Cambridge, MA, 1997), p. 26.

35 Ibid., p. 25.

36 John Richardson, *Sacred Monsters, Sacred Masters* (London, 2001), p. 248.

2 Andrew Carnegie

1 Andrew Carnegie quoted in David Nasaw, *Andrew Carnegie* (New York, 2006), p. 229.

2 Andrew Carnegie, 'Variety versus Uniformity', in Carnegie, *Problems of Today: Wealth – Labor – Socialism* (New York, 1908), pp. 144–5.

3 Andrew Carnegie quoted in Nasaw, *Andrew Carnegie*, p. 229.

4 Andrew Carnegie to the President and Trustees of the Carnegie Institute, October 1897, quoted in Joseph Frazier Wall, *Andrew Carnegie* (Pittsburgh, PA, 1989), p. 817.

5 Andy Warhol, *The Philosophy of Andy Warhol (From A to B and Back Again)* (New York, 1977), pp. 100–101.

6 Ibid.

7 Andrew Carnegie, 'Best Uses of Wealth' [1895] in *Miscellaneous Writings of Andrew Carnegie*, ed. Burton J. Hendrick (New York, 1923), p. 210.

8 Andrew Carnegie, 'The Gospel of Wealth', in Carnegie, *The Gospel of Wealth and Other Timely Essays* (New York, 1901), p. 36, quoted in Neal, *A Wise Extravagance*, p. 5.

9 Andrew Carnegie quoted in Hendrick, ed., *Miscellaneous Writings*, p. 11.

10 Or there may well have been another motive. This is how Diana Strazdes explains Carnegie's patronage of institutions for the social betterment of his workers: 'As a businessman, [Carnegie] had a vested interest in encouraging

a mobile labour force, because it would allow him to avoid dealing with the demands of lifetime workers in the increasingly semi-skilled steelworking jobs, whose labour costs he wished to minimize. The lavish spending on culture may well have been Carnegie's attempt to repair his reputation with Pittsburgh workers. Even so, Carnegie's sponsorship of such a comprehensive vehicle for self-betterment was in keeping with the views of an employer whose solution to a low-paying job was for the individual worker to progress to a better-paying type of work.' Diana Strazdes, 'Andrew Carnegie's Art Museum for the Masses', in *Journal of the History of Collections* (forthcoming), MS pp. 6–7.

11 Andrew Carnegie, quoted ibid., p. 16.

12 Dale Kent, *Cosimo de' Medici and the Florentine Renaissance: The Patron's Oeuvre* (New Haven, CT, 2000), p. 345.

13 One version of this difference is summarized by Dale Kent: the Catholic 'cult of the saints, "the very special friends", which created an unbroken chain of association between the protection and authority of earthly fathers, friends, and patrons, and those who dwelt in heaven, is fundamental to understanding the quality of political patronage and the government built upon its relationships in Mediterranean societies from antiquity through the Renaissance to the present. This mode of thinking has been marginalized by modern political theory, which arose on mainly northern European, post-Reformation foundations. Insisting on the individual's direct relationship to authority and the Word, and removing the sanction of the saints for a society of orders, the Protestant Church provided no model of the function of mediation, which had been the cement of pre-modern Catholic society.' Ibid., p. 368.

14 Michael Baxandall, *Painting and Experience in Fifteenth-century Italy: A Primer in the Social History of Pictorial Style* (Oxford, 1988), p. 34.

15 For one good discussion of that history see Neal, *A Wise Extravagance*, pp. 1–22.

16 Homer Saint-Gaudens, *The American Artist and his Times* (New York, 1941), pp. 7–8.

17 Max Weber, *The Protestant Ethic and the Spirit of Capitalism* (New York, 1958).

18 Homer Saint-Gaudens quoted in Susan Platt, 'Gambling, Fencing and Camouflage: Homer Saint-Gaudens and the Carnegie International, 1922–1950', in *International Encounters: The Carnegie International and Contemporary Art, 1896–1996*, ed. Vicky A. Clark (Pittsburgh, PA, 1996), p. 66.

19 Andrew Carnegie to William Frew, 1894, quoted in Wall, *Andrew Carnegie*, p. 819.

20 Carnegie, 'Variety versus Uniformity', pp. 145–6.

21 Carnegie, 'The Best Use of Wealth', pp. 209–10, quoted in Neal, *A Wise Extravagance*, p. 4.

22 Carnegie, *The Gospel of Wealth*, p. 12.

23 Andy Warhol and Pat Hackett, *POPism: The Warhol Sixties* (New York and London, 1980), p. 16.

24 Andy Warhol, 8 October 1984, entry in Andy Warhol, *The Warhol Diaries*, ed. with Pat Hackett (New York, 1991), p. 606.

25 Gretchen Berg, 'Andy: My True Story', *Los Angeles Free Press* (17 March 1967), p. 3.

26 Duane Michals quoted by Stein in *Edie: An American Biography*, ed. Jean Stein and George Plimpton (New York, 1982), p. 184.

27 Benjamin H. D. Buchloh, 'Andy Warhol's One-dimensional Art: 1956–1966', in *Andy Warhol: A Retrospective*, exh. cat, Museum of Modern Art, New York (1989), reprinted in Annette Michelson, ed., *Andy Warhol* (Cambridge, MA, 2001), pp. 36–7.

28 Matthew Josephson, *The Robber Barons: The Great American Capitalists, 1861–1901*, reprint edn (New York, 1962), p. 362.

29 'CALLS ON CARNEGIE TO HELP IMMIGRANTS; Baron von Hesse-Wartegg Also Appeals to Rockefeller to Give Attention to Ellis Island', *The New York Times* (25 June 1911).

30 Norman Mailer, 'The White Negro: Superficial Reflections on the Hipster', in Mailer, *Advertisements for Myself* (Cambridge, MA, 1992), p. 345.

31 This, of course, was not so different from other forms of oppression, such as (even if it was far less extreme) the experience of Jews in the wake of the Holocaust. This is a point made by Andrea Levine: '"The White Negro"'s fetishization of an aggressive African American response to a history of persecution is in part an effort to obscure the image of the cowed, impotent Jew, going meekly to the gas chamber: an image that nonetheless haunts the essay.' Andrea Levine, 'The (Jewish) White Negro: Norman Mailer's Racial Bodies', *MELUS*, XXVIII/2 (Summer 2003), pp. 59–81.

32 See Jennifer Gilley and Stephen Burnett, 'Deconstructing and Reconstructing Pittsburgh's Man of Steel: Reading Joe Magarac against the Context of the 20th-century Steel Industry', *The Journal of American Folklore*, CXI/442 (Autumn 1998), pp. 392–408.

3 Shirley Temple

1 See the reports from various family members and friends regarding Warhol's childhood enthusiasm for mass culture and particularly Shirley Temple cited in Fred Lawrence Guiles, *Loner at the Ball: The Life of Andy Warhol* (London, 1990), p. 14, David Bourdon, 'Warhol Interviews Bourdon' [1962–3], in *I'll Be Your Mirror: The Selected Andy Warhol Interviews, 1962–1987*, ed. Kenneth Goldsmith (New York, 2004), p. 13; Victor Bockris, *The Life and Death of Andy Warhol* (New York, 1989), pp. 14–22.

2 This from her entry in the 'St James Encyclopedia of Pop Culture', at www.highbeam.com.

3 'Peewee's Progress', *Time* (27 April 1936), cover, pp. 36–44.

4 Ibid. A writer in *Ladies' Home Journal* commented, 'When she was born the doctor had no way of knowing the celestial script called for him to say, not "It's a girl" but "It's a gold mine"'. Quoted in Charles Eckert, 'Shirley

Temple and the House of Rockefeller' [1974], in *Jump Cut: Hollywood, Politics and Counter Cinema*, ed. Peter Steven (New York, 1985), p. 46.

5   Bourdon, 'Warhol Interviews Bourdon', p. 17; Bockris, *Life and Death*, p. 41; Shirley Temple Black, *Child Star: An Autobiography* (New York, 1988), p. 51.

6   Lawrence Grobel, *Conversations with Capote* (New York, 1985), p. 187.

7   Truman Capote quoted in *Edie: An American Biography*, ed. Jean Stein and George Plimpton (New York, 1982), p. 196. Capote also reports receiving fan letters from Warhol every day, often including illustrations from of his stories, and Warhol regularly standing outside his building waiting to see him come and go. The catalyst for Warhol's shift in affections was a poster-size blow-up of Capote's sexualized portrait from the back cover of his novel *Other Voices, Other Rooms* (1948). Bockris, *Life and Death*, p. 22; Bourdon, *Warhol*, p. 17.

8   Bockris, *Life and Death*, pp. 39, 44; Guiles, *Loner at the Ball*, p. 15.

9   Bockris, *Life and Death*, p. 46.

10   Ibid., p. 30.

11   The citation on her Juvenile Oscar in 1934, for example, declared her to be the 'one great towering figure in the cinema game in 1934, one artiste among artists, one giant among troupers'. Robert Windeler, *The Films of Shirley Temple* (Secaucus, NJ, 1978), p. 26.

12   Gilbert Seldes, 'Two Great Women', *Esquire* (July 1935), p. 86.

13   Marjorie Rosen, *Popcorn Venus: Women, Movies and the American Dream* (New York, 1973), p. 183.

14   Simon Watney, 'Queer Andy', in *Pop Out: Queer Warhol*, ed. Jennifer Doyle et al., (Durham, NC, 1996), p. 22; Guiles, *Loner at the Ball*, p. 15; Bockris, *Life and Death*, p. 30.

15   'Because, as gays, we grew up isolated not only from our heterosexual peers but also from each other, we turned to the mass media for information and ideas about ourselves; [because the isolation] made the need to escape more keen for us than some other social groups; [because] we could pilfer from straight society's images of the screen such that it would help us build up a subculture; [and because] one of the things you learn fastest if you are gay is the ability to pass for straight, to perform, to make illusions', and cinema 'offered us, unconsciously no doubt (for it as well as for us), an endless examination of this vital part of our everyday lives'. Richard Dyer, 'Introduction', *Gays and Film* (New York, 1984), pp. 1–2.

16   Leo Bersani describes this cross-gender identification in more general terms: 'In a heterosexual society,' a society in which available positive images of gay male sexuality are limited, 'women play a major role, at once psychic and corporeal, in teaching the gay man how to frame and to stage his sexuality.' Leo Bersani, *Homos* (Cambridge, MA, 1995), pp. 60–61.

17   Michael Moon, 'Flaming Closets', *October*, 51 (Winter 1989), p. 44.

18   Support for this conclusion and the drive to legislate content restrictions that were realized in the 1934 Production Code came from many corners. The Catholic Legion of Decency mounted the best-organized and largest religious campaign throughout the early 1930s; much of the popular press,

including the entire Hearst media empire, provided regular support; and, in 1933, twelve research studies funded through the Motion Picture Research Council were published. These studies, 'Movies and Conduct', 'Movies, Delinquency and Crime', 'The Emotional Responses of Children to the Motion Picture Situation', 'Motion Pictures and Standards of Morality' and so on, collectively known as the Payne Fund Studies, all focussed in one way or another on the ways in which the spectator was transformed by movies.

19 Columbia University professor Walter Pitkin, for example, argued against the assumption that Hollywood depictions of gangsters were no different from news reports by making the outstanding claim that when 'we can measure psychic intensities . . . more precisely, we shall find that the picture version [of an underworld event] is even 1,000,000,000 times more effective than the printed'. Walter B. Pitkin, 'Screen Crime vs. Press Crime', *The Outlook*, XXIX (July 1931), quoted in Andrew Bergman, *We're in the Money: Depression America and Its Films* (New York, 1971), p. 4. See also Lea Jacobs, 'Reformers and Spectators: The Film Education Movement in the Thirties', *Camera Obscura*, XXII (January 1990), pp. 30–33.

20 Robert Warshow, *The Immediate Experience: Movies, Comics, Theatre and Other Aspects of Popular Culture* (Garden City, NY, 1962), pp. 127–9.

21 In Warshow's analysis the affective contradiction between the euphoria and the desperation took on a pathological dimension the more these two emotions pressed against each other, making the gangster drama over into a social symptom. In the end the 'whole meaning' of the movie gangster's life, Warshow writes, 'is a drive for success'. As he progressively distances himself from the law, 'his activity becomes a kind of pure criminality' with 'brutality' becoming 'at once the means to success and the content of success'. The affective appeal for the moviegoer was drawn both from an identification with the subcultural freedom of the gangster, who beat the dominant culture at its own game by pursuing its economic principles to the logical endpoint, and from an identification with the political law that ultimately crushes the gangster for his transgression. As such, the moviegoer was given licence to participate vicariously in both the capitalist-gangster's sadism and, shifting sides at the film's conclusion, in an embodiment of the law as that sadism is 'turned against the gangster himself'. Ibid., pp. 131–2.

22 As one Hays office lieutenant put it, 'With crime practically denied them, with box office figures down, with high-pressure methods being employed back home to spur the studios to get in a little more cash', the studios resorted to another 'sure-fire' audience-getter: sex. Quoted in Marybeth Hamilton, *When I'm Bad, I'm Better: Mae West, Sex, and Entertainment* (Berkeley, CA, 1997), pp. 177–8.

23 *Variety* (17 October 1933), p. 19; quoted in Marybeth Hamilton, 'Goodness Had Nothing to Do with It: Censoring Mae West', in *Movie Censorship and American Culture*, ed. Francis G. Couvares (Washington, DC, 1996), p. 187.

24 'The very man who will guffaw at Mae West's performance as a reminder of the ribald days of his past', a Production Code Administration office

memo stated, 'will resent her effect upon the young, when his daughter imitates the Mae West wiggle before her boyfriends and mouths "Come up and see me sometime"'. Ibid., p. 202.

25 Quoted in Pamela Robertson, *Guilty Pleasures: Feminist Camp from Mae West to Madonna* (Durham, NC, 1996), p. 39.

26 Cited in Leonard J. Leff and Jerold L. Simmons, *The Dame in the Kimono: Hollywood, Censorship, and the Production Code from the 1920s to the 1960s* (New York, 1990), pp. 23–4.

27 Quoted in Robertson, *Guilty Pleasures*, p. 39.

28 Quoted in Ramona Curry, *Too Much of a Good Thing: Mae West as Cultural Icon* (Minneapolis, MN, 1996), p. 18. Garbo, Dietrich and West all realized their tremendous screen presence and authority through a type of androgyny. The distinctive sexual charge of both Garbo and Dietrich was founded in particular on their deep, husky voices, their regular cross-dressing and the autoerotic play back and forth between the temptress and vampire, aggressor and supplicant, male and female halves of their personas. West's charms were different.

29 Rosen, *Popcorn Venus*, p. 154.

30 Mark W. Booth, *Camp* (London and New York, 1983), p. 134.

31 Mae West, 'Sex in the Theatre', *Parade* (September 1929), pp. 12–13, quoted in Curry, *Too Much of a Good Thing*, p. 3.

32 Quoted in Robertson, *Guilty Pleasures*, p. 46.

33 Ibid., p. 39. See also Hamilton, *When I'm Bad, I'm Better*, pp. 187–211.

34 Seldes, 'Two Great Women', p. 86.

35 Ibid.

36 David Parkinson, ed., *The Graham Greene Film Reader: Mornings in the Dark* (Manchester, 1993), p. 106.

37 Ibid., p. 128.

38 Ibid., pp. 233–4.

39 Ibid., p. 234.

40 It was Cagney who was given the leading role in Warner Brothers's *G Men* of 1935.

41 The solution developed by Busby Berkeley, it might be argued, was simply cumulative. Instead of an excessively sexual Mae West he put together as many young women who just passed the test as he could fit on stage at any one time. The abstract and spectacular sexual form that had made Mae West so successful comes to be rendered in Berkeley's films in geometric arrangements of bodies coordinating themselves into a combined excess for the viewer's pleasure.

42 See, for example, *Bright Eyes* (1934), *Little Miss Marker* (1934), *Curly Top* (1935), *Captain January* (1935), *Poor Little Rich Girl* (1936).

43 The hit *Captain January* (1935), for example, included a dance number which originally presented Temple as 'a nubile island maiden' complete with 'hula skirt and brassiere of slippery seaweed fronds'. When the film was previewed by reviewers from the Mothers Clubs of America, who 'gasped in horror', the scene was quickly rewritten and refilmed, with trousers and no fronds. Perhaps the most fantastic moment of interest in

Temple piqued by such category confusion occurred when, after reports in British tabloids suggested that the child star was no child at all but instead a 30-year-old midget, the official Vatican newspaper, *L'Osservatore Romano*, dispatched a Church prelate all the way from Rome to investigate. Temple Black, *Child Star*, pp. 128, 184.

44 Molly Haskell, *From Reverence to Rape: The Treatment of Women in the Movies* (Chicago, 1987); Bret Wood, 'Lolita Syndrome', *Sight & Sound*, IV/6 (June 1994), p. 34.

45 In the context of discussion about and development of the welfare state, all three functioned critically and ideologically. 'So strongly overdetermined is Shirley's capacity for love', Eckert argues, 'that she virtually exists within it [with] no id, ego or superego. She is unstructured reification of the libido.' Eckert goes on to discuss various ways in which Temple's image of unrestricted generosity was complicit with the New Deal liberal ideology of compassion. 'Shirley's acts of softening, interceding and the rest are spontaneous ones, originating in her love of others. Not only do they function as condensations of all the mid-depression schemes for the care of the needy, but they repress the concept of duty to give or of a responsibility to *share* (income tax, federal spending) . . . Shirley and her burden of love appeared at a moment when the official ideology of charity had reached a final and unyielding form and when the public sources of charitable support were drying up.' Eckert, 'Shirley Temple and the House of Rockefeller', pp. 45, 47.

46 Bourdon, 'Warhol Interviews Bourdon', p. 13.

47 Gretchen Berg, 'Andy Warhol: My True Story', *The East Village Other* (1 November 1966), reprinted in *I'll Be Your Mirror: The Selected Andy Warhol Interviews, 1962–1987*, ed. Kenneth Goldsmith (New York, 2004), p. 85.

48 Invulnerable in a manner not unrelated to Mae West: 'She proudly mocked her sexiness even as she exploited men's interest in sex. Unlike glamour girls and sex goddesses before and after, she was nice-tough, good humored and forthright – which made her invulnerable.' William Safire, 'I Remember Mae', *The New York Times* (22 May 2000), p. A23.

4 Aubrey Beardsley

1 Quoted in Jean Stein and George Plimpton, eds, *Edie: An American Biography* (New York, 1982), p. 185.

2 Ellis Hanson, *Decadence and Catholicism* (Cambridge, 1997), p. 18.

3 Eagleton, *The Gatekeeper* [AQ: quoted in Adams, 'Idol Curiosity' as before?], pp. 32, 35–6.

4 Michael Azkoul, *The Influence of Augustine of Hippo on the Orthodox Church* (Lewiston, NY, 1990), p. 198.

5 Hanson, *Decadence and Catholicism*, pp. 86, 38.

6 Ibid, p. 7.

7 Viva quoted in Stein and Plimpton, eds, *Edie*, p. 226.

8 Christopher Makos, *Warhol: A Personal Photographic Memoir* (New York, 1988), p. 53.

9 Jules Cheret, Dudley Hardy and Aubrey Beardsley, 'The Art of Hoarding', *New Review* (July 1894), p. 54; quoted in Bridget J. Elliott, 'Sights of Pleasure: Beardsley's Images of Actresses and the New Journalism of the Nineties', in *Reconsidering Aubrey Beardsley*, ed. Robert Langenfeld (Ann Arbor, MI, 1989), p. 94.

We do not need to go quite so far as Chris Snodgrass, that 'ultimately the grotesqueness of his figures (and configurations) is but the incarnation of a fundamental erosion of categorical distinctions', or even Bridget J. Elliot, that 'Beardsley was violating fundamental cultural assumptions that defined art as the property of a social elite and amusement as the popular recreation of the masses', to agree that the categorical claims made on behalf of art were put to question, ibid., p. 97; Chris Snodgrass, 'Beardsley's Oscillating Spaces: Play, Paradox, and the Grotesque', in *Reconsidering Aubrey Beardsley*, ed. Langenfeld, p. 40.

10 'Pop Art? Is It Art? A Revealing Interview with Andy Warhol', *Art Voices* (December 1962), reprinted in *I'll Be Your Mirror: The Selected Andy Warhol Interviews, 1962–1987*, ed. Kenneth Goldsmith (New York, 2004), p. 5.

11 Aubrey Beardsley, 'The Ballad of a Barber', available at www.cypherpress.com/beardsley.

12 Hanson, *Decadence and Catholicism*, p. 37.

13 Quoted in Stein and Plimpton, eds, *Edie*, p. 239.

14 Wayne Koestenbaum, 'Afterword: Warhol's Interviews', in *I'll Be Your Mirror*, ed. Goldsmith, p. 396.

15 Arthur Symons, *Aubrey Beardsley* (London, 1898), p. 26.

16 John Updike, 'Fast Art: The Sweatless Creations of Andy Warhol', *The New Republic* (27 March 1989), available at www.tnr.com.

17 Hanson, *Decadence and Catholicism*, p. 10.

18 Robert Ross, *Aubrey Beardsley* (London and New York, 1909), p. 32.

19 Gretchen Berg, 'Andy Warhol: My True Story', *The East Village Other* (1 November 1966), reprinted in *I'll Be Your Mirror: The Selected Andy Warhol Interviews, 1962–1987*, ed. Kenneth Goldsmith (New York, 2004), p. 3.

5 Ben Shahn

1 David Bourdon, 'Warhol Interviews Bourdon' [1962–3], in *I'll Be Your Mirror? The Selected Andy Warhol Interviews, 1962–1987*, ed. Kenneth Goldsmith (New York, 2004), p. 8.

2 Ibid., p. 8.

3 Gregory Battcock, interviewed in 1978 by Patrick S. Smith, in Smith, *Andy Warhol's Art and Films* (Ann Arbor, MI, 1981), p. 216.

4 Bourdon, 'Warhol Interviews Bourdon', p. 21. After his freshman year Warhol was dropped from Carnegie Tech because he had failed one of his academic requirements and the school needed to make room for returning

veterans who wanted to study under the GI Bill. He won his way back into the programme by filling a sketchbook with drawings of daily life from the Pittsburgh slums done in a speed-sketching style he had learned during his first year at Carnegie. One classmate said of this group of drawings: 'In a very simple manner he really got the essence of the depressed side of life.' Smith, *Andy Warhol's Art and Films*, p. 11. Another classmate commented more generally on the way Warhol styled himself during this period as follows: 'Like Courbet, who came from peasant stock and was on the upwardly mobile road via art, Andy wore his peasant heritage like a badge of honour. His use of the working-class vernacular was part of it.' Victor Bockris, *The Life and Death of Andy Warhol* (New York, 1989), p. 38. The mix of social subject-matter and style taken from warm-up exercises used for figure drawing classes provided an aesthetic charge for Warhol's audience. The drawings amounted to a major early success: not only did they get him reinstated into Carnegie Tech, they also won him a $40 prize for the best work done over the summer and were exhibited in a prominent school gallery. They also gained him the recognition of the faculty and entry into a bright group of mostly older students, led by Phillip Pearlstein.

5 Greenberg summed up his view as follows: 'This art is not important, is essentially beside the point as far as ambitious present-day painting is concerned, and is much more derivative than it seems at first glance. There is a poverty of culture and resources, a pinchedness, a resignation to the minor, a certain desire for "quick" acceptance – all of which the scale and cumulative evidence of the present show make more obvious.' *Clement Greenberg: The Collected Essays*, vol. II: *Arrogant Purpose, 1945–1949*, ed. John O'Brian (Chicago and London, 1986), p. 174; Francis K. Pohl, *Ben Shahn: New Deal Artist in a Cold War Climate, 1947–1954* (Austin, TX, 1989), p. 72.

6 Robert Lepper, letter to Rainer Crone, 3 January 1974, box 2, ff 7, Robert L. Lepper Papers, 1920–1989; Bulk Dates 1938–1965, Carnegie Mellon University Archives, Staff and Faculty Papers. The Shahn retrospective opened the autumn season of 1947 at the Museum of Modern Art.

7 'We used him primarily because he had a style and a technique that was very reminiscent of Ben Shahn, [who] was a lot more expensive and [who was] not available', said one, 'it was such an obvious knock-off of Ben Shahn'. 'Ben Shahn did a lot of work for [the Upjohn Company]', said another, 'and they looked upon Andy as a cheaper Ben Shahn . . . people used him when they couldn't get Ben Shahn'. 'Andy Warhol had the visual impact I wanted', said still another, 'There's a gritty quality about the style . . . Shahn brought the same thing to it; that's why I cast Andy in that role.' Peter Palazzo and George Klauber, interviewed by Patrick Smith in Smith, *Warhol: Conversations About the Artist* (Ann Arbor, MI, 1988), pp. 108, 28; Lou Dorfsman quoted in Donna De Salvo et al., *'Success is a Job in New York . . .': The Early Art and Business of Andy Warhol*, exh. cat., Grey Art Gallery, New York University, Carnegie Museum of Art (1989), p. 53.

8 The high visibility of this campaign provided exposure and the blotted-ink drawing style and social issue subject-matter cast Warhol in the mould of Shahn as an artist with ethical purpose and critical sensibility who also happened to do commercial illustration. As Lou Dorfsman, the art director at CBS who hired him, put it: 'There's a gritty quality about the style . . . Shahn brought the same thing to it; that's where I cast Andy in that role . . . [I] wouldn't give Andy Warhol or Ben Shahn the "Dick van Dyke Show" or "Mary Tyler Moore Show" to do . . . Warhol was at a higher level than prime time entertainment.' Quoted in De Salvo et al., *'Success is a Job'*, p. 36. The award was the Art Director's Club Medal for Newspaper Advertising Art presented 13 May 1952 to Andrew Warhol, Artist; Lou Dorfsman, Art Director; CBS Radio, Advertiser. Sometime later Warhol inscribed on the cover of the envelope containing this award, 'Andrew Warhol, her medal'. Trevor Fairbrother, 'Tomorrow's Man', in De Salvo et al., *'Success is a Job'*, p. 72.

9 Ben Shahn, 'If I Had to Begin My Art Career Today', from an art school student symposium, Andover, Massachusetts, 15 September 1949, excerpted in *Ben Shahn*, ed. John D. Morse (New York and Washington, DC, 1972), pp. 94–5.

10 Frances K. Pohl, *Ben Shahn* (San Francisco, 1993), p. 5.

11 Ibid., p. 3.

12 Diego Rivera, foreword to the pamphlet for the Shahn exhibition at the Downtown Gallery in New York, 2–20 May 1933.

13 One fellow student reports that Lepper's course was a particularly crucial influence on Warhol's artistic development. See Bockris, *Life and Death* p. 43.

14 Robert Lepper, Department of Painting and Design, 'Processes in Professor Lepper's Courses in Pictorial Design', typed manuscript, August 1948, Robert L. Lepper Papers, Carnegie Mellon University, box 2, ff 57, p. 1.

15 Ibid., pp. 3–5.

16 Ibid., p. 6.

17 Ibid.

18 Lepper had previously assigned several different novels, all of which focus on a single male protagonist struggling to find his way in a rapidly changing world. These included Ernest Hemingway's account of an American volunteer to the anti-Franco forces in the Spanish Civil War in *For Whom the Bell Tolls* (1940), James T. Farrell's story about the plight of a youth amid Depression-era urban squalor, *Young Lonigan* (1932), and Theodore Dreiser's study of the moral and psychological repercussions of market-driven values in *An American Tragedy* (1925). The particular novel chosen for Warhol's class and illustrated in Warhol's drawing, Robert Penn Warren's 1946 Pulitzer Prize-winner *All the King's Men* was, like the others, a story about coming of age in very specific, very modern social and historical circumstances.

19 Share Our Wealth called for a radical redistribution of wealth with a platform that included a minimum family income, a cap on the individual wealth any individual could accumulate, a federal pension plan, a limited

work week and equal opportunity in education for all. For a recent assessment of the (substantial) influence of the Share Our Wealth society on the New Deal, see Edwin Amenta, Kathleen Dunleavy and Mary Bernstein, 'Huey Long's "Share Our Wealth" and the Second New Deal', *American Sociological Review*, LIX/5 (October 1994), pp. 678–90.

20 See David Caute, *The Fellow-Travellers: A Postscript to the Enlightenment* (New York, 1973).

21 The novel met with great critical success, winning the Pulitzer Prize for 1947. It was made into a movie by King Vidor in 1949 which, in turn, won three Academy Awards, including Best Picture and Best Actor (Broderick Crawford).

22 Nan Rosenthal notes that 'Moholy's New Bauhaus, or Institute of Design in Chicago, was a fashionable, in the sense of hip . . . in the 1940s. Aspiring artists knew about it the way they knew about Cal Arts in the early 1970s or Yale in the 1960s.' Nan Rosenthal, 'Let Us Now Praise Famous Men: Warhol as Art Director', in *The Work of Andy Warhol*, ed. Gary Garrels (Seattle, 1989), p. 40. See also David Deitcher's excellent essay 'Unsentimental Education: The Professionalization of the American Artist', in which he writes, 'the transformation of art, design, and their instruction in America . . . [in] the 1930s and 1940s . . . by Bauhaus teaching, aimed at a practically Hegelian transformation of art and design . . . Pop artists . . . experienced a unique, transitory moment in the history of American art instruction, when a singularly rational approach to teaching unprecedented numbers of students the skills of pictorial organization and commercial design was united with a still romantic belief in the inherent beneficence of art and science.' In Donna De Salvo et al., eds, *Hand-painted Pop: American Art in Transition, 1955–62*, exh. cat., Museum of Contemporary Art, Los Angeles (1992), pp. 115–16.

23 For one account of the persistence of the culture of the 1930s after the end of the decade, see Michael Denning, *The Cultural Front: The Laboring of American Culture in the Twentieth Century* (London, 1998).

24 For a discussion of Moholy-Nagy's influence on Lepper, see Richard Guy Wilson, 'Robert Lepper and the Machine Age', *Carnegie Magazine* (May/June 1987), pp. 12–19.

25 Robert Lepper, 'Comments on a Vulgar Art', *Architectural Forum* (May 1940), p. 350.

26 This gesture, as it is depicted in Warhol's drawing, has been repeatedly interpreted as a Nazi salute, and the meaning of Warhol's drawing limited to a comparison between Willie Stark/Huey Long and Nazis. See for example Rainer Crone, *Andy Warhol: A Picture Show by the Artist* (New York, 1986). While certainly the association would have been a very strong one in 1948, to limit the meaning of the drawing in this way does not adequately account for the ambivalence of the character in the story or in the drawing, nor does it account for the emergence of Soviet communism as a replacement evil for the defeated Nazis.

27 Robert Penn Warren, *All The King's Men* (New York, 1946), p. 13.

28 If we look at his career as a whole, Warhol was a self-portraitist perhaps

more than any other artist in history. All his early successes involved self-portraits. A sophomore-year exhibition of drawings of daily life in the Pittsburgh slums that gained him recognition and kept him from flunking out of Carnegie included a prominently placed, oversize self-portrait. His first *succès de scandale* was a painting often referred to as *Nosepicker* but whose full title is *The Broad Gave Me My Face But I Can Pick My Own Nose*. And the card announcing the exhibition at the Stable Gallery in 1962 that launched his career as a fine artist in New York was a self-portrait. Throughout the remainder of his career Warhol would pose for thousands of self-portraits, society photographs, promotional photographs and photographs recording life at the Factory. In many he would pose alongside other public figures: Marilyn, Elvis, the Pope, Mickey Mouse and so on. This tendency to picture himself generally, and to picture himself specifically in the context of celebrity, is fully consistent with his career as a whole and with the widely agreed-on assumption that his persona was one of Warhol's greatest artistic accomplishments.

29 Diana Trilling, 'Fiction in Review', *The Nation* (24 August 1946), p. 220.

30 Another reviewer put it this way: 'How much of reasonably recent political state history Mr. Warren may have had in mind, the reader can decide for himself.' W.K.R., review of *All the King's Men*, *Christian Science Monitor* (4 September 1946), p. 14.

31 *The New York Times Magazine* (2 May 1948); *Life* (5 January 1948).

32 Author unidentified, 'Foreign News', *Time* (17 November 1947), p. 33.

33 David Shub, *Lenin: A Biography* (New York, 1948).

34 Robert L. Lepper, 'An Outline of an Attitude', *The Charette*, xiii/4–5 (April–May 1933), p. 3.

35 'Art and the Social Entity', press release based on an interview with Lepper by an unspecified member of the Public Relations department at Carnegie Tech, 1948, Lepper archive, Carnegie Mellon University, box 3, ff. 80.

36 Robert L. Lepper, 'Designer's Dilemmas', *Art Education Bulletin*, xiv/6 (September 1957), p. 7.

37 Further, it needs to be noted, communism was an ongoing theme for Warhol in a way that it was not for any other modernist of his generation. There are many and varied indications of this enthusiasm throughout his career and it is not necessary to dig very deep for evidence. There was, for example, the attempt in the early 1960s to have his work known as 'Communist Art' (rather than 'Pop Art') because it played on the word communist (Smith, *Andy Warhol's Art and Films*, p. 67) or his famous claim to Gene Swenson in 1963 about the similar effects on subjects of capitalism and communism (that what Russia is doing 'under strict government' is 'happening here all by itself' – 'Everybody looks alike and acts alike, and we're getting more and more the same way.' (Gene Swenson, 'What is Pop Art? Interviews with Eight Painters (Part 1)', *Artnews*, 62, no. 7, November 1967, p. 734.) There was the hammer-and-sickle series and the Mao series, and then in 1982 there was the trip to China to see the Great Wall, about which Warhol said the following (with uncharacteristic affect): 'I went to see the Great Wall. You know you read about it for years.

And actually it was great. It was really really really great.' Paul Taylor, 'Andy Warhol: The Last Interview', *Flash Art*, CXXXIII (April 1987), p. 44. There were many other efforts, too, to reflect on the political history of the twentieth century: the *Flash* series of 1968, focusing on Kennedy's assassination, and many of the Jackies, for example, or the *Zeitgeist* series of 1982. My intention in pointing out the exceptional recurrence of such political themes in Warhol's work is not to claim that it indicates a conventional form of criticality – that, for example, he was really a manner of latter-day Social Realist concerned to 'dramatiz[e] the breakdown of commodity exchange' with 'a kind of history painting' (Thomas Crow, 'Saturday Disasters: Trace and Reference in Early Warhol', *Reconstructing Modernism: Art in New York, Paris, and Montreal, 1945–1964*, ed. Serge Guilbaut, Cambridge, MA, and London, 1990, pp. 313, 320). Nor is this simple observation meant to suggest that he sought only to profit from the cultural capital of such imagery with 'all the mindless shallowness that America has to offer', as another, very different sort of apologist has claimed, against the views of 'Old World, neo-Marxist navel-gazers' (such as, presumably, Crow) who 'actually believe Warhol was a heavyweight, subtly exposing the iniquities of American life' (Ferdinand Protzman, 'The Embellished Andy Warhol: Corcoran Exhibit Tries to Add Bang to Pop Phenomenon', *The Washington Post*, 6 December 2000. See also the letter in the *Post* in response to this position by H. Perry Chapman, which takes the author to task for the haughtiness of his dismissal of academic 'navel-gazers' and for his refusal to support his claims with any serious or substantive analysis of the work in question; 'Warhol's Art', 16 December 2000, and the catalogue for the exhibition that spurred these responses: Jonathan P. Binstock, *Andy Warhol: Social Observer*, Philadelphia, PA, 2000). In a sense, my aim here is more modest: to explain how Warhol was an artist of a moment and how his work tells us much about that moment. He was a product of a complex set of conflicting influences and aims and the politics of the position he eventually came to represent so effectively and influentially carried with it all the ambivalence and contradiction of that history. To emphasize either Social Realist or Capitalist Realist positions seems too strong, by my account, and flattens out the complex history and expressive forcefulness that his work represents. More importantly, to do so misses the very substantial legacy that Warhol and his work continue to have for us today.

38 Curtis Daniel MacDougall, *Gideon's Army* (New York, 1965), vol. II, p. 402.

39 Letter from Philip Pearlstein to Rainer Crone, Robert L. Lepper Papers.

6 Andy Paperbag

1 Gene R. Swenson, 'What is Pop Art? Interviews with Eight Painters (Part 1)', *Artnews*, 62, no. 7 (November 1967), p. 734.

2 'He has that terrific look of looking very young and very old at the same time this look is really important to what he does sort of . . . he promotes a

very sophisticated mystery, and people read a lot of fantasies into it.' Fred Hughes interviewed by John Wilcox, in Wilcox, *The Autobiography and Sex Life of Andy Warhol* (New York, 1971), n.p.

3 Barbara Goldsmith, 'Affectless but Effective', *The New York Times* (14 September 1975), p. 238. See also Kelly M. Cresap, *Pop Trickster Fool: Warhol Performs Naiveté* (Urbana, IL, and Chicago, 2004) which takes this issue as its main theme. Here is one further characteristic statement by an interviewer that illustrates some of the rushing in referred to by Goldsmith and noted by most observers: 'You are a paradox of endless combinations. There's the human and the mystical, there's the passive and the active, there's the sexual and the anti-sexual, there's the masculine and the feminine. And yet what is most often heard about you is praise about your love and tolerance of people. Do you feel that you have any kind of negative influence over any of the people who have surrounded you?' The concluding question, of course, refers to one of the other characteristics often associated with Warhol, even though the interviewer is polite enough to not say so directly. Claire Demers, 'An Interview with Andy Warhol: Some Say He's the *Real* Mayor of New York', *Christopher Street* (September 1977), reprinted in *I'll Be Your Mirror: The Selected Andy Warhol Interviews, 1962–1987*, ed. Kenneth Goldsmith (New York, 2004), pp. 271–2.

4 'Warhol was the black hole in space, the vortex that engulfed all, the still epicenter of the psychological storm. He wound the key to the motor of the merry-go-round, as the kids on the outside spun faster and faster and, no longer able to hang on, flew off into space.' Ultra Violet, *Famous for 15 Minutes: My Years with Andy Warhol* (New York, 1988), p. 3.

5 Gerard Malanga interviewed by Patrick S. Smith, in Smith, *Andy Warhol's Art and Films* (Ann Arbor, MI, 1981), pp. 405–6.

6 Andy Warhol and Pat Hackett, *POPism: The Warhol Sixties* (New York and London, 1980), pp. 47, 40.

7 Bosley Crowther, 'Screen: *The Carpetbaggers* Opens: Adaptation of Book by Robbins in Debut', *The New York Times* (2 July 1964), available at www.nytimes.com/movies.

8 Murray Schumach, 'The Gaudy Career of Jonas Cord Jr.', *The New York Times* (25 June 1961), p. BR24.

9 The record is a little sketchy here (as far as I have been able to track it down).

10 Clive Barnes and Bert Andrews, 'Theater: Two-Character *The Beard*: Billie Dixon and Bright in McClure's Play', *The New York Times* (25 October 1967), p. 40; Bert Andrews, 'The Theater: A Reptilian Mating Fugue', *Wall Street Journal* (26 October 1967), p. 18.

11 Ultra Violet interviewed in Wilcox, *Autobiography and Sex Life*, n.p.

12 Michael McClure, 'Suicide and Death', in McClure, *Meat Science Essays* (San Francisco, 1963), p. 45.

13 Victor Bockris and Gerard Malanga, *Up-tight: The Velvet Underground Story* (London, 1983), pp. 71, 88.

14 Warhol and Hackett, *POPism*, pp. 170–71.

15 Norman Mailer, 'Foreword', in Michael McClure, *'The Beard' & 'VKTMS': Two Plays by Michael McClure* (New York, 1985), p. 5. For an inquiry into the prehistory of this later form of seriality, see Blake Stimson, *The Pivot of the World: Photography and Its Nation* (Cambridge, MA, 2006).
16 The concept of creative destruction was developed in 1942 by Joseph Schumpeter in his *Capitalism, Socialism and Democracy* and has since become a mainstay of neoliberal social and economic theory.
17 Roland Barthes, 'That Old Thing, Art . . .', in Barthes, *The Responsibility of Forms* (New York, 1985), p. 200.
18 Jackie Curtis in Smith, *Andy Warhol's Art and Films*, p. 238.
19 Emile de Antonio in Smith, *Andy Warhol's Art and Films*, p. 294.
20 Tina S. Fredericks, 'Remembering Andy/An Introduction', in Jesse Kornbluth, *Pre-Pop Warhol* (New York, 1988), p. 10.
21 For a note on his use of 'André' see 'Pre-Pop', at www.warholstars.org, page one, and on 'Morningstar', page six. For a discussion of 'what the cat dragged in', see Eleanor Ward interviewed in Wilcox, *Autobiography and Sex Life*, n.p. 'Andy Paperbag' and 'Raggedy Andy' are referred to in many sources. See Nathan Gluck in Smith, *Andy Warhol's Art and Films*, p. 324 for the reported name-change plan.
22 Gregory Battcock in Smith, *Andy Warhol's Art and Films*, p. 216.
23 Charles Lisanby in Smith, *Andy Warhol's Art and Films*, p. 386.
24 Wayne Koestenbaum, *Andy Warhol* (London, 2001), p. 1.
25 Ibid., p. 204.
26 Joseph Giordano in Patrick S. Smith, *Warhol: Conversations About the Artist (Studies in the Fine Arts: The Avant Garde, No 59)* (Ann Arbor, 1988), p. 129.
27 Giovannina Conchiglia, Gennaro Della Rocca and Dario Grossi, 'When the Body Image becomes "Empty": Cotard's Delusion in a Demented Patient', *Acta Neuropsychiatrica*, xx/5 (October 2008), pp. 283–4.
28 Charles Henri Ford interviewed in Wilcox, *Autobiography and Sex Life*, n.p.
29 Bob Colacello, *Holy Terror: Andy Warhol Close Up* (New York, 1990), p. 344.
30 Victor Bockris, 'Dinner with Andy and Bill, February 1980', *Blueboy* (October 1980), reprinted in Goldsmith, ed., *I'll Be Your Mirror*, p. 280.
31 Vito Giallo, 'On Working with Warhol in the Early Years', in John O'Connor and Benjamin Liu, *Unseen Warhol* (New York, 1996), p. 22.
32 Gerard Malanga interviewed in Wilcox, *Autobiography and Sex Life*, n.p.
33 Sam Green interviewed in Wilcox, *Autobiography and Sex Life*, n.p.
34 Giallo, 'On Working with Warhol', p. 20.
35 Charles Lisanby in Smith, *Andy Warhol's Art and Films*, p. 378.
36 P. T., 'Exhibition at Bodley Gallery', *Art News* (December 1956), p. 59, quoted in Richard Meyer, *Outlaw Representation: Censorship and Homosexuality in Twentieth-century American Art* (Oxford, 2002), pp. 107–8.
37 Quoted in Victor Bockris, *The Life and Death of Andy Warhol* (New York, 1989), p. 177.

38 'The tremendous importance the individual accords to the sexual instinct is not a result of its importance for the species, but arises because procreation is the real achievement of the individual and consequently his highest interest, his highest expression of power (not judged from the consciousness but from the center of the whole individuation'. Friedrich Nietzsche, *The Will to Power*, trans. Walter Kaufmann and R. J. Hollingdale (New York, 1968), section 680, p. 360.

39 Herbert Marcuse, *One-Dimensional Man: Studies in the Ideology of Advanced Industrial Society* (New York, 1964), p. 76.

7 The Nothingness Himself

1 Michael Fried, 'Art and Objecthood', *Artforum*, v (June 1967), p. 20.

2 Andy Warhol and Pat Hackett, *POPism: The Warhol Sixties* (New York and London, 1980), p. 3.

3 Benjamin H. D. Buchloh, 'Andy Warhol's One-Dimensional Art', in *Andy Warhol*, ed. Annette Michelson (Cambridge, MA, 2001), pp. 5–6.

4 Andy Warhol, *The Philosophy of Andy Warhol (From A to B and Back Again)* (New York, 1975), p. 10.

5 Asger Jorn, 'The End of the Economy and the Realization of Art', first published in *Internationale Situationniste*, IV (June 1960), available excerpted and in translation at www.infopool.org.uk.

6 David Bourdon, 'Warhol Interviews Bourdon' [1962–3], in *I'll Be Your Mirror: The Selected Andy Warhol Interviews, 1962–1987*, ed. Kenneth Goldsmith (New York, 2004), p. 11.

7 Wayne Koestenbaum, *Andy Warhol* (London, 2001), p. 215.

8 Text 'The Personality of the Artist' by Gene Swenson, in the announcement shown here as illus. 59.

9 Victor Bockris, *The Life and Death of Andy Warhol* (New York, 1989), p. 395; quoted in Jonathan Flatley, 'Liking Things', in John W. Smith et al., *Possession Obsession: Andy Warhol and Collecting* (Pittsburgh, PA, 2002), p. 103.

10 Warhol, *Philosophy*, p. 144.

11 Ibid., p. 146–7.

12 Wayne Koestenbaum, *The Queen's Throat: Opera, Homosexuality, and the Mystery of Desire* (New York, 1993), pp. 51, 62.

13 Rachel Cooke, 'Overexposed and over here: The travelling show of ultimate Andy Warhol trivia has hit town. But please don't all rush at once . . .: Andy Warhol: Other Voices, Other Rooms: Hayward Gallery, London', *The Observer* (12 October 2008), p. 19.

14 Warhol, *Philosophy*, p. 196.

15 Ibid., p. 143.

16 Naomi Levine interviewed in John Wilcox, *The Autobiography and Sex Life of Andy Warhol* (New York, 1971), n.p.

17 Ultra Violet, *Famous for 15 Minutes: My Years with Andy Warhol* (New York, 1988), p. 156.

18 Charles Henri Ford interviewed in Wilcox, *Autobiography and Sex Life*, n.p.

19 Gretchen Berg interviewed in Wilcox, *Autobiography and Sex Life*, n.p.

20 'Artists feel that anyone who doesn't enjoy their work does not really experience it. So we are insulated, we have this happy space of ours.' Jeff Wall in Jacques Herzog and Jeff Wall, *Pictures of Architecture/Architecture of Pictures* (Vienna and London, 2004), p. 68. See Jeff Wall, *Dan Graham's Kammerspiel* (Toronto, 1991). See also my 'The Artiste', *Oxford Art Journal*, XXX (2007), pp: 101–15.

21 Ultra Violet interviewed in Wilcox, *Autobiography and Sex Life*, n.p.

22 Werner Bamberger, *The New York Times* (21 January 1959): 'CONTAINERS CITED AS SHIPPING "MUST": Industry Officials Say Use Will Be Limited Only by Challenge of Labor', p. 62; *The New York Times* (8 November 1959), p. F9.

23 'Text of the President's Message to Congress on Nation's Transportation Problems', *The New York Times* (6 April 1962), p. 18; Morris Forgash, 'The Roll and Rock of Containerization in Transport Economics', *Annals of the American Academy of Political and Social Science*, CCCXLV (January 1963), p. 121.

24 Marc Levinson, *The Box: How the Shipping Container Made the World Smaller and the World Economy Bigger* (Princeton, NJ, 2006), p. 11.

25 'Better by the Box', *Time*, LXXXVII/8 (25 February 1966), p. 95; 'Engineer's Esthetic', *Time*, LXXXVII/22 (3 June 1966), p. 64.

26 Theodor Adorno, *Aesthetic Theory*, trans. Robert Hullot-Kentor (Minneapolis, MN, 1997), p. 349.

27 Quoted in Norman Webster, 'My 15 minutes with Warhol; What is Art? Ask Canadian Customs Inspectors', *The Gazette* (Montreal, 9 November 2008), p. A15.

28 Susan Sontag, 'On Self', *The New York Times* (10 September 2006), available at www.nytimes.com.

8 Drella

1 Mario Amaya in John Wilcox, *The Autobiography and Sex Life of Andy Warhol* (New York, 1971), n.p.

2 Gene R. Swenson, 'What is Pop Art?' Answers from Eight Painters (Part 1)', *Artnews*, 62, no. 7 (November 1963), p. 60.

3 For example, in 1972, Andrea Feldman committed suicide by jumping out of her family's apartment window on Fifth Avenue after arranging for several former boyfriends to be waiting for her on the street below. In 1986, *Interview* contributor Tinkerbelle (Jeri Lee Veronica Visser) jumped to her death from a fifth-floor apartment on West 111th Street. See www.warhol-stars.org/tinkerbelle.html.

4 Alain Jouffroy, untitled essay in *Warhol* (Paris, 1964), n.p., my translation.

5 Swenson, 'What is Pop Art?', p. 60.

6 Grace Glueck, 'We Threw Andy Out of Our Orgy', *The New York Times* (20 November 1988), available at www.nytimes.com.

7   Victor Bockris, *Warhol: The Biography* (New York, 2003), p. 236; Ultra
     Violet, *Famous for 15 Minutes: My Years with Andy Warhol* (New York,
     1988), p. 28.

8   See '1966', at www.warholstars.org. A similar account of the phone call is
     provided by Danny Williams's mother in the film *A Walk into the Sea:
     Danny Williams and the Warhol Factory* (Thatgrl Media, 2007) made by
     Williams's niece, Esther Robinson.

9   Paul Morrissey's film *Andy Warhol's Dracula* (or *Blood for Dracula*), 1973,
     and Warhol's silkscreen paintings of Dracula of 1981.

10   Talia Schaffer, '"A Wilde Desire Took Me": The Homoerotic History of
     Dracula', ELH, LXI/2 (Summer 1994), p. 398. See also Christopher Craft,
     '"Kiss Me with those Red Lips": Gender and Inversion in Bram Stoker's
     Dracula', *Representations*, VIII (Autumn 1984), pp. 107–33.

11   Maurice Richardson, 'The Psychoanalysis of Ghost Stories', *Twentieth
     Century*, CLXVI/ 994 (December 1959), pp. 426–9.

12   Bram Stoker, *Dracula* (New York, 1897), pp. 282, 319.

13   Sigmund Freud, *Civilization and Its Discontents* (New York, 2005), p. 121.

14   Stoker, *Dracula*, p. 320.

15   Ibid., p. 19.

16   'If the flâneur has disappeared as a specific figure, it is because the percep-
     tive attitude which he embodied saturates modern existence, specifically, the
     society of mass consumption . . . In the flâneur, concretely, we recognize our
     own consumerist mode of being-in-the-world.' Susan Buck-Morss, 'The
     Flâneur, the Sandwichman and the Whore: The Politics of Loitering', *New
     German Critique*, XXXIX (Autumn 1986), pp. 104–5.

17   See Howard Junker, 'Andy Warhol, Movie Maker', *The Nation* (22
     February 1965), p. 207. Quoted in Callie Angell, *Andy Warhol Screen
     Tests: The Films of Andy Warhol Catalogue Raisonné*, vol. 1 (New York,
     2006), p. 14.

18   Angell, *Andy Warhol Screen Tests*, p. 14. Here is an earlier and more
     lengthy explication by the same author: 'sometimes people were instructed
     to hold completely still and not even blink, in the hopes that the resulting
     film would be so static and unmoving that it would be indistinguishable from
     an actual photograph, as a kind of joke on the viewer. But what happens in
     these films, of course, is that this performance requirement makes people
     very uncomfortable; it's very hard to hold still for three minutes, and it's
     nearly impossible not to blink (although a couple of people did manage it),
     and so instead of pseudo-photographs, what you get are some very intense
     performances, performances which emerge from the tension that is created
     when people are asked to behave as if they were their own image. In a
     sense, the Screen Tests are like little documentaries about what it is like to
     sit for your portrait, and what you see in these films are people engaged
     in direct physical conflict with the idea of their own image.' Callie Angell,
     'Doubling the Screen: Andy Warhol's *Outer and Inner Space*', *Millennium
     Film Journal*, XXXVIII (Spring 2002), available at www.mfj-online.org.

19   Ellis Hanson, 'Undead', in *Inside/Out: Lesbian Theories, Gay Theories*,
     ed. Diana Fuss (New York, 1991), p. 325.

20 Franco Moretti, *Signs Taken for Wonders: Essays in the Sociology of Literary Forms* (London, 1983), p. 84. 'Our hoarder is a martyr to exchange-value, a holy ascetic seated at the top of a metal column. He cares for wealth only in its social form, and accordingly he hides it away from society. He wants commodities in a form in which they can always circulate and he therefore withdraws them from circulation. He adores exchange-value and he consequently refrains from exchange. The liquid form of wealth and its petrification, the elixir of life and the philosophers' stone are wildly mixed together like an alchemist's apparitions. His imaginary boundless thirst for enjoyment causes him to renounce all enjoyment. Because he desires to satisfy all social requirements, he scarcely satisfies the most urgent physical wants.' Karl Marx, 'Critique of Political Economy' (1859), available at www.marxists.org.

21 Karl Marx, *Capital*, vol. I: *A Critique of Political Economy* (New York, 1977, p. 342.

22 Michael Warner, 'Introduction', in Warner, *Fear of a Queer Planet: Queer Politics and Social Theory* (Minneapolis, MN, 1993), p. xxxi.

23 Marx, *Capital*, pp. 163–4.

24 Moretti, *Signs Taken for Wonders*, p. 101.

25 Pat Hackett, 'Introduction', in Hackett, *The Andy Warhol Diaries* (New York, 1989), p. xii.

26 'Paul Morrissey: The director of Warhol's best-known and most commercial films goes on record about their work and his old partner's talents and weaknesses', Nelson Lyon, *Interview*, XXXVIII/5 (June–July 2008), p. 107.

27 Philip Lewis, *Seeing Through the Mother Goose Tales: Visual Turns in the Writings of Charles Perrault* (Stanford, CT, 1996), p. 11.

28 Ibid., p. 20.

29 Gretchen Berg, 'Andy Warhol: My True Story', *The East Village Other* (1 November 1966), reprinted in *I'll Be Your Mirror: The Selected Andy Warhol Interviews, 1962–1987*, ed. Kenneth Goldsmith (New York, 2004), p. 3.

30 Mario Amaya in Wilcox, *Autobiography and Sex Life*, n.p.

31 Ibid.

32 Wayne Koestenbaum, *Andy Warhol* (London, 2001), p. 5.

33 Andy Warhol, *The Philosophy of Andy Warhol (From A to B and Back Again)* (New York, 1975), p. 56.

34 Quoted in Victor Bockris, *The Life and Death of Andy Warhol* (New York, 1989), p. 210.

35 Warhol, *Philosophy*, p. 26.

36 Étienne Gilson, *The Arts of the Beautiful* (New York, 1965), p. 142.

37 See John Palmer, Henry Romney, Andy Warhol, Gerard Malanga, Marie Desert and Jonas Mekas, 'Empire Conversation' (1964), in 'Articles', at www.warholstars.org.

38 Jeff Rian, 'Vito Acconci: I Never Wanted to be Political; I Wanted the Work to be Politics', interview, *Flash Art* (January / February 1994), pp. 84–5.

39 While all Warhol's activities functioned in this way, it was the films and, later, *Interview* magazine that more than any other served as the frontroom

draw that was the engine for his high-profile career and backroom, high-margin sales. Everyone he met who was more than a little bit famous or more than a little bit attractive (or, in some cases early on, more than a little bit crazy), would be invited for a screen test in the mid-'60s or promised a cover of *Interview* in the 1970s and '80s.

40 Susan Sontag, 'On Self', *The New York Times* (10 September 2006), available at www.nytimes.com.

41 Gene R. Swenson, 'What is Pop Art? Interviews with Eight Painters (Part 2)', *Art News*, LXII/10 (February 1964).

9 Citizen Warhol

1 Pat Hackett, ed., *The Andy Warhol Diaries* (New York, 1991), p. xviii.

2 Introduction to 'Love Me, I'm a Liberal', recorded on *Phil Ochs in Concert* (Elektra Records, 1966), album.

3 The commentator was Dave Hickey and he is quoted from the film in Ed Halter, '240 Minutes of Fame: Epic Doc Traces an Intellectual History of Warhol', *The Village Voice* (22 August 2006), available at www.villagevoice.com.

4 Bram Stoker, *Dracula* (New York, 1897), p. 49.

5 'And Andy works as hard as anybody I know . . . Whenever he'd ask me how many songs I'd written that day, whatever the number was Andy would say, "you should do more".' Victor Bockris and Gerard Malanga, *Up-tight: The Velvet Underground Story* (London, 1983), p. 128.

6 See Hal Foster's delineation of a position very close to this, focussed on the following in Warhol's work and persona: 'a traumatic notion of the real, a contemporary version of the optical unconscious, a historical confusion between private fantasy and public reality, a hysterical relay between mass subject and mass object, a forging of a psychic nation through mass-mediated disaster and death.' Hal Foster, 'Death in America', *October*, 75 (Winter 1996), pp. 36–59.

7 Jorge Luis Borges, 'An Overwhelming Film', originally published in *Sur*, 83 (August 1941), English translation *October*, 15 (Winter 1980), p. 13.

8 Ultra Violet, *Famous for 15 Minutes: My Years with Andy Warhol* (New York, 1988), p. 26.

9 *Village Voice* (10 February 1966).

10 Bob Colacello, *Holy Terror: Andy Warhol Close Up* (New York, 1990), p. 308.

11 Glenn O'Brien, 'Pat Hackett: Andy Warhol's Gal Friday Talks about her Boss's Odd Work Habits and Her Career as Amanuensis, Screenwriter, and Co-author', *Interview* (June–July 2008), p. 106.

12 Viva interviewed in John Wilcox, *The Autobiography and Sex Life of Andy Warhol* (New York, 1971), n.p.

13 Paul Morrissey interviewed ibid.

14 Billy Name in John O'Connor and Benjamin Liu, *Unseen Warhol* (New York, 1996), p. 40.

15 John Giorno, 'Andy Warhol Interviewed by a Poet', in *I'll Be Your Mirror: The Selected Andy Warhol Interviews, 1962–1987*, ed. Kenneth Goldsmith (New York, 2004), p. 26.

16 Wayne Koestenbaum, *Andy Warhol* (London, 2001), p. 179.

17 Ultra Violet, *Famous for 15 Minutes*, p. 231.

18 Susan Sontag, 'Jack Smith's *Flaming Creatures*', *Against Interpretation and Other Essays* (New York, 1966), p. 229.

19 Geldzahler in *Superstar: The Life and Times of Andy Warhol*, dir. Chuck Workman (Shout Factory Theater, 1990).

Angell, Callie, *Andy Warhol Screen Tests: The Films of Andy Warhol Catalogue Raisonné*, vol. I (New York, 2006)
——, 'Doubling the Screen: Andy Warhol's *Outer and Inner Space*', *Millennium Film Journal*, XXXVIII (Spring 2002)
Binstock, Jonathan P., *Andy Warhol: Social Observer* (Philadelphia, PA, 2000)
Bockris, Victor, *The Life and Death of Andy Warhol* (New York, 1989)
——, *Warhol: The Biography* (New York, 2003)
——, and Gerard Malanga, *Up-tight: The Story of the Velvet Underground* (London, 1983)
Buchloh, Benjamin H. D., 'Andy Warhol's One-dimensional Art, 1956–1966', in *Andy Warhol: A Retrospective*, exh. cat. ed. Kynaston McShine, Museum of Modern Art, New York (1989)
Colacello, Bob, *Holy Terror: Andy Warhol Close Up* (New York, 1990)
Cresap, Kelly M., *Pop Trickster Fool: Warhol Performs Naiveté* (Urbana, IL, and Chicago, 2004)
Crimp, Douglas, 'Getting the Warhol We Deserve: Cultural Studies and Queer Culture', *InVisible Culture*, I (Winter 1999)
Crow, Thomas, 'Saturday Disasters: Trace and Reference in Early Warhol', *Reconstructing Modernism: Art in New York, Paris, and Montreal, 1945–1964*, ed. Serge Guilbaut (Cambridge, MA, and London, 1990)
Danto, Arthur, 'The Artworld', *The Journal of Philosophy*, LXI/19 (15 October 1964)
De Salvo, Donna, et al., eds, *Hand-painted Pop: American Art in Transition, 1955–62*, exh. cat., The Museum of Contemporary Art, Los Angeles (1992)
——, et al., '*Success is a Job in New York . . .': The Early Art and Business of Andy Warhol*, exh. cat., Grey Art Gallery, New York University, Carnegie Museum of Art (1989)
Dillenberger, Jane Daggett, *The Religious Art of Andy Warhol* (New York, 1998)
Dyrud, Keith P., *The Quest for the Rusyn Soul: The Politics of Religion and Culture in Eastern Europe and in America, 1890–World War I* (Philadelphia, PA, 1992)
Foster, Hal, *The Return of the Real: The Avant-garde at the End of the Century* (Cambridge, MA, 1996)

Garrels, Gary, ed., *The Work of Andy Warhol* (Seattle, 1989)

Geldzahler, Henry, 'The Recording Angel', in *Andy Warhol: A Memoir*, exh. cat., Dia Art Foundation, Bridgehampton, New York (1987)

Goldsmith, Barbara, 'Affectless but Effective', *The New York Times* (14 September 1975)

Goldsmith, Kenneth, ed., *I'll Be Your Mirror: The Selected Andy Warhol Interviews, 1962–1987* (New York, 2004)

Guiles, Fred Lawrence, *Loner at the Ball: Life of Andy Warhol* (London, 1990)

Halter, Ed, '240 Minutes of Fame: Epic Doc Traces an Intellectual History of Warhol', *The Village Voice* (22 August 2006)

Jouffroy, Alain, untitled essay in *Warhol*, ed. John Ashbery, Alain Jouffroy and Jean-Jacques Lebel (Paris, 1964)

Kattenberg, Peter, *Andy Warhol, Priest: 'The "Last Supper" Comes in Small, Medium, and Large'* (Leiden, 2001)

Koestenbaum, Wayne, *Andy Warhol* (London, 2001)

——, *The Queen's Throat: Opera, Homosexuality, and the Mystery of Desire* (New York, 1993)

Kornbluth, Jesse, *Pre-Pop Warhol* (New York, 1988)

Makos, Christopher, *Warhol: A Personal Photographic Memoir* (New York, 1988)

Meyer, Richard, *Outlaw Representation: Censorship and Homosexuality in Twentieth-century American Art* (Oxford, 2002)

Michelson, Annette, ed., *Andy Warhol*, (Cambridge, MA, 2001)

O'Brien, Glenn, 'Pat Hackett: Andy Warhol's Gal Friday Talks about her Boss's Odd Work Habits and Her Career as Amanuensis, Screenwriter, and Co-author', *Interview* (June–July 2008)

O'Connor, John, and Benjamin Liu, *Unseen Warhol* (New York, 1996)

Protzman, Ferdinand, 'The Embellished Andy Warhol: Corcoran Exhibit Tries to Add Bang to Pop Phenomenon', *The Washington Post* (6 December 2000)

Smith, John W. et al., *Possession Obsession: Andy Warhol and Collecting* (Pittsburgh, PA, 2002)

Smith, Patrick S., *Andy Warhol's Art and Films* (Ann Arbor, MI, 1981)

——, 'Warhol: Conversations About the Artist', *Studies in the Fine Arts: The Avant Garde*, 59 (Ann Arbor, MI, 1988)

Stein, Jean, and George Plimpton, eds, *Edie: An American Biography* (New York, 1982)

Stimson, Blake, 'Andy Warhol's Red Beard', *Art Bulletin*, LXXXIII/3 (September 2001)

Swenson, Gene R., 'What is Pop Art?', *Artnews*, 62, no. 7 (November 1963)

Taylor, Paul, 'Andy Warhol: The Last Interview', *Flash Art*, CXXXIII (April 1987)

Updike, John, 'Fast Art: The Sweatless Creations of Andy Warhol', *The New Republic* (27 March 1989)

Violet, Ultra, *Famous for 15 Minutes: My Years with Andy Warhol* (New York, 1988)

Warhol, Andy, and Pat Hackett, *POPism: The Warhol Sixties* (New York and London, 1980)

——, *The Philosophy of Andy Warhol (From A to B and Back Again)* (New York, 1975)

——, *The Warhol Diaries*, ed. with Pat Hackett (New York, 1991)

Warhola family, 'Andy's Mother', The Andy Warhol Family Album, at www.warhola.com

Warzeski, Walter C., 'The Rusin Community in Pennsylvania', in *The Ethnic Experience in Pennsylvania*, ed. John E. Bodnar (Lewisburg, PA, 1973)

Watney, Simon, 'Queer Andy', in *Pop Out: Queer Warhol*, ed. Jennifer Doyle et al. (Durham, NC, 1996)

Webster, Norman, 'My 15 Minutes with Warhol; What is Art? Ask Canadian Customs Inspectors', *The Gazette* (Montreal, 9 November 2008)

Wilcox, John, *The Autobiography and Sex Life of Andy Warhol* (New York, 1971)

Workman, Chuck, dir., *The Life and Times of Andy Warhol Superstar* (Shout Factory Theater, 1990)

ACKNOWLEDGEMENTS

I am grateful to Micki McCoy, Lindsay Riordan, Nicoletta Rousseva, Matthew Weseley and Betsy Stepina for their generous help with various research duties, editorial improvements and intellectual conundrums, and to Leah Theis, Lisa Zdybel and Betsy Stepina for their gracious assistance with images and picture research. Thank you too for the thoughtful and substantial report, commissioned by the Publisher, from an anonymous reader. Research and writing benefited from a sabbatical from the University of California, Davis, and publication has been assisted by funding from the University of Illinois, Chicago. Finally, my thanks are owed to Michael Leaman, Publisher at Reaktion Books, for accommodating my shifting schedule.

Much of the material in chapters Three and Five was previously published in an earlier state as 'Andy Warhol's Red Beard', Art Bulletin, LXXXIII / 3 (September 2001), pp. 527–47. This book has benefited from the responses of many readers to my initial article.

PHOTO ACKNOWLEDGEMENTS

The author and publishers wish to express their thanks to the following sources of illustrative material and/or permission to reproduce it. Some locations are also supplied here for reasons of brevity.

All Warhol Artworks: © 2013 The Andy Warhol Foundation for the Visual Arts, Inc./Artists Rights Society (ARS), New York

© 2013 Vito Acconci / Artists Rights Society (ARS), New York: 69; photo Archives Study Center, Andy Warhol Museum, Pittsburgh, © 2013 Ken Heyman: 62; from *Art Instruction* (October 1938): 44; © 2013 Banco de México Diego Rivera Frida Kahlo Museums Trust, Mexico, D.F. / Artists Rights Society (ARS), New York: 5; photo © Bettmann / CORBIS: 45; Boca Raton Museum of Art, Florida (gift of Bob Adelman, 2009.3 – photo courtesy of Bob Adelman): 72; photo Bridwell Library Special Collections, Perkins School of Theology, Southern Methodist University: 75; The Carnegie Museum of Art, Pittsburgh: 4 (gift of the artist, 49.24), 22 (Richard M. Scaife American Painting Fund, 81.107), 24 (gift of Elizabeth Hampsey, 93.191.14), 42, 43 (gift of Russell G. Twiggs); from Milton Friedman, *Capitalism and Freedom* (University of Chicago Press, 1962), reproduced by kind permission of the University of Chicago Press: 77; Collection Froehlich, Stuttgart: 20, 30; Donation Jorn, Silkeborg / Artists Rights Society (ARS), New York/ COPY-DAN, Copenhagen: 54; courtesy of the Gropper family: 26; from the *Index librorum prohibitorum Typographia reverendæ Cameræ apostolicæ* (Rome, 1758): 75; from *Interiors* (June 1952): 60; photo Jim.henderson: 16; photo Penny King (http://stchrysostoms.wordpress.com/2011/09/14/postcard-from-czestochowa-poland/): 14; © 2013 Barbara Kruger (courtesy Mary Boone Gallery, New York): 9; Kunstsammlung Nordrhein-Westfalen, Düsseldorf: 65; photo Library of Congress, Washington, DC (Prints and Photographs Division, Carl Van Vechten Collection): 29; locations not known: 38, 40, 47; photo courtesy of MacDougall Auctions: 13; from Margarita Madrigal, *Madrigal's Magic Key to Spanish* (Garden City, NY, 1951): 27, 51; Christopher Makos 1982 makostudio.com : 1, 11; Milwaukee Museum of Art: 55 (gift of Mrs Harry Lynde Bradley, M1975.172); Musées Royaux des Beaux-Arts at Brussels: 70; photo Jon Naar (copyright 1965, 2013): 17; photos © Billy Name: 7, 37; from Robert Nathan, *Mobilizing for Abundance* (New York:

McGraw Hill, 1944): 8; courtesy *The New York Times*: 61; Öffentliche Kunst-sammlung Basel (Kupferstichkabinett): 41; from E. J. Pace, *101 Christian Cartoons* (Philadelphia, 1922): 19; The Phillips Collection, Washington, DC: 10; from Allan Pinkerton, *Strikers, Communists, Tramps and Detectives* (New York, 1878): 23; from the *Pittsburgh Gazette Times* (10 April 1907): 21; private collections: 18, 56; San Francisco Art Institute: 5; © 2013 Estate of Ben Shahn / Licensed by VAGA, New York: 40; from David Shub, *Lenin* (New York and Toronto: Mentor Books, 1948): 46; Smithsonian American Art Museum, Washington, DC: 57 (gift of Container Corporation of America, 1984.124.150); 58 (gift of Container Corporation of America, 1984.124.247); Stedelijk Museum Amsterdam © 2013 Asger Jorn / Artists Rights Society (ARS), New York: 54; Collection Mrs John F. Steiner, on loan to the Andy Warhol Museum, Pittsburgh: 35; photo Blake Stimson: 55; from Andy Warhol, *America* (New York, 1985): 2; from Andy Warhol, *Andy Warhol's Index (Book)* (New York, 1967): 76; The Andy Warhol Museum, Pittsburgh (Founding Collection, Contribution The Andy Warhol Foundation for the Visual Arts, Inc.): 6, 25, 33, 52, 53, 66, 68, 74; photo by John Warhola: 12; Collection Paul Warhola Family, Pittsburgh: 15.

Every effort has been made to contact unacknowledged copyright holders. Any copyright holders we have been unable to reach or to whom inaccurate acknowledgements have been made please contact Reaktion Books, and corrections will be made in any subsequent printing.

INDEX